Lecture Notes in Computer Science 4569

Commenced Publication in 1973
Founding and Former Series Editors:
Gerhard Goos, Juris Hartmanis, and Jan van Leeuwen

Andreas Butz   Brian Fisher
Antonio Krüger   Patrick Olivier
Shigeru Owada (Eds.)

Smart Graphics

8th International Symposium, SG 2007
Kyoto, Japan, June 25-27, 2007
Proceedings

 Springer

Volume Editors

Andreas Butz
Ludwig-Maximilians-Universität, Institut für Informatik
Amalienstrasse 17, 80333 Munich, Germany
E-mail: butz@ifi.lmu.de

Brian Fisher
Simon Fraser University at Surrey
13450 102 Ave., Surrey, BC V3T 5X3, Canada
E-mail: brian.fisher@acm.org

Antonio Krüger
University of Münster, Institute for Geoinformatics
Robert-Koch-Str. 26-28, 48149 Münster, Germany
E-mail: antonio.krueger@uni-muenster.de

Patrick Olivier
University of Newcastle upon Tyne, Informatics Research Institute
Newcastle upon Tyne, NE1 7RU, UK
E-mail: p.l.olivier@ncl.ac.uk

Shigeru Owada
Sony Computer Science Laboratories, Inc.
Takanawa Muse Bldg. 3-14-13, Higashigotanda
Shinagawa-ku, Tokyo 141-0022, Japan
E-mail: sowd@acm.org

Library of Congress Control Number: Applied for

CR Subject Classification (1998): I.3, I.2.10, I.2, I.4, I

LNCS Sublibrary: SL 6 – Image Processing, Computer Vision, Pattern Recognition,
and Graphics

ISSN   0302-9743
ISBN-10   3-540-73213-6 Springer Berlin Heidelberg New York
ISBN-13   978-3-540-73213-6 Springer Berlin Heidelberg New York

Springer is a part of Springer Science+Business Media

springer.com

© Springer-Verlag Berlin Heidelberg 2007
Printed in Germany

Typesetting: Camera-ready by author, data conversion by Scientific Publishing Services, Chennai, India
Printed on acid-free paper   SPIN: 12080496   06/3180   5 4 3 2 1 0

Preface

The International Symposium on Smart Graphics 2007 was held during June 25–27, 2007 in Kyoto, Japan. It was the eighth event in a series which originally started in 2000 as a AAAI Spring Symposium and has taken place every year since then in Europe and North America. The 2007 Symposium was our first to reach out to the Asian Smart Graphics community. As a result the number of submissions has again increased and the acceptance rate dropped to 31–36% (depending on category).

The core idea behind the Smart Graphics symposia is to bring together researchers and practitioners from the field of computer graphics, artificial intelligence, cognitive science, graphic design and the fine arts. Each of these disciplines contributes to what we mean by the term "smart graphics": the intelligent process of creating effective, expressive and esthetic graphical presentation. While artists and designers have been creating communicative graphics for centuries, artificial intelligence focuses on automating this process by means of the computer. While computer graphics provides the tools for creating graphical presentations in the first place, the cognitive sciences contribute the rules and models of perception necessary for the design of effective graphics. The exchange of ideas between these four disciplines has led to many exciting and fruitful discussions, and the smart graphics symposia draw their liveliness from a spirit of open minds and the willingness to learn from and share with other disciplines.

Many Smart Graphics symposia emphasize a particular aspect of the field in the call for papers. Since we had received an increasing number of papers related to smart interaction in recent years, this became the focus for the 2007 call. As a consequence, one third of all the papers in the 2007 symposium were on the topic of smart interaction. In order to create synergies with the local community, we co-located SG with the domestic Japanese Visual Computing / Graphics and CAD symposium, which took place in Osaka during June 23–24.

We would like to thank all authors for the effort that went into their submissions, the Program Committee for their work in selecting and ordering contributions for the final program, and of course the participants who made Smart Graphics 2007 such a success.

June 2007

Andreas Butz
Brian Fisher
Antonio Krüger
Patrick Olivier
Shigeru Owada

Organization

Organization Committee

Andreas Butz (University of Munich, Germany)
Brian Fisher (University of British Columbia, Canada)
Antonio Krüger (University of Münster, Germany)
Patrick Olivier (University of Newcastle Upon Tyne, UK)
Shigeru Owada (Sony Computer Science Laboratory)

Program Committee

Elisabeth André (University of Augsburg)
William Bares (Millsaps College)
Marc Cavazza (Teesside University)
Marc Christie (University of Nantes)
Sarah Diamond (Ontario College of Art and Design)
Steven Feiner (Columbia University)
Knut Hartmann (University of Magdeburg)
Hiroshi Hosobe (National Institute of Informatics, Japan)
Rainer Malaka (University of Bremen)
Jun Mitani (University of Tsukuba)
W. Bradford Paley (Columbia University; didi)
Bernhard Preim (University of Magdeburg)
Thomas Rist (University of Applied Sciences, Augsburg)
Takafumi Saito (Tokyo University of Agriculture and Technology)
Shigeo Takahashi (The University of Tokyo)
Lucia Terrenghi (University of Munich)
Gabriel Zachmann (University of Clausthal)
Massimo Zancanaro (FBK-irst)
Michelle Zhou (IBM T.J. Watson Research Center)

Secondary Reviewers

Ragnar Bade (University of Magdeburg)
Alexandra Baer (University of Magdeburg)
Arno Krüger (University of Magdeburg)
Konrad Mühler (University of Magdeburg)
Christian Tietjen (University of Magdeburg)

Supporting Institutions

The Smart Graphics Symposium 2005 was held in cooperation with Eurographics, AAAI, ACM Siggraph and ACM Sigchi.

Table of Contents

Interaction

Lifelike Characters and Affective Computing

Kowledge-Based Graphics Generation and Interaction

Visualization and Graphics Algorithms

Posters and Demos

A Sketch-Based Interface for Modeling Myocardial Fiber Orientation

Kenshi Takayama[1], Takeo Igarashi[2], Ryo Haraguchi[3], and Kazuo Nakazawa[3]

[1] Department of Computer Science, The University of Tokyo,
Bunkyo-ku, Tokyo, Japan
kenshi@ui.is.s.u-tokyo.ac.jp
[2] Department of Computer Science, The University of Tokyo / PRESTO, JST
takeo@acm.org
[3] National Cardiovascular Center Research Institute
Suita, Osaka, Japan
{haraguch, nakazawa}@ri.ncvc.go.jp

Abstract. This article proposes a sketch-based interface for modeling muscle fiber orientation of a 3D virtual heart model. Our target was electrophysiological simulation of the heart and fiber orientation is one of the key elements to obtaining reliable simulation results. We designed the interface and algorithm based on the observation that fiber orientation is always parallel to the surface of the heart. The user specifies the fiber orientation by drawing a freeform stroke on the object surface. The system first builds a vector field on the surface by applying Laplacian smoothing to the mesh vertices and then builds a volumetric vector field by applying Laplacian smoothing to the voxels. We demonstrate the usefulness of the proposed method through a user study with a cardiologist.

1 Introduction

Many people suffer from abnormal heart rhythm, and effective treatment is much desired. One approach to understanding the mechanism of this disease is electrophysiological simulation of the heart (Fig. 1a). Various parameters are required for this simulation, and orientation of myocardial fiber (i.e., muscle fiber of heart as shown in Fig. 1b) is one of the key elements that determines the behavior of signal propagation [1] [2].

In order to study the direct influence of the myocardial fiber orientation on the simulation result, it is necessary for physicians to manually design various models of fiber orientation based on their expert knowledge. A simple method is to have the user set orientations on discrete slices, but it is very difficult to design complicated orientation fields using such crude methods. To support this process, we present a sketch-based interface for designing a volumetric vector field that represents myocardial fiber orientation inside of a given 3D heart model. We designed the system based on the observation that the fiber orientation is parallel to the model's surface. This makes it possible to use simple sketching on the

A. Butz et al. (Eds.): SG 2007, LNCS 4569, pp. 1–9, 2007.

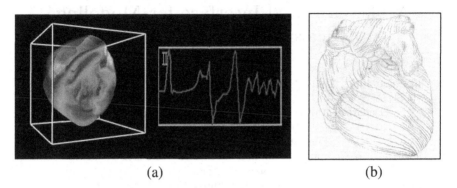

(a)   (b)

Fig. 1. (a) Electrophysiological simulation of the heart [7]. (b) A schematic view of myocardial fibers (drawn by the author using [6] as a guide).

surface as input and to use a two-step interpolation (surface and volume) scheme for the construction of the volumetric vector field.

Figure 2 is a snapshot of our prototype system. The user can draw strokes on the model with a common 2D input device such as a mouse or pen. The system applies two-step interpolation to these user-drawn strokes to obtain the volumetric vector field. We used the Laplacian smoothing method for the interpolation to enable interactive trial-and-error design. Using our method, the user can design volumetric vector fields quickly and easily.

We asked a cardiologist to test our system and received positive feedback. He appreciated the ability to design fiber orientations quickly and confirmed that the proposed system can be a useful tool for practical applications. We also ran a sample electrophysiological simulation using the myocardial fiber model he had created to demonstrate the capability of the system.

2   Related Work

Various studies have been conducted on *analyzing* and *visualizing* vector fields of various kinds [5]. However, studies on the *design* of vector fields are relatively few. Here we introduce some of the existing methods for designing vector fields.

Salisbury et al. [9] made a simple tool for designing vector fields on a 2D plane for the purpose of rendering a 2D image with orientable textures. Its interface was more like that of ordinary Paint applications, with operations such as draw, blur and fill. Praun et al. [8] and Turk [11] used vector fields on surfaces of 3D models to synthesize textures on surfaces. In those studies, they let the user specify vector values on some of the vertices of the 3D models and assigned interpolated vector values to the remaining vertices. Praun et al. [9] used Gaussian radial basis functions technique for interpolation, whereas Turk [11] applied a mesh hierarchy technique. The topology of a vector field is often very important for certain applications, and Zhang et al. [12] demonstrated a novel method for designing vector fields on 2D planes and 3D surfaces taking topology into consideration.

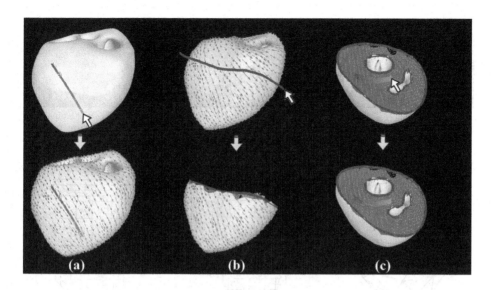

Fig. 2. Designing fiber orientations by sketching. (a) Drawing a stroke on the surface to specify the orientations on the surface. (b) Cutting the model to see the orientations inside the model. (c) Drawing a stroke on the cross-sectional surface to further control the orientation inside the model.

To our knowledge, however, no previous study has reported on the design of volumetric vector fields. We propose a sketch-based interface for designing volumetric vector fields using a two-step approach.

3   User Interface

The system first loads a 3D polygonal model specified by the user. After several precomputations, including polygon-to-voxel conversion and calculation of Laplacian matrices, the user can design volumetric vector fields using the sketch-based interface.

The user draws free-form strokes on the surface of the model to specify the local fiber orientation on the surface (Fig. 2a). The user can draw an arbitrary number of strokes on the surface to specify the fiber orientation field in detail. The user can cut the model by drawing a cross stroke. The stroke is extruded to the viewing direction, and the system hides the part of the model on the left-hand side of the extruded surface (Fig. 2b). The user can also draw strokes on this cross-sectional surface to specify the fiber orientation inside of the model (Fig. 2c). Cutting is also useful for drawing strokes on internal surfaces (Fig. 3).

Receiving these user-drawn strokes as inputs, the system performs two-step Laplacian smoothing to obtain the resulting volumetric fiber orientation field. The computation takes only a few seconds, and the user can incrementally add or remove strokes until obtaining a satisfactory result.

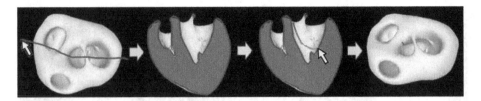

Fig. 3. Drawing a stroke on the internal surface by cutting off the interfering part of the surface

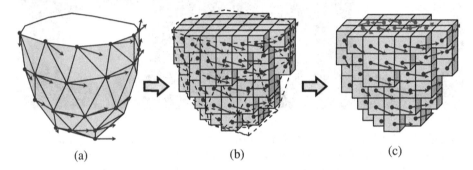

(a)   (b)   (c)

Fig. 4. The overview of the two-step interpolation. (a) Smoothing on the surface. (b) Applying vectors on the surface to the boundary voxels. (c) Smoothing on the volume.

4   Algorithm

4.1   Overview

When the 3D model is loaded, the system first converts the surface model into voxels using a standard scanning method. Note that each boundary voxel is associated with its neighboring polygon, which is required when setting constraints on the vector field of the volume from the vector field of the surface.

The vector field of the surface consists of the unit orientation vectors associated with the mesh vertices, whereas the vector field of the volume comprises the unit orientation vectors associated with the voxels. After receiving user-drawn strokes as input, the system performs two-step interpolation to obtain the volumetric vector field (Fig. 4). The system first sets the orientation vector of the mesh vertices near the stroke in the direction parallel to the nearest stroke direction (Fig. 5). The system then applies Laplacian smoothing to the surface mesh by using the vertices near the input strokes as constraints (Fig. 4a). The system then applies the vector field of the surface to the vector field of the volume (Fig. 4b) by setting the orientation vector of boundary voxels to the blending of nearby mesh vertices (Fig. 6). The strokes drawn on the cross sections are also mapped to the neighboring voxels (Fig. 7). The system finally applies Laplacian smoothing to the inside voxels to obtain the final volumetric vector field (Fig. 4c).

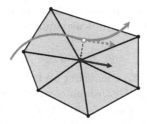

Fig. 5. The orientation vector of mesh vertices near the input stroke is set parallel to the stroke and used as constraints for applying interpolation to the surface

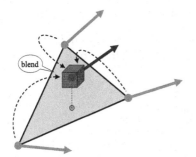
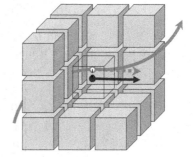

Fig. 6. Setting the vector of a boundary voxel to the blending vector of its neighboring vertices

Fig. 7. The orientation vector of voxels near the stroke drawn on the cross section is set parallel to the stroke and used as additional constraints for applying interpolation to the volume

Note that our system does not take into account the magnitudes of vectors because its purpose is only to design orientation. Therefore, the system normalizes all of the vectors after each smoothing. The interpolated vectors on the surface may not be tangential to the surface. The system therefore projects the vectors associated to the mesh vertices to their tangential planes after each interpolation on the surface.

4.2 Laplacian Smoothing

Here we briefly describe how the Laplacian smoothing works in our case (more details about this technique are available in [10]). Let $x_1, \cdots, x_n$ be orientation vectors associated with mesh vertices or voxels. Then the Laplacian of x_i is defined as

$$\delta_i = x_i - \sum_{j \in N_i} w_j^i x_j \tag{1}$$

where N_i is the neighbors of x_i (i.e., 1-ring of the i-th mesh vertex or voxels adjacent to the i-th voxel). We simply set weights as $w_j^i = \frac{1}{|N_i|}$, meaning that

δ_i is the difference between x_i and the average of its neighbors. Our goal was to minimize these Laplacians in the least-squares sense while satisfying given constraints:

$$x_{k_i} = b_i \quad (i = 1, \cdots, m) \tag{2}$$

where k_i is the index of the i-th constraint and m is the number of constraints. In the case of the mesh vertices, constraints were given at the vertices near the input strokes (Fig. 5). In the case of the voxels, constraints were given at the voxels near the surface (Fig. 6), as well as those near the additional strokes drawn on the cross sections (Fig. 7).

This goal can be rewritten using vectors and matrices as

$$\text{minimize} \left| \begin{pmatrix} L \\ C \end{pmatrix} \boldsymbol{x} - \begin{pmatrix} \mathbf{0} \\ \boldsymbol{b} \end{pmatrix} \right|^2$$

where $\boldsymbol{x} = (x_1, \cdots, x_n)^{\mathrm{T}}$ and $\boldsymbol{b} = (b_1, \cdots, b_m)^{\mathrm{T}}$ are vectors, and $L = (l_{ij})$ and $C = (c_{ij})$ are $n \times n$ and $m \times n$ matrices, respectively, defined by

$$l_{ij} = \begin{cases} -1 & (i = j) \\ w_j^i & (j \in N_i) \\ 0 & (\text{otherwise}) \end{cases}$$

$$c_{ij} = \begin{cases} 1 & (j = k_i) \\ 0 & (\text{otherwise}) \end{cases}$$

This corresponds to solving the following system

$$A^{\mathrm{T}} A \boldsymbol{x} = A^{\mathrm{T}} \begin{pmatrix} \mathbf{0} \\ \boldsymbol{b} \end{pmatrix} \tag{3}$$

where $A = \begin{pmatrix} L \\ C \end{pmatrix}$. Matrix $A^{\mathrm{T}} A$ and vector $A^{\mathrm{T}} \begin{pmatrix} \mathbf{0} \\ \boldsymbol{b} \end{pmatrix}$ can be rewritten in a simple form as

$$A^{\mathrm{T}} A = (L^{\mathrm{T}} \ C^{\mathrm{T}}) \begin{pmatrix} L \\ C \end{pmatrix}$$

$$= L^{\mathrm{T}} L + C^{\mathrm{T}} C$$

$$A^{\mathrm{T}} \begin{pmatrix} \mathbf{0} \\ \boldsymbol{b} \end{pmatrix} = (L^{\mathrm{T}} \ C^{\mathrm{T}}) \begin{pmatrix} \mathbf{0} \\ \boldsymbol{b} \end{pmatrix}$$

$$= C^{\mathrm{T}} \boldsymbol{b}$$

Note that the k_i-th diagonal element in $C^{\mathrm{T}} C$ is 1 and the k_i-th element in $C^{\mathrm{T}} \boldsymbol{b}$ is b_i (for $i = 1, \cdots, m$) and all the other elements in $C^{\mathrm{T}} C$ and $C^{\mathrm{T}} \boldsymbol{b}$ are 0.

The system solves (3) for the mesh vertices every time the user draws a stroke on the surface. Because the Laplacian matrix L remains constant for a given mesh, we can precompute $L^{\mathrm{T}} L$ and add 1 to the constrained diagonal elements when solving. In the case of Laplacian smoothing for the voxels, $A^{\mathrm{T}} A$ remains constant as long as the user draws strokes only on the mesh surface; it changes only slightly when the user adds a stroke on a cross section. This matrix is sparse enough to apply an optimized algorithm for sparse matrices. We currently use a fast sparse matrix solver based on LU decomposition [3].

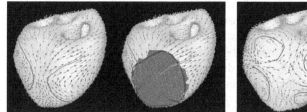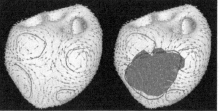

Fig. 8. Example fiber orientations designed using the system

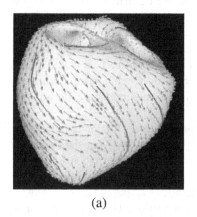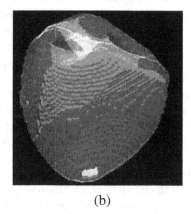

(a)   (b)

Fig. 9. (a) Myocardial fiber orientation designed by the physician using our system. (b) Sample result of electrophysiological simulation using (a).

5   Results and User Experience

The current prototype system is implemented in C++ using OpenGL and runs on Windows PCs. Figure 8 shows some fiber orientations that have been designed using the system. It took about 3 s total to compute a volumetric vector field from user-specified strokes for a heart model with 1,992 vertices and 7,646 voxels using a PC with a 2.1-GHz CPU and 2.0-GB RAM.

To obtain feedback, we asked a physician in the field of cardiac electrophysiology to try our system, with which he designed a fiber orientation for a given heart model. We performed the test using a standard laptop PC and a mouse. We used a commercially available 3D polygonal model of the heart as a sample model for the test. We first gave the physician a brief tutorial on using the system, and he became familiar with it in about 10 min. He then started to design a complete myocardial fiber orientation and finished it in about 8 min. Figure 9 shows the fiber orientation he designed and a sample result of electrophysiological simulation based on [4] using this model.

We then interviewed the physician and obtained the following feedback. He evaluated our system as an important contribution to his area of research, because it is the first system that allows the user to directly design 3D fiber structures. Existing methods force the user to work on 2D slices to specify a 3D vector field, which is very tedious. He was pleased with the resulting myocardial fiber orientation he created using the system, as it successfully represented the typical twisted structure of myocardial fibers. He stressed that our system is definitely faster than existing methods, even if the calculation time increases with the increasing number of voxels.

He also noted the importance of our method in defining the volumetric vector field using 3D surface geometry and strokes because this approach would make it possible for a user to quickly generate another volumetric vector field from the existing one by simply deforming the geometry (a feature that is not yet supported in the current implementation).

He gave us some suggestions for further improvements and noted that it would be helpful if the user could design myocardial fiber orientation using some sample images of actual medical data mapped onto the model's surface. This would allow the user to create far more realistic fiber orientation by tracing sample images. He noted that *tracing* is an important operation in a medical sense because it achieves human filtering of noisy medical data.

He also pointed out that cross-sectioning is not suitable for visualizing myocardial fiber orientation because an actual myocardial fiber consists several layers parallel to the surface, and researchers usually associate myocardial fiber orientations with such layers and not with cross sections. He proposed a *peeling* interface, with which the user can perceive the gradual change in fiber orientation by continuously peeling layers in the depth direction. He also noted that such visualization techniques would enhance further intuitive design.

6   Conclusion

In this article, we presented a novel method for designing a volumetric fiber orientation field filling a 3D heart model using a sketch-based interface. We applied two-step Laplacian smoothing on the surface and on the volume to obtain a smoothly varying 3D fiber orientation field from user-specified constraints on the surface. We asked a cardiologist to try our prototype system and confirmed the effectiveness of our method. Many improvements still need to be made, and we plan to continue working on resolving these problems.

Acknowledgements

We thank Dr. Takashi Ashihara of Shiga University of Medical Science for cooperating in our user study and providing valuable feedback. This research was partially supported by the Ministry of Education, Science, Sports and Culture, Grant-in-Aid for Scientific Research (B) 18300157 and Leading Project for Biosimulation. This work was partially supported by grants from PRESTO/JST (Japan Science and Technology Agency).

References

1. Ashihara, T., Namba, T., Ikeda, T., Ito, M., Kinoshita, M., Nakazawa, K.: Breakthrough waves during ventricular fibrillation depend on the degree of rotational anisotropy and the boundary conditions: A simulation study. Journal of Cardiovascular Electrophysiology 12(3), 312–322 (2001)
2. Ashihara, T., Namba, T., Yao, T., Ozawa, T., Kawase, A., Ikeda, T., Nakazawa, K., Ito, M.: Vortex cordis as a mechanism of postshock activation: Arrhythmia induction study using a bidomain model. Journal of Cardiovascular Electrophysiology 14(3), 295–302 (2003)
3. Davis,T. A.: A column pre-ordering strategy for the unsymmetric-pattern multifrontal method. ACM Trans. Math. Softw. 30(2), 165–195 (2004)
4. Haraguchi, R., Igarashi, T., Owada, S., Yao, T., Namba, T., Ashihara, T., Ikeda, T., Nakazawa, K.: Electrophysiological heart simulator equipped with sketchy 3-d modeling. In: Wu, J.L., Ito, K., Tobimatsu, S., Nishida, T., Fukuyama, H. (eds.) Complex Medical Engineering, Springer, Heidelberg (2007)
5. Hauser, H., Laramee, R.S., Doleisch, H.: State-of-the-art report 2002 in flow visualization (2002)
6. Kahle, W., Leonhardt, H., Platzer, W.: Taschenatlas der Anatomie 2. Innere Organe. Prosa, Essays, Briefe. Thieme, Stuttgart (2003)
7. Nakazawa, K.,Suzuki, T.,Ashihara, T., Inagaki, M., Namba, T., Ikeda, T.,Suzuki, R.: Computational analysis and visualization of spiral wave reentry in a virtual heart model. In: Yamaguchi, T. (ed.) Clinical Application of Computational Mechanics to the Cardiovascular System. Springer, Japan.
8. Praun, E., Finkelstein, A., Hoppe, H.: Lapped textures. In: SIGGRAPH '00: Proceedings of the 27th annual conference on Computer graphics and interactive techniques, pp. 465–470. ACM Press/Addison-Wesley Publishing Co, New York, NY, USA (2000)
9. Salisbury, M.P., Wong, M.T., Hughes, J.F., Salesin, D.H.: Orientable textures for image-based pen-and-ink illustration. In: Michael, P., Salisbury, M.T., Wong, J.F. (eds.) SIGGRAPH '97: Proceedings of the 24th annual conference on Computer graphics and interactive techniques, pp. 401–406. ACM Press/Addison-Wesley Publishing Co, New York, NY, USA (1997)
10. Sorkine, O., Cohen-Or, D., Lipman, Y., Alexa, M.,R&#246, C., Seidel, H.-P.: Laplacian surface editing. In: SGP '04: Proceedings of the 2004 Eurographics/ACM SIGGRAPH symposium on Geometry processing, pp. 175–184. ACM Press, New York, NY, USA (2004)
11. Turk, G.: Texture synthesis on surfaces. In: SIGGRAPH '01: Proceedings of the 28th annual conference on Computer graphics and interactive techniques, pp. 347–354. ACM Press, New York, NY, USA (2001)
12. Zhang, E., Mischaikow, K., Turk, G.: Vector field design on surfaces. ACM Trans. Graph. 25(4), 1294–1326 (2006)

NPR Lenses: Interactive Tools
for Non-photorealistic Line Drawings

Petra Neumann, Tobias Isenberg, and Sheelagh Carpendale

Department of Computer Science, University of Calgary, Canada
{pneumann,isenberg,sheelagh}@cpsc.ucalgary.ca

Abstract. NPR Lenses is an interactive technique for producing expressive non-photorealistic renderings. It provides an intuitive visual interaction tool for illustrators, allowing them to seamlessly apply a large variety of emphasis techniques. Advantages of 3D scene manipulation are combined with the capabilities of viewer-aligned lenses by inserting 2D lens controls into the 3D rendering pipeline. By using lenses that are spatially explicit and constrained we enable object-independent adjustments in 3D. Regions of emphasis can be easily created by adjusting lens parameters and any combination of line style, type, shape, and position of computer-generated lines. NPR Lenses support the creation of effects similar to those found in many existing hand-drawn illustrations and allow creative freedom through interactive control at the same time.

1   Introduction

For hundreds of years, humans have been creating illustrations by hand for scientific, medical, technical, artistic, and entertainment purposes. Non-Photorealistic Rendering (NPR, [1,2]) research deals with the computer-based development of techniques to create such illustrations. While now a large number of NPR techniques exist, they have not yet been widely adopted by the illustration community. NPR research tends to focus on the difficult technical problems that can make these techniques viable. In contrast, few NPR techniques have been developed which provide creative freedom for the illustrator using them. For example, they tend to provide access to a single technique at a time, while many hand-drawn illustrations often incorporate several style variations within a single drawing. The development of such interactive tools is necessary to help illustrators leverage NPR techniques more frequently and successfully. We address this problem of creating tools to support illustrators and present an interactive tool called NPR Lenses that allows artists and illustrators to interactively apply and explore emphasis effects to line drawings similar to those in hand-drawings.

Recent developments in computer-based techniques for line drawings and other NPR methods allow artists to automatically create illustrations. However, many illustrative and expressive techniques common in hand-drawn illustrations remain unexplored in electronic systems. For instance, emphasis has been used over many centuries in art, cartography, and illustration as a means of giving

A. Butz et al. (Eds.): SG 2007, LNCS 4569, pp. 10–22, 2007.
© Springer-Verlag Berlin Heidelberg 2007

importance and guiding attention. Most hand-made illustrations provide this emphasis by adjusting one or more of many different aspects of the illustration of an object such as shape, lighting, style, etc. Such adjustments perform important functions such as conveying the intended meaning, implying relative importance of certain parts, providing room for additional information, and creating humor. These techniques may use variant lines styles and weights, spatial distortion for exaggeration (as in caricatures), or even selective inclusion or exclusion of lines to reveal hidden or internal information. Many of these emphasis techniques have already received research attention, however, previous solutions often *(1) have a global effect (on the entire image)*: illustrators may want explicit control of how the emphasis technique spreads into the rest of the image; *(2) create discontinuities*: illustrators, in part, create their desired impact by how emphasis in one region is integrated with the rest of the illustration; *(3) require knowledge of end goals*: an illustrator may not know a priori what degree of emphasis will achieve the intended result; and *(4) lack intuitive interaction techniques and speed*: to be able to create illustrations just as they envision them, illustrators need ease and freedom of interactive control and immediate visual response.

Inspired by professional illustrations and drawings, we developed a collection of tools called NPR Lenses to address these problems. To address the first problem, our NPR Lenses facilitate the application of both global and local effects. If desired, they can have a global effect but they can also be localized in a variety of different way such as: localized spatially, localized to chosen objects, localized to parts of objects, and even localized to specific sets of lines. Our solution allows illustrators to modify line properties locally by adjusting line shape, style, and presence independent from a scene-building object hierarchy. To address the second problem, our technique also provides visual integration between regions of emphasis thus avoiding visual discontinuities. To address the last two problems of freedom of intent and intuitive interaction, we integrated a 3D scene manipulation environment with 2D viewer-aligned lenses to support interactive creation of emphasis effects and dynamic exploration of the application of these effects. Our technique allows illustrators to explore line renderings of a 3D model by manipulating the view of a scene itself and to creatively play with the lenses and their effects until a desired illustration result is achieved.

The NPR Lenses approach differs from existing research and technology in the following ways: (1) NPR Lenses use 2D input to apply emphasis to line renditions that reside in a 3D rendering environment; (2) NPR Lenses allow artists to seamlessly apply a large variety of emphasis techniques, both locally and globally, independently of a scene hierarchy; (3) NPR Lenses all employ a common interaction approach, giving an illustrator freedom of chosen effects within a single interface; and (4) NPR Lenses support the creation of a variety of emphasis effects similar to those found in many existing hand-drawn illustrations.

The remainder of the article is structured as follows: We first discuss research related to NPR Lenses in Sec. 2. Sec. 3 describes the interaction framework on which NPR Lenses are based. Sec. 4 contains examples of expressive effects possible with NPR Lenses. We provide implementation details in Sec. 5 and a discussion of our approach in Sec. 6. Sec. 7 summarizes our contributions.

2   NPR Lenses in Context

NPR Lenses relate to previous work in several research areas and, in particular, to interactive NPR stylization within a 3D graphics environment. We first introduce concepts and terminology that influenced our development of emphasis techniques for illustration and then discuss related research.

=NPR Lenses are *spatially explicit and constrained, view-dependent 3D scene adjustments.* An adjustment to a 3D scene is *spatially-explicit* if the adjustment caused by the lens is located in the 3D world space. Thus, moving the model into or across the location of the lens affects the model accordingly. That means a single object may be partly within the adjustment space and partly not, thus allowing effects to be applied only to regions of a given object. A *view-dependent* adjustment is attached to the viewpoint and follows its movement in the 3D scene. A *constrained* adjustment has a region of influence that can be set to less than the full resulting image.

Fig. 1 shows different types of spatially explicit scene adjustments. One, the NPR Lens, extends "cone-like" from the viewpoint into the view frustum. Another lens, the Cube Lens as used in 3D Magic Lenses, exists at a specific location in the scene and influences objects in a cubed region in 3D [3]. The third example, the Half-Plane Lens, partitions the view-frustum into an area of influence and one area that is not influenced [4]. All of these adjustments have a spatial explicit description and objects in the scene are either partially or fully in their influence ranges.

Spatially explicit emphasis is important for NPR line drawing since it is often seen in hand-drawn examples. Making NPR Lenses also viewer-aligned ensures that their effects are always visible. Related to this spatially explicit, viewer-aligned emphasis is the WYSIWYG-NPR system [5] that lets users add detail strokes and stylization directly to the scene from their view perspective. The primitives drawn on the image plane are projected onto the model and attached to it so that they remain on the surface when the model is rotated. This spatially explicit and view-dependent way to add detail only affects the top-most layer of the model similar to painting onto physical objects.

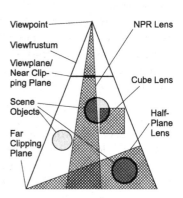

Fig. 1. Spatially explicit scene adjustments (crosshatched) in a 3D view frustum. Scene objects are partially in (darker) or out of their influence range. NPR Lenses are a subset of these and other possible spatially explicit scene adjustments.

In NPR research, most stylization effects in 3D have been restricted to influence whole objects at a time. A popular technique for emphasizing model parts *independently* from the object structure is depth cueing, i.e., varying line attributes with respect to depth. Other examples that allow a much wider range of object-independent stylization effects include use of lighting conditions, viewing direction, specific axes in 3D space, or the relation to a 3D point of interest

[4]. NPR Lenses add new possibilities to apply such object-independent emphasis. Our approach also relates to 3D Magic Lenses [3] where spatially explicit
lenses are placed in a 3D virtual environment. This technique has been extended
for real-time rendering and arbitrarily shaped spatially explicit lenses [6].

Spatial distortion is an emphasis technique that has received wide research
attention but is usually not integrated with additional line stylization for creating emphasis. Morphing or warping are likely the most well-known techniques.
These are commonly applied in image-space where pixels are shifted according
to the manipulation of coordinate grid points or feature lines [7]. As an object-
based technique, spatial deformation is often used in animation to change the
appearance of objects or transform one object into another [7]. Spatial distortion of the viewing space has been used for centuries in varying portrayals of
depth such as in medieval art, renaissance art, or cubism. Recent viewing-space
approaches in NPR distort scene geometry based on the manipulation of camera
and viewing parameters to create expressive renditions [8,9,10,11]. While NPR
Lenses incorporate spatial distortion, it is only one of the possible emphasis
techniques. None of these require explicitly specified deformation functions or
warping points. NPR Lenses, thus, have the added benefit of simple interaction
and specification of a number of effects using one common interaction approach.

Our goal of making the NPR Lens interaction technique as familiar as the
common interaction with 2D input devices such as mice or touch pads and
successfully applying this to the manipulation of 3D scenes is a difficult problem.
The difficulty results from correlation issues between the 2D mouse movement
and object movement in the 3D virtual world [12]. Common 2D mouse interaction
makes it difficult to exactly place or select an object in a 3D scene since the
exact z-location of the cursor is not fully specified. Using a 3D input device to
manipulate an object could help in specifying an exact z-location. However, the
projection of the objects to the 2D screen and missing depth cues often makes it
difficult to correctly analyze the position of 3D object parts and the 3D cursor
in relation to each other.

3   NPR Lens Interaction Framework

We present an interaction framework that addresses 3D interaction difficulties by
integrating 2D interaction and 3D application of effects. Our technique allows
illustrators to interactively modify illustrations created by an otherwise fully
automated line rendering process. The interaction has the feel of a 2D manipulation within a 3D graphics environment and provides the direct and expected
3D visual response. This interaction framework does not introduce the previously
mentioned difficulties associated with interaction in 3D and achieves this without
converting the 3D world to a 2D image. Thus, we can retain the advantages of
3D viewing, scene rotation, and line generation and provide simple interaction.

A metaphor will clarify how we integrate 2D and 3D interaction for NPR
Lenses. Metaphorically, an NPR Lens parallels our use of a hand-held magnifying
lens in the physical world. If you are examining a 3D physical scene with your
magnifying lens you can move the lens freely over the scene or you can move

objects in and out of your view. Your lens and scene are entirely independent but for the lens to be effective it must be placed between the eyes and the scene. NPR Lenses are similar and work on the same spatial principles but can achieve many different effects as well as magnification. The 3D rendering environment has a 3D scene that can be influenced by an NPR Lens. The lens operates on the viewplane and, like a physical magnifying lens, affects the entire portion of the 3D scene that is projected into its region of influence on the viewplane.

Since NPR Lenses integrate interaction in both 2D and 3D spaces, they have both a 2D and a 3D manifestation which is spatially explicit (Fig. 2). Their 2D manifestation on the viewplane (here shown on the near clipping plane) is defined by the lens' parameters. The 3D manifestation results from being projected from the viewplane into the 3D scene, called the *lens frustum* as in 3D Magic Lenses [3]. The lens frustum's shape is defined by the type of 3D projection and the chosen lens parameters (Fig. 2). In a perspective view frustum the NPR Lens is viewpoint-aligned whereas in an orthogonal view frustum the lens is view-direction-aligned. The lens parameters defined by the 2D manifestation extend consistently into the lens frustum according to the projection used.

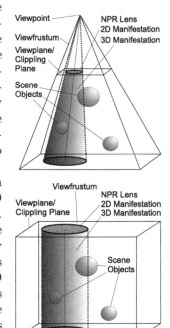

Fig. 2. Physical manifestation of NPR Lenses: perspective & orthogonal frusta

Instead of having to adjust single scene entities, specify algorithms based on lighting or depth cues, or specify distortion functions to create emphasis effects we can freely position the NPR Lens' 2D manifestation on the viewplane and interactively manipulate it. Changing the location of the emphasis effects only requires moving the lens across the screen. This is independent of the objects in the scene and resembles moving a search light within a physical environment (Fig. 3). The view-alignment ensures that the lens provides the expected visual response as it will only affect objects within its lens frustum. The adjustments are

applied in 3D in a process transparent to the users. Being able to freely manipulate the viewpoint, users can place a lens on the screen and then rotate the model or camera to create the desired effects. Exploration of the model is possible and creative play with the lens and emphasis parameters allows for an interactive trial-and-error design process to achieve the final illustration.

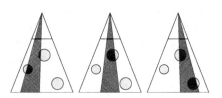

Fig. 3. Adjusting the 2D manifestation to move an NPR Lens in 3D

We can also add any number of NPR Lenses to influence a 3D scene. Each lens can then be controlled and manipulated independently of the other lenses and the objects in the scene. When lenses intersect, both effects are integrated.

4   NPR Lens Effects

The following describes several of the effects possible with NPR Lenses. Within the NPR Lens framework many other effects can easily be conceived and implemented. Here, we will describe Line-Style Lenses, Hidden-Line Lenses, Spatial-Distortion Lenses, the application of object-based constraints, and the use of lenses in combination. It is important to notice that while an NPR Lens exists in 2D on the viewplane, its 3D manifestation, as projected into the 3D scene, operates on the entire set of 3D lines that have been extracted.

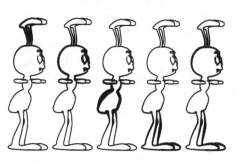

Fig. 4. Integrated local change of line style guides a viewer's attention

The lenses have attributes such as a center, a type of effect, a degree of effect (DOE), a region of maximum effect, a region of influence, and an attenuation style. In designing a specific NPR Lens, one chooses lens attributes and what NPR line parameters to affect. The style of attenuation can be used, e. g., to create seamless integration from the affected region to those regions that are not. Alternatively, this factor can be ignored and an abrupt transition or distinct change from the lens region to the rest of the model may be created. While these factors are adjustable for all lenses, there are reasonable defaults that allow using lenses without constantly attending to such details. The interactivity of the lenses and their ability to provide seamless integration into the unmodified part of the image is a significant advantage of our method over previous object-independent stylization techniques.

Fig. 5. Integrated local change of line color with two and three Line-Style lenses

Line-Style Lenses can locally influence the line style of extracted strokes including aspects such as width, saturation, transparency, color, etc. In hand-drawn illustrations artists often use different line weights to place an emphasis on certain parts of an object and de-emphasize others. For example, varying line thickness can change the emphasis placed on particular aspects of the line renditions as shown in Fig. 4. Note how the emphasis on different body parts changes the impact of the images and can direct the attention of the viewer. This parallels effects described in [13,14] as being capable of influencing the viewer. Similarly, Fig. 5 shows how color can be used to highlight chosen aspects and to create localized lighting effects.

The *Hidden-Lines Lens* displays silhouette or feature lines of the underlying model that would not normally be visible from the current viewpoint and thus reveals otherwise hidden information. A distinct style such as a dotted line can be used to make these extra lines clearly distinguishable from regular lines (Fig. 6). This effect is similar

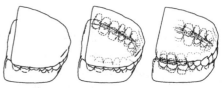

Fig. 6. None, one, and two Hidden-Line Lenses applied to a medical model

to the wireframe lens mentioned as future work in the original magic lens paper [15] and similar to effects possible with 3D Magic Lenses [3]. In contrast to these techniques, we allow an individually adjustable views of hidden lines, blended into the surrounding context, while Magic Lenses work as filters that have strong visual contrast at the edges of the lenses. One advantage of this blended filtered view of hidden lines—as opposed to always displaying them—lies in avoiding a cluttered display by showing hidden lines only where needed. The Hidden-Lines Lens can also be used to display other types of invisible lines, e. g., wireframe edges. The effects possible with such a lens are often seen in medical illustrations where objects behind the skin or other organs is made visible to guide learning in context.

The effects of a *Spatial-Distortion Lens* resemble the effects created with other fisheye lenses. Such distortions can often be found in traditional hand-drawn illustrations where artists adjust chosen surface features or regions of particular importance to place an emphasis on aspects of an object's appearance. Also, carefully applied

Fig. 7. Spatial distortion yields expressive line drawings (right; left: undistorted)

geometric distortions can give the resulting image a caricature or comic-like appearance. As such, the Spatial-Distortion Lens can be a valuable NPR tool. It allows to interactively change the appearance of line renditions to give them character according to one's intentions (Fig. 7). It can also be used as an interactive tool to examine aspects of an object that would otherwise remain unnoticed. In contrast to traditional zoom techniques, an examination of 3D model information is possible while still being able to view contextual information. Also, no modification of the model itself is necessary. An examination can take place via the lines created from these models.

Lenses as discussed so far have been applied to selected contiguous image regions. However, for any lens type, object-space constraints can be applied to restrict its application, to preserve some aspects of the model as unaffected or to choose to only affect particular parts of the

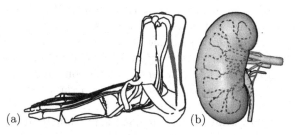

(a)   (b)

Fig. 8. Lens effect constrained in object-space

model or selected objects. The objects to pass to the lens can be chosen in the graphical user interface. Fig. 8 shows two examples where the application of emphasis effects has been constrained: to the Achilles tendon of the foot in Fig. 8(a) and to the region of blood supply of the kidney in Fig. 8(b).

To improve the flexibility of the setup, all presented lenses as well as the object-space constraints can be combined in one lens manifestation. Fig. 8(a), e.g., demonstrates how a lens can influence both line color and thickness to emphasize the Achilles tendon of a foot. Here, a single lens in the interface applies several types of effects. Alternatively, one can choose to use several lens manifestations that each apply similar or different effects at different parts of the rendition as shown for line color in Fig. 5 and hidden lines in Fig. 6. Each of these manifestations can be individually controlled and parameterized.

5 Implementation

To generate line renderings from polygonal models we use the OPENNPAR framework [16]. The line rendering process is modeled in a pipeline consisting of a series of rendering nodes. These nodes manage vertex coordinates and the edge data connecting these vertices (Fig. 9).

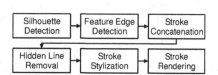

Fig. 9. Traditional pipeline

The pipeline takes a 3D model as input and first extracts silhouettes and feature lines. Next, these lines are concatenated to longer strokes and hidden line data is stored for each vertex. Stroke stylization determines a line's rendering style including texture, thicknesses, and color. The pipeline may contain optional steps to, e.g., remove artifacts or to add parameterization data (e.g., object IDs) to later modify the strokes' appearance. All stroke coordinates are kept in 3D to render them onto the underlying model.

NPR Lenses are used to manipulate line rendering styles. This can be done coherently by using *G-strokes* [17]. This concept separates geometry information from stylization parameters, allowing pipeline nodes to specify and change stylization parameters for line segments. G-strokes are used in our work to capture the line style parameters' changes applied using lenses.

NPR Lenses are also based on the EPF framework [18] which places a 2D data representation onto a base plane that itself is located in the x-y-plane in 3D space. The base plane is viewed from above, perspectively projected. Different presentation styles can be created by manipulating the base plane. These manipulations (*EPF Lenses*) are functions that can be parameterized to produce the desired effects. We use this flexible and fast means to specify and compute 2D emphasis effects and, in particular, the fact that the DOE is known for any location within the lens, making it possible to affect factors other than location.

To apply lens techniques to line drawings rendered from 3D models we have to adjust the traditional rendering pipeline (Fig. 9). In the first step, as usual, silhouettes or feature lines are extracted from the model. Next, these lines are

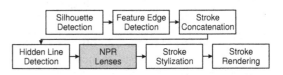

Fig. 10. Modified line rendering pipeline

concatenated to form long stokes and their visibility is determined. At this point the line data is available for the lens to modify. To add these new steps, NPR Lens nodes are inserted into the pipeline. They are applied before the line stylization and rendering stage so that the effects of the lens can be reflected in these two stages (Fig. 10). With this setup each lens takes geometric information as input and influences stylization and rendering of the lines. Each NPR Lens node introduced in the line rendering pipeline comprises four steps: (1) take a 3D input Point $P(x, y, z)$ from the list of calculated silhouette or feature line points, (2) project P to image-space yielding $P(wx, wy, wz)$, (3) obtain values from an EPF lens using wx and wy yielding a new point $P'(wx', wy', wz)$ and a degree of effect factor *doe* for this point, and (4) use all or just a subset of these values obtained from EPF as input for a specific NPR Lens.

This sequence represents a hybrid image- and object-space approach. To allow illustrators to apply emphasis effects as if a lens would be moved over a 2D line rendition, the emphasis effect has to be applied in 2D coordinates. Hence, each 3D vertex is first projected to image-space where the emphasis is applied. Then, the vertices are back-projected into 3D world-space coordinate. We need to maintain the world coordinate stroke pipeline because some further stroke processing requires world coordinates. The *doe* and new coordinate information is then used by an NPR Lens as input for modifying the style of the given line rendition to create expressive variations or to allow exploration of the model.

The computational impact of this additional pipeline step is small since only the extracted strokes have to be processed. Thus, its rendering time depends on the complexity of the processed lines and not that of the model from which the lines are derived. In fact, the bottleneck of the stroke pipeline usually lies in the silhouette edge extraction and hidden line removal and not the following stroke processing. We found that meshes suitable for line rendering (i. e., not producing too many lines that would overly clutter the image) are rendered at interactive to real-time frame rates. Thus, NPR Lenses typically do not impact the system's interactivity; only for very detailed strokes with several lenses applied the lens computation is noticeable but interactive frame rates are still maintained.

The NPR Line-Style Lens uses only the degree of effect *doe* to control the line style parameter by multiplying or adding *doe* to the previous value, resulting in changing the line style parameter's G-stroke. Adding *doe* creates more subtle effects than multiplying. The extent of the desired influence is user-controlled through setting the usual lens parameters. Similarly, we use the computed *doe* value to reveal hidden model information within the influence range of the lens by only processing vertices that have a raised *doe* value. For these vertices we now render otherwise hidden layers of the image such as hidden lines, either on top of the regular visible lines or instead of them. The new layers are smoothly blended into the surrounding context according to the *doe* to achieve visual continuity and can be given a certain (e. g., dotted) line style.

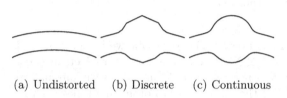

(a) Undistorted   (b) Discrete   (c) Continuous

Fig. 11. Addressing the artifacts from strong discrete distortion (b) with adaptive subdivision (c)

For creating a Spatial-Distortion Lens the 3D positions of the stroke vertices obtained from the geometric model are projected to image-space and subjected to the spatial distortion as described above. The discrete, object-space nature of this processing may introduce artifacts since the topology of the strokes is not modified: large *doe* factors result in the stepwise linear character of edges to become visible (Fig. 11(b)). This effect could be avoided by working with parametric curves between vertex positions. This in turn may result in the lines deviating too much from the expected object shape and being visually awkward. Real continuous distortion, on the other hand, is computationally impossible. It can only be emulated by using a dense set of vertices in the original strokes. This, however, increases the required storage capacity and slows down processing. Moreover, a dense vertex sampling is only required in regions with high *doe* values. Thus, we use *adaptive stroke subdivision* to approximate continuous distortion in magnified regions (Fig. 11(c)). This keeps the vertex density roughly constant and the number of additional vertices at the necessary minimum.

Object-space constraints are applied during the feature and silhouette line generation. An ID parameter is generated for each vertex that indicates from which object in the scene or model it was extracted. Based on this ID value, filtering can be applied in the NPR Lens node and only objects that are passed through the filter will be influenced by the lenses.

6   Discussion and Future Work

We suggested a number of example domains such as medical illustration (Fig. 8 and 12(a)), technical illustration (Fig. 12(b)), or even caricature (Fig. 7) where

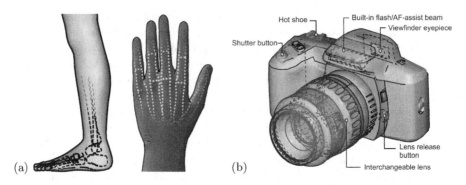

Fig. 12. Medical (a) and technical illustrations (b) using lens combinations and background shading, the latter with added annotations. Components are highlighted using color lenses and components inside the camera are shown using the Hidden-Lines Lens.

NPR Lenses can be used to create expressive effects. While we have introduced and discussed several different types of NPR Lenses, many other effects are possible with our framework. Possible other lenses could include the manipulation of line transparency or texture and the application to other line types such as hatching or stippling. Lenses could be used as brushes to add lines where desired or as erasers to remove or hide lines where they are not wanted.

NPR Lenses were built to be a useful tool for the creation of static illustrations for print-reproduction or use in electronic media. They are better suited for creating still images rather than line drawing animations. When the 3D scene is moved under a placed NPR Lens, the effects resulting from that lens do not rotate with the model but affect the new parts of the model in the influence range of the lens. This is a direct result of our spatially explicit scene adjustment approach. Making effects stay on the the objects is one possible direction of future work. Another potential direction is to apply emphasis not only to extracted lines but to the underlying mesh as well by applying a distortion to the mesh vertices and moving them in 3D space while keeping the mesh's topology. Our lenses could provide an intuitive 2D interaction method for polygonal modeling that applies effects in 3D. Preliminary results are promising (Fig. 13).

(a) Undistorted mesh

(b) One distortion step

(c) Several iterations

Fig. 13. Mesh distortion with NPR Lenses

Although we have not yet formally evaluated NPR Lenses, they have been tried by students and a professional artist. Generally, they found the tool easy to use and enjoyed adjusting and distorting the rendered line drawings. Often one person using the tool would attract attention from others and instigate more usage. Future work will include more thorough studies to assess how useful our tool is to, e. g., professional illustrators and what features they require for their work.

7 Conclusion

This paper introduces the NPR Lens interaction framework built for an easy and intuitive creation of expressive line renderings for illustration. The emphasis techniques provided in our framework are used frequently in art and illustration as a means to express emotional content, guide the user's attention, or articulate an artist's or illustrator's view of the depicted scene. NPR Lenses were developed with the intent of providing illustrators with a tool that allows for creative freedom in the illustration process. This is achieved by using 2D lens controls inside the 3D rendering pipeline, thereby integrating the advantages of 3D scene manipulation with the capabilities of spatially-explicit, viewer-aligned lenses.

NPR Lenses make four main contributions: (1) they integrate 2D input and 3D application of effects to make the application of emphasis effects with NPR Lenses as simple as the common interactions with a mouse, touchpad, or stylus; (2) they allow the seamless application of emphasis effects both locally and globally independent of a scene hierarchy; (3) they provide a common interaction approach, thereby, allowing a creative exploration of the application of effects without a priori knowledge of end goals; and (4) they support the creation of a variety of emphasis effects common in hand-drawn illustration in a single extensible interface. We hope that this research will spark new interest in the creation of NPR tools targeted at the illustration community, so that NPR techniques will be used more frequently and successfully in the future.

References

1. Gooch, B., Gooch, A.: Non-Photorealistic Rendering. A K Peters, Natick (2001)
2. Strothotte, T., Schlechtweg, S.: Non-Photorealistic Computer Graphics. In: Modelling, Animation, and Rendering, Morgan Kaufmann Publishers, San Francisco (2002) http://doi.acm.org/10.1145/544522
3. Viega, J., Conway, M.J., Williams, G., Pausch, R.: 3D Magic Lenses. In: Proc. of UIST 96, pp. 51–58. ACM Press, New York (1996) http://doi.acm.org/10.1145/237091.237098
4. Isenberg, T., Masuch, M., Strothotte, T.: 3D Illustrative Effects for Animating Line Drawings. In: Proc. of IV 2000, pp. 413–418. IEEE, Los Alamitos (2000) http://doi.ieeecomputersociety.org/10.1109/IV.2000.859790
5. Kalnins, R.D., Markosian, L., Meier, B.J., Kowalski, M.A., Lee, J.C., Davidson, P.L., Webb, M., Hughes, J.F., Finkelstein, A.: WYSIWYG NPR: Drawing Strokes Directly on 3D Models. In: ACM Transactions on Graphics, vol. 21(3), pp. 755–762. ACM Press, New York (July 2002) http://doi.acm.org/10.1145/566654.566648
6. Ropinski, T., Hinrichs, K.: Real-Time Rendering of 3D Magic Lenses Having Arbitrary Convex Shapes. Journal of WSCG 12(1–3), 379–386 (2004) http://wscg.zcu.cz/wscg2004/Papers_2004_Full/D03.pdf
7. Parent, R.: Computer Animation Algorithms and Techniques. Morgan Kaufmann, San Francisco (2002)

8. Rademacher, P.: View-Dependent Geometry. In: Proc. of SIGGRAPH 99, pp. 439–446. ACM Press, New York (1999) http://doi.acm.org/10.1145/311535.311612

9. Martín, D., García, S., Torres, J.C.: Observer Dependent Deformations in Illustration. In: Proc. of NPAR 2000, pp. 75–82. ACM Press, New York (2000) http://doi.acm.org/10.1145/340916.340926

10. Singh, K.: A Fresh Perspective. In: Proc. of GI 2002, pp. 17–24. A K Peters, Natick (2002) http://www.graphicsinterface.org/proceedings/2002/152/

11. Coleman, P., Singh, K.: RYAN: Rendering Your Animation Nonlinearly Projected. In: Proc. of NPAR 2004, pp. 129–138. ACM Press, New York (2004) http://doi.acm.org/10.1145/987657.987678

12. Foley, J.D., van Dam, A., Feiner, S.K., Hughes, J.F.: Computer Graphics: Principles and Practice in C, 2nd edn. Addison-Wesley, Reading (1990) http://doi.acm.org/10.1145/83821

13. Strothotte, T., Preim, B., Raab, A., Schumann, J., Forsey, D.R.: How to Render Frames and Influence People. Computer Graphics Forum 13(3), 455–466 (1994) http://dx.doi.org/10.1111/1467-8659.1330455

14. Winkenbach, G.A., Salesin, D.H.: Computer-Generated Pen-and-Ink Illustration. In: Proc. of SIGGRAPH 94, pp. 91–100. ACM Press, New York (1994) http://doi.acm.org/10.1145/192161.192184

15. Bier, E.A., Stone, M.C., Pier, K., Buxton, W., DeRose, T.D.: Toolglass and Magic Lenses: The See-Through Interface. In: Proc. of SIGGRAPH 93, pp. 73–80. ACM Press, New York (1993) http://doi.acm.org/10.1145/166117.166126

16. Halper, N., Isenberg, T., Ritter, F., Freudenberg, B., Meruvia, O., Schlechtweg, S., Strothotte, T.: OpenNPAR: A System for Developing, Programming, and Designing Non-Photorealistic Animation and Rendering. In: Proc. of Pacific Graphics 2003, pp. 424–428. IEEE Computer Society, Los Alamitos (2003)

17. Isenberg, T., Brennecke, A.: G-Strokes: A Concept for Simplifying Line Stylization. Computers & Graphics 30(5), 754–766 (2006) http://dx.doi.org/10.1016/j.cag.2006.07.006

18. Carpendale, S., Montagnese, C.: A Framework for Unifying Presentation Space. In: Proc. of UIST 2001, pp. 61–70. ACM Press, New York (2001) http://doi.acm.org/10.1145/502348.502358

A Sketch-and-Spray Interface for Modeling Trees

M Nordin Zakaria and Siti Rokhmah M Shukri

Universiti Teknologi Petronas, Malaysia
{nordinz,siti_rokhmah}@petronas.com.my

Abstract. We introduce in this paper an interface for modeling botanical trees that we term a sketch-and-spray interface. In using the interface, a user would sketch out various types of strokes to construct the main structures of a tree. A user could use a branch stroke to draw a single branch, a leaf stroke to draw a single leaf or a stem of leaves, or a copy stroke to draw a whole branch together with all its sub-branches and leaves. A user could also use various editing strokes to modify the tree structure. Finally, a user could spray particles upon it to 'grow' the overall shape of the tree. We illustrate the utility of our interface using a number of examples throughout this paper.

Keywords: Sketch-based modeling, tree modeling.

1 Introduction

A botanical tree is inspiring in the sense that it is ubiquitous, structured yet highly complex, and in a timeless way, beautiful. Trees have graced the Earth and have supported civilizations since the beginning of time, and in very much more recent time we have found its virtual replication to be a necessary concern in computer graphics applications such as landscape walkthrough, computer games and movie scenes. Many methods have been proposed for creating virtual tree models, and yet to this day, due to its complexity and beauty, it remains a challenge to produce a virtual tree model with plausibility close to that found in nature.

There are currently three competing approaches for producing tree models. The first approach relies on the specification of rules or procedures that describe the structure or growth of a tree, and is implemented in formalisms such as L-systems [15] and AMAP [17]. The second method relies on a library of generic models or components and allows the user to parameterize and arrange each to obtain a tree. The third approach, pioneered very recently by Okabe et al [13] in 2005, allows the user to simply sketch the tree. While the third approach is the simplest from an end-user point of view, its modeling power remains to be improved to match the complexity of trees in nature. In this paper, we build upon this third approach by introducing three simple yet effective ideas to improve the state-of-the-art in this specific modeling form.

Our first idea is to generalize the notion of a stroke in sketching a tree so that a drawing stroke need not always represent just a single branch. We refer to a stroke that represents a single branch as a *branch stroke*. A stroke could also represent a copy of another branch together with all of that branch's descendents and leaves. We

A. Butz et al. (Eds.): SG 2007, LNCS 4569, pp. 23–35, 2007.

refer to such a stroke as a *copy stroke*. It could be used to easily and controllably duplicate many of the branches in the tree. Further, a stroke could also represent a single leaf, simple or compound or clustered, that has been previously modeled. We refer to such a stroke as a *leaf stroke*. It could be used to easily deform and add individual leaves on the branches.

Fig. 1. The 'spray' in our interface

Our second idea derives from our observation that modeling a structure as complex as that of a typical leafy tree tends to be a tiring process, even if the modeling process involves just stroke-drawings. Frequently, a user is interested only in hand-modeling a few visually important branches. She does not really care about other branches as they tend to be hidden by the leaves or they are simply to be viewed from a certain distance. At the same time, the user has an idea about the overall shape to be formed by the foliages of the tree. To fulfill this need, our system supports leaf spraying – the user simply sprays leaves onto the tree model, and the system will grow branches to support the shape indicated by the spraying. Figure 1 shows the result of this spraying operation.

Our third idea is that a sketch-based modeler should allow the use of simple actions to perform a number of small yet significant (in the context of tree modeling) changes to the structure being modeled. For example, our system let the user model a simple form of buttress on the tree trunk using just a single freeform stroke. Also, our system allows the user to deform a branch stroke or a leaf blade by drawing a single stroke. Finally, our system offers the user a 'micro' version of the example-based editing described by Okabe et al [13]. While the system described by Okabe el al automatically suggest entire configurations of leaves and branches based on initial user strokes and a number of preprogrammed suggestive routines, our system implements an approach whereby the user will place sample sub-branches and leaves along a branch and the system will then interpolate further sub-branches and leaves along the branch based on the samples.

In all, the prototype system that we build as a proof-of-concept offers an interface comprising of two main interaction elements: sketching and spraying. We refer to this form of interface as a sketch-and-spray interface, and we will illustrate its benefit, using a number of examples, throughout this paper and also in the accompanying video clips.

We organize the rest of this paper as follows: In section 2, we describe prior work related to ours. In section 3, we describe the general operation of our interface. In section 4, we describe the tree-drawing interface, while in section 5, we concentrate on leaf drawing. Finally we conclude our paper in section 6. We note that in this paper, we focus primarily on describing the user interface of our system, discussing the implementation details only where the underlying algorithms we consider to be less than obvious.

2 Related Work

Prior to the work by Okabe et al [13], there were two general approaches to modeling plants. One approach focuses on visual plausibility rather than biological correctness. Linterman and Deussen [11] for example described a predefined library of components, from which a plant may be modeled. Weber and Penn [21] parameterized the description of a plant geometrically such that modeling a plant involves only specifying mostly numerical parameters describing plant attributes such as range of length and radius of branches at different branching levels. While this approach allows for relatively easy modeling, the choice of plants that can be modeled is limited by the content of the library used or the range of parameters values that can be tweaked by the user.

The second approach focuses on biological correctness. In using this approach both the programmer and the user need a substantial knowledge in plant botany (especially morphology). The L-system [15], for example, requires the user to code a grammar description of the structure of the plant to be modeled. This is far from trivial. One could attempt to start by playing around and tweaking the example L-system grammar specifications given in [15] for example, but the results obtained are generally difficult to predict and control. Ijiri et al in [8] proposed a sketch-based system to control the generation of tree structure from L-system. In their system, the user specifies the central axis of a plant by drawing a stroke. The stroke is used to determine the depth of recursion in interpretating L-system grammars. However, a grammar must still be specified by the user. Nevertheless, despite the inherent difficulty in producing grammar specifications, the L-system is a powerful tool that has be used extensively for biological studies (see the *AlgorithmicBotany* web page [1] for example).

Sketch-based modeling of plants is an example of domain-specific sketch-based interface. Aside from modeling trees, Ijiri et al [7] has also shown the utility of sketch-based modeling for the modeling of flowers while Anastacio et al [2] illustrate its use in controlling the formation of phyllotactic patterns in specific plant structures. There was relatively more work done before on general-domain sketch-based modeling. Zeleznik et al [23] in describing the SKETCH system showed how a library of sketch-based gestures could be used to simplify conventional CSG-like shape creation. Igarashi et al [5] in introducing Teddy showed how free-form models could be elegantly obtained from sketches none of which require sophisticated computer vision algorithm for interpretation. Murakawa et al [12] and Tsang et al [20] explored the use of images to guide the sketching process. Karpenko and Hughes [9] explored enhancements that allow for more sophisticated sketching strokes. Owada et al [14] discussed how 'handles' stroke could be used for copy-paste synthesis of 3D geometry. This work in particular inspires the formulation of our copy stroke and leaf stroke.

3   The User Interface

The user interface for our system, as shown in Figure 2, comprises of a tree editor and a leaf editor. A user uses the tree editor to create a tree, and the leaf editor to create a leaf. The two windows appear side by side when a user starts the application, the separation between the two windows implicitly modularizing the modeling tasks.

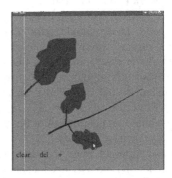

Fig. 2. Our user interface

A series of buttons at the bottom of the tree editor allows the user to go into certain editing modes. In the bending mode ("Bend" button in Figure 2), a user could bend parts of the tree. In the leaf mode ("Leaf"), a user could draw leaves on the tree. In this mode, the user could use a single leaf stroke to represent a single leaf or a cluster of leaves. The user could also spray particles upon a tree, each of which will then be replaced by a single leaf or leave cluster. In the copying mode ("Paste" and "Drag"), a user could duplicate the branches of the tree. In the buttress mode ("Buttress"), a user could deform the trunk of the tree to form simple buttress shape. In the focusing mode ("fOCUS"), a user could adjust her viewpoint to focus at a particular segment of a tree. This mode is especially useful in drawing small structures.

In both editors, we provide as well a button labeled '+'. This button when triggered creates a new branch or leaf on a selected branch based on an interpolation of existing branches or leaves on the branch. We provide as well in both editors buttons for typical operations such as clearing the screen and undoing operations.

4   Basic Interaction with the Tree Editor

To draw a tree, a user starts off using the left mouse button to draw a single freeform stroke that represents the tree trunk. A user may choose to have the resulting structure rendered with either line strokes or with shaded generalized cylinders. A double click anywhere on the background and anytime throughout the interactive session toggles between the two rendering modes. Further, a user may override the default radius of a generalized cylinder created by drawing a stroke using the middle mouse button over parts of a branch. The length of the stroke (rendered as a straight line delimited by 2 perpendicular short lines) will be used as a radius value to be interpolated along the cylinder.

With the trunk drawn, the user can then draw further strokes to create branches up to an arbitrary number of levels. While Okabe et al [13] allow the user to draw in 2D and relies on the system to automatically project the drawing into 3D space, our system allows the user to rotate the tree drawing before drawing further branches. Branches drawn will always be on the plane perpendicular to the viewing direction. Hence, the user is not restricted to directly specifying a set of branches that lie on a single flat plane.

4.1 Deforming a Branch

To deform a branch, the user first switches to the bending mode. Any further strokes drawn then that starts from a branch or trunk would be drawn as a vector stroke. The vector stroke defines the direction of an offset applied to the part of the branch from which it starts. The range of influence of the stroke on the points along the affected branch is proportional to the length of the bending stroke. A longer vector stroke affects a greater portion of the branch, and shorter one a shorter range. Figure 3 illustrates a bending operation. The rightmost picture in the figure shows the final result.

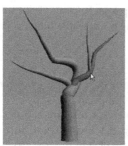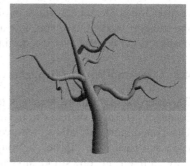

Fig. 3. Bending a Branch

An alternative approach would be to let the user simply drag the end point or certain other points on the branch and to use nonlinear least squares optimization [22] to appropriately transform other parts of the branch in a manner that preserves details and other attributes such as total length of the branch. Yet another possible approach would be to let the user redraw the branch stroke. The branch would then assume the shape of the new stroke. To preserve the details present in the original sketch, one may then adapt the surface detail transfer approach described by [19]. We do not implement either of these alternative approaches as we found our stroke deformation method to be intuitive enough in the context of tree modeling and relatively more straightforward to implement.

4.2 Adding Buttress

Our system also enables the formation of simple buttress from the main trunk. In the buttress mode, a stroke drawn starting from the trunk will be used to modify the trunk appropriately in order to extrude a simple buttress-like shape. To form this extrusion, vertices in the mesh forming the trunk are offset in the direction of corresponding points in the buttress stroke. An example buttress formation operation is shown in Figure 4.

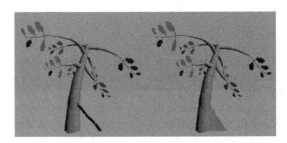

Fig. 4. Forming a buttress

An alternative approach to model a simple buttress would be to adopt the cross-sectional over-sketch described in [4]. A user would then redraw the cross-section of the trunk to modify its shape. The approach we implemented in our system however enables better control over the starting point of the buttress in the trunk.

4.3 Copy-and-Paste of Branches

The user may add more branches to a tree simply by copying and pasting existing branches. The user switches to the appropriate mode to be able to do copy-and-paste. Our system currently allows for two forms of copy-and-paste. With the first form of copy-and-paste (the "Paste" button), the user selects an existing branch, and then draws a freeform copy stroke anywhere else in the tree structure. The copy stroke will act as a deformation stroke. The selected branch along with its children branches will be deformed according to the shape of the copy stroke and placed at the new location. What actually happens with this form of copy-and-paste is that the system duplicates the data contained within the selected original branch and deforms it appropriately. When building a large tree containing many branches, memory may be an issue, however. Therefore, with the second form of copy-and-paste (the "Drag" button), the original selected branch along with its children will be uniformly rotated, scaled and translated according to the end-to-end length and direction of the copy stroke but it would not be deformed. Hence, the new branch will be just an instance of the original branch. The user can then create many more of such branches without as much worry about memory consumption.

Fig. 5. Copy-and-paste of a branch

Figure 5 shows an example copy-and-paste operation. In the leftmost picture of Figure 5, the user having selected an existing branch, draws a copy stroke. The copy stroke automatically becomes a deformed copy of the selected branch as shown in the middle picture. The rightmost picture in Figure 5 shows a rotated view, while Figure 6 shows the same tree after several repetitions of the copy-and-paste operation. Note that the tree in Figure 6 was obtained very quickly (few minutes).

Fig. 6. A tree after several copy-and-paste

4.4 Example-Based Editing

As for example-based editing, our system offers a simpler yet effective version of the functionality similar in spirit to that described in Okabe et al [13]. Suppose the user wants to draw many sub-branches on a particular branch. Using our system, the user will then draw a few sample branch strokes at sample locations along the 'mother' branch. The system will then interpolate, using a Catmull-Rom spline, the parameters of the sample strokes along the mother branch. The parameters interpolated are namely the lengths of the branch strokes, and the angle each make with the mother branch. When the user clicks on the "+" button, a new branch will be formed based on the interpolation of these characteristics.

Figure 7 shows an example use of the example-based interpolation. The leftmost picture in the figure shows the initial configuration. The middle picture shows the result after several branch strokes were added using the interpolation operation, while that on the right shows the same result rendered using cylinders. Note that there may be collision between a newly added branch and another branch in the tree. Our current implementation does not take any automated action in the event of such, leaving it to the user to either delete any of the offending branches, or leave it all as is.

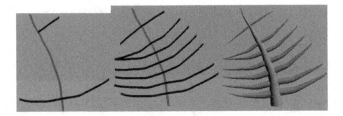

Fig. 7. Example-based interpolation

Another possible approach to implement example-based editing would be to let the user draw a graph that specifies the variation of parameters along the selected branch. A similar approach was described in [11,16]. We have not, however, implemented this approach in our system.

5   Drawing Leaves

Before a user can draw leaf strokes in the tree editor, she must first model a leaf in the leaf editor. As shown in Figure 8, to draw a leaf, she would first draw a closed contour in the leaf editor with the desired shape. The system then triangulates the contour drawn and displays a shaded leaf.

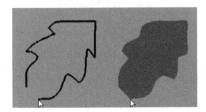

Fig. 8. Drawing a leaf contour

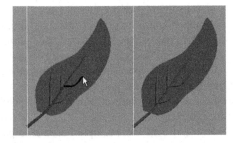

Fig. 9. Drawing secondary veins

The user proceeds to modeling a vein by drawing a stroke that starts from outside the leaf blade and ends inside it. This vein would be the primary vein and is constructed geometrically. The user can proceed on by drawing more veins. These secondary veins would be drawn as flat textures attached to the leaf blade. The algorithm we use for this vein painting is a simplified version of the texture painting algorithm described by Igarashi [6]. An example result of this vein painting operation is shown in Figure 9. For more complex venation structure with many fine tertiary veins, it may be more feasible to use a biologically-inspired approach such as that proposed by Runions et al [18].

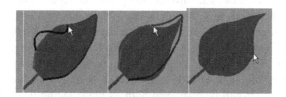

Fig. 10. Wave perturbation of leaf contour

Fig. 11. Leafy examples

Real leaves in nature tend to be crumpled rather than flat. Our current implementation allows a simple crumpling effect by letting the user specify a bend stroke at the silhouette of the leaf blade. The bend stroke is similar to that used in the tree editor, and has a similar effect on the leaf contour. The user could also bend the main vein of the leaf using a similar bend stroke. A different form of deformation happens when the user draws a wavy stroke at the silhouette of the leaf blade, as shown in Figure 11. The amplitude of the wavy stroke is interpretated to be the amplitude of a sine wave. The wavelength of the wave is computed to be a pre-defined function of the amplitude. The computed sine wave is then applied to the silhouette edges of the leaf blade.

To model leaflets or simply a stem of leaves arranged in a certain way, the user would first draw stroke representing a leaf stem at any other part of the leaf editor. The user would then draw leaf strokes along the stem, each of which defines a deformation of the base leaf model along its main vein. To implement the deformation, we adopted the algorithm described by Kho and Garland [10].

Note, however, a stroke defines a curve while a leaf blade defines a surface with a certain orientation. To tackle this disparity, our system assumes that a leaf blade is always consistently oriented with the stem to which it is attached. When the leaf object is first created, it will be displayed with its blade facing the user, and attached to a virtual stem – a vertical white line that passes through the starting tip of the main vein. This displays the default orientation of the leaf relative to any stem or branch it is to be attached to. To change this orientation, a user would simply select the leaf blade or its main vein, and use the mouse right button to rotate the leaf about an axis pointing along the base of its main vein.

Once a leaf has been modeled, we can now add leaves to a tree in the tree editor by simply drawing leaf strokes, each of which representing either a single leaf or a stem of leaves depending on the current user selection in the leaf editor.

5.1 Spraying Leaves

We can also add leaves to a tree by simply spraying points or particles upon it, as shown in Figure 1. In the leaf mode, the user begins this operation by starting a mouse drag from the background. Static particles then appear that after a few seconds, become actual leaves attached to actual branches that the system grows to accommodate the shape of the particles deposit. The miscellaneous leafy examples shown in Figure 10 all had their leaves grown using this tool.

We implement leaf spraying as follows: We first group the 2D particles into clusters such that each cluster is associated with the closest branch in 2D screen space coordinate. We do the required nearest branch search by first building a kd-tree over the points making up the branch strokes of the tree projected to screen space. Using the kd-tree, we find for each particle P, the closest point, b, on the closest branch stroke, B, and assign to it a depth value in screen space equals to that for b. The particle is then placed into the cluster, C, associated with B.

With the particles now clustered, the next step is to extrude them into 3D. The extrusion should be such that the shape of a cluster in 3D is approximately rounded. Particles near the center of a cluster should be projected further away along the viewing axis compared to a particle near the edge of a cluster. Further no two particles should be too close together. To do this extrusion, we first transform the particles to object space and then we perform a few iterations of particle dynamic simulation in which particles within a cluster C tend to repel one another over a short distance, and the particles depending on their distance from the center c of C, will tend to move away from the center. The detail of this dynamic simulation is similar to that in a typical particle simulator (see for example [3]).

We next place the clusters into a queue, Q. The aim is now to process each cluster one after another until Q is empty. We process each cluster, C_j, as follows: We iterate through the particles contained within the cluster, and for each particle, P_i, we compute its distance from the nearest point, b, on the associated branch stroke, B. If there is any distance computed that is more than a threshold *leaf_branch_distance*, we generate a new branch B_{new} starting from B with an angle *branch_angle*, and we split C_j into 2 subclusters, C_{j1} and C_{j2}. C_{j1} is associated with the original branch B and hence contained particles closer to B than to B_{new}, while C_{j2} is associated in a similar way with B_{new}. We then add the 2 new subclusters to the back of Q and proceed on to the next cluster, C_{j+1} in Q.

If a cluster C_j is not split, it means that all its particles are within the prescribed distance threshold. We then replace each point, P_i, in C_j with a leaf (or leaf stem), L_i, with a size, *leaf_size*. We place the tip of L_i at the position occupied by P_i. The base of L_i is placed at a position along the branch B that results in an angle Φ that is closest to a preset value *leaf_branch_angle*.

The variables *leaf_branch_distance*, *branch_angle*, *leaf_size*, and *leaf_branch_angle* could each be set to a default value or set according to the relevant characteristics of initial leaf strokes drawn by the user. We further note that the leaf placement algorithm could be made to be more sophisticated in order that the appearance of the final foliages appears more natural. We leave this, however, as our future work.

It would also be convenient to allow the user to simply draw a tree contour as done in [13] and then sample leaf points within the contour. We have not implemented this. But we note that spraying allows for more complex foliage shape formation than simple contouring, and has a feel to it that is similar to when one uses the spraying functions commonly implemented in drawing applications such Microsoft Paint.

6 Conclusion

We have described a user interface that incorporates a number of simple yet effective ideas for sketch-based modeling of trees. In using our user interface, a single open stroke need not just represent a single branch, but it could also represent a leaf or a collection of branches and/or leaves. Further not everything needs to be expressed in the form of sketches. A spray metaphor could be an equally expressive form of interaction when it comes to adding leaves to a tree drawing. Finally, we introduced a number of simple yet effective sketching tools to enhance the modeling process.

In the future, we intend to investigate better algorithms to improve the output from the spraying process. Also, we intend to start a user study to study the effectiveness of our user interface in modeling real trees.

References

1. Algorithmic Botany website: www.algorithmicbotany.org
2. Anastacio, F., Sousa, M.C., Samavati, F., Jorge, J.: Modeling Plant Structures Using Concept Sketches. In: 4th International Symposium on Non Photorealistic Animation and Rendering (NPAR '06) Annecy, France (June 2006)
3. Baraff, D., Witkin, A.: Physically Based Modeling. In: SIGGRAPH 2001 course notes (2001)
4. Cherlin, J.J., Samavati, F., Sousa, M.C., Jorge, J.A.: Sketch-based Modeling with Few Strokes. In: 21st Spring Conference on Computer Graphics (SCCG 2005) Budmerice, Slovak Republic (May 2005)
5. Igarashi, T., Matsuoka, S., Tanaka, H.: Teddy: A Sketching Interface for 3D Freeform Design. In: Proceedings of SIGGRAPH 1999, pp. 409–416 (1999)
6. Igarashi, T.,Cosgrove, D.: Adaptive Unwrapping for Interactive Texture Painting, ACM Symposium on Interactive 3D Graphics, ACM I3D'01 Research Triangle Park, NC, pp. 209–216 (March 19-21, 2001)
7. Ijiri, T., Okabe, M., Owada, S., Igarashi, T.: Floral Diagrams and Inflorescences: Interactive Flower Modeling using Botanical Structural Constraints, ACM Transactions on Computer Graphics. In: ACM SIGGRAPH 2005, vol. 24(3), Los Angels, USA (2005)
8. Ijiri, T., Owada, S., Igarashi, T.: The Sketch L-System: Global Control of Tree Modeling Using Free-form Strokes, Smart Graphics 2006, pp. 138–146. Vanvcouver, Canada (2006)
9. Karpenko, O.A., Hughes, J.F.: SmoothSketch: 3D Free-Form Shapes from Complex Sketches, ACM Transactions on Graphics. In: Proceedings of ACM SIGGRAPH 2006, vol. 25(3), pp. 89 – 598 (July 2006)
10. Kho, Y., Garland, M.: Sketching Mesh Deformations. In: Proceedings of the ACM Symposium on Interactive 3D Graphics, pp. 147–154 (April 2005)
11. Lintermann, B., Deussen, O.: Interactive Modeling of Plants. IEEE Computer Graphics and Applications 19(1), 56–65 (1999)
12. Murakawa, J., Hong, T., Yoon, I., Lank, E.: Parts, Image, and Sketch based 3D Modeling Method. In: Proceedings of Sketch-Based Interfaces and Modeling, SBIM 2006 (2006)
13. Okabe, M., Owada, S., Igarashi, T.: Interactive Design of Botanical Trees Using Freehand Sketches and Example-based Editing, Computer Graphics Forum. In: Eurographics 2005, Aug 29 - Sep 02, vol. 24(3), Trinity College, Dublin, Ireland (2005)
14. Owada, S., Nielsen, F., Nakazawa, K., Igarashi, T.: Copy-paste Synthesis of 3D Geometry with Repetitive Patterns. In: Smart Graphics 2006, LNCS, vol. 4073, pp. 184–193. Springer-Verlag, Heidelberg (2006)
15. Prusinkiewicz, P., Lindenmayer, A.: The Algorithmic Beauty of Plants. Springer, Heidelberg (1996)
16. Prusinkiewicz, P., Mündermann, L., Karwowski, R., Lane, B.: The Use of Positional Information in the Modeling of Plants. In: Proceedings of SIGGRAPH 2001, pp. 289-300 (2001)
17. Reffye, P.d., Edelin, C., Francon, J., Jaeger, M., Puech, C.: Plant Models Faithful to Botanical Structure and Development, Computer Graphics, vol. 22(4) (August 1988)
18. Runions, A., Fuhrer, M., Lane, B., Federl, P., Rolland-Lagan, A.-G., Prusinkiewicz, P.: Modeling and Visualization of Leaf Venation Patterns. ACM Transactions on Graphics vol. 24(3), pp. 702–711
19. Sorkine, O., Cohen-Or, D., Lipman, Y., Alexa, M., Rössl, C., Seidel, H.-P.: Laplacian Surface Editing, 2004 Eurographics/ACM SIGGRAPH symposium on Geometry processing, July 08-10. Nice, France (2004)

20. Tsang, S., Balakrishnan, R., Singh, K., Ranjan, A.: A Suggestive Interface for Image Guided 3D Sketching. In: Proceedings of the 2004 conference on Human factors in computing systems, pp. 591–598. Vienna, Austria (2004)
21. Weber, J., Penn, J.: Creation and Rendering of Realistic Trees. In: SIGGRAPH '95 Proceedings, pp. 119–128 (August 1995)
22. Weng, Y., Xu, W., Wu, Y., Zhou, K., Guo, B.: 2D Shape Deformation using Nonlinear Least Squares Optimization. Visual Computer 22, 653–660 (2006)
23. Zeleznik, R.C., Herndon, K.P., Hughes. J.F.: SKETCH: An Interface for Sketching 3d Scenes.In: Proceedings of SIGGRAPH 1996, pp. 163–170 (1996)

Sketching-Out Virtual Humans: A Smart Interface for Human Modelling and Animation

Chen Mao, Sheng Feng Qin, and David Wright

School of Engineering and Design, Brunel University, Uxbridge, UB8 3PH, UK
{Chen.Mao, Sheng.Feng.Qin, David.Wright}@brunel.ac.uk

Abstract. In this paper, we present a fast and intuitive interface for sketching out 3D virtual humans and animation. The user draws stick figure key frames first and chooses one for "fleshing-out" with freehand body contours. The system automatically constructs a plausible 3D skin surface from the rendered figure, and maps it onto the posed stick figures to produce the 3D character animation. A "creative model-based method" is developed, which performs a human perception process to generate 3D human bodies of various body sizes, shapes and fat distributions. In this approach, an anatomical 3D generic model has been created with three distinct layers: skeleton, fat tissue, and skin. It can be transformed sequentially through rigid morphing, fatness morphing, and surface fitting to match the original 2D sketch. An auto-beautification function is also offered to regularise the 3D asymmetrical bodies from users' imperfect figure sketches. Our current system delivers character animation in various forms, including articulated figure animation, 3D mesh model animation, 2D contour figure animation, and even 2D NPR animation with personalised drawing styles. The system has been formally tested by various users on Tablet PC. After minimal training, even a beginner can create vivid virtual humans and animate them within minutes.

Keywords: sketching interface, human modelling and animation, creative model-based method, multi-layered generic model, morphing.

1 Introduction

Human modelling and animation has been an essential theme of computer graphics for many decades. Nowadays, their application has penetrated a great variety of fields, including industry, military, biomedicine, and education. In today's public entertainment, virtual humans are playing a particularly remarkable role when engaged in 3D games, Hollywood films, and multimedia (virtual human presenter).

Current virtual human generation methods can be classified into three major categories: creative [1][2], reconstructive [3][4], and interpolated [5][6]. Although these approaches are capable of creating highly realistic human body models with various appearances and motions, they require extensive expertise, special equipment (traditional/video camera, 3D body scanner, motion capture system, etc), and proficient computer skills. Therefore, it is extremely difficult for regular users (2D

A. Butz et al. (Eds.): SG 2007, LNCS 4569, pp. 36–48, 2007.

artists/designers and ordinary users) to participate and create their own 3D virtual human models.

Sketching, however, is probably one of the most popular and approachable ways to quickly rough out characters and their motions. Since ancient times, from the proficient to novice, people have, with ease and familiarity, drawn their imaginary or real characters with pencil and paper. Hence, developing a sketch-based tool is crucial. It can transfer ordinary users into the 3D animation world via their favoured medium - *sketching*.

Regarding sketch-based human modelling and animation, two categories of related work can be basically identified: *sketch-based 3D freeform modelling* and *sketch-based character animation*. The former research category represented by [7][8] transfers users' 2D freehand drawings into 3D freeform surfaces of stuffed toys, simple clothes, car/furniture models, etc, in various ways. However, sketch-based 3D human body modelling has remained a difficult undertaking, which has rarely been addressed before. Since the human body has an irregular and complex surface and our eyes are especially sensitive to the human figure, current modelling techniques constrained by their underlying construction schemes, are inadequate for obtaining plausible results. Moreover, these interfaces accept mainly single and clean stroke input and enforce a "part-by-part" drawing routine, where one sketch stroke often specifies the shape of an entire object part and modelling an object is more like assembling a handcraft toy than real freehand sketching.

The current research on sketch-based character animation is demonstrated by various sketching interfaces for articulated figure animation [9][10], motion doodling [11], cartoon storyboarding [12], etc. Although impressive, many of these systems deal with simple characters, rather than sophisticated human characters with realistic and various appearances. Moreover, none of them has delivered a complete picture of "sketch-based modelling and animation", including key framing, figure pose recognition, 2D-3D surface modelling, and the resulting animations performed by various levels of characters.

In this paper, we present our new method and a novel sketching interface, which enable anyone who can draw to "sketch-out" 3D virtual humans and animation. Our sketching interface can automatically transfer users' 2D figure sketches into 3D human bodies of various body sizes, shapes and fat distributions. It supports a natural drawing process and allows rough and sketchy 2D figure input (with multi-stroke profiles, missing body contours, and drawing imperfections). Users can incrementally modify their 3D models by over-sketching 2D figure. The resulting animations can be delivered in various forms, including articulated figure animation, 3D mesh model animation, 2D contour figure animation, and even 2D NPR animation with personalised drawing styles.

Fig. 1 illustrates the graphical pipeline of this virtual human sketching interface. Users first draw stick figure key frames to define a specific motion. Then, they can "flesh-out" any existing stick figure with body profiles to portray an imaginative character. The system can automatically "perceive" the body size (skeleton proportion) and shape (body profile and fat distribution) from the sketched figure, and transfer it into a 3D virtual character through continuous graphical comparisons and generic model morphing (*rigid morphing, fatness morphing,* and *surface fitting*). Our anatomical generic model is created from Visible Human cross-section images [13], which are encapsulated with three distinct layers: skeleton, fat tissue, and skin for undertaking both geometric and physical morphing. The resulting 3D skin surface can be mapped onto each of the posed stick figure key frames [16], which can be further interpolated as final 2D/3D animations. Here, the 3D poses are reconstructed from 2D stick figure sketches through a "multi-layered back-front ambiguity clarifier" [10].

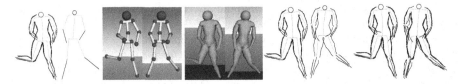

Fig. 1. Sketching out a virtual human and animating it in both 2D and 3D world

2   Sketch-Based Human Modelling and Animation Pipeline

As in [14], humans are accustomed to doing the reverse projection of sketched geometry from 2D back into 3D. It is, however, mathematically indeterminate and very difficult to emulate computationally. To decompose the complexity of direct 3D modelling and animation from 'noisy' figure sketches (featured by foreshortening, contour over-tracing, body part overlapping, shading/shadow, etc.), we designed a "Stick Figure [10]→Fleshing-out→Skin Mapping" pipeline (described in Section 1). This is inspired by the drawing sequence recommended by many sketch books. In principle, it echoes the modelling and animation pipeline in commercial packages (e.g. 3DS MAX, Maya). Regarding our current design, functionalities at different levels are gained for different users. Thus they can choose to make simple stick figures, create delicate 3D surface models, or explore further to animate these sketch-generated creatures. Moreover, models can be exported to commercial packages at any level to be refined by their function kits.

3   Creative Model-Based 3D Body Generation Scheme

As discussed earlier, humans are capable of instinctively perceiving a 'noisy' 2D figure sketch as a realistic 3D body. Thus, understanding this perception process is essential for realising the automatic 2D-to-3D reconstruction. Since we see and interact with people everyday, our brain has been familiarised with various body shapes and the correlations between 2D flat features and their real 3D counterparts [14]. Therefore, when observing a raw figure sketch, our brain can automatically clean-up the distracting 'noises', perceive the body size and shape, recall an associated body shape from memory, and then morph it and fit it into the 2D drawing to obtain the final 3D image. Theoretically, if given a range of pre-stored morphable template bodies, a computer is able to perform this as well, through performing the similar 'thinking', 'recalling', and morphing routines.

In terms of the 3D body templates, the statistically parameterised models generated from [5][6] may provide a rich resource of realistic human body shapes. However, each figure sketch depicts an imaginative character, which has a unique and even unrealistic body shape that often blends the features of many different bodies, together with its individualised attributes. Thus, it is very hard to find a matching model from the existing body geometries through a fixed number of sizing parameters. Since the human brain is able to morph the body shape both geometrically and physically to fit-in the 2D sketch, it is necessary to introduce more physical layers (i.e. fat, muscle) into the current two-layered (skeleton-skin) digital template [5][6], to match it more flexibly into the 2D drawing with plausible effects. In our system, we adopted a three-layered (skeleton-fat tissue-skin) anatomical model, because compared with muscle, the fat condition is more variable and dominant in affecting the overall body shape.

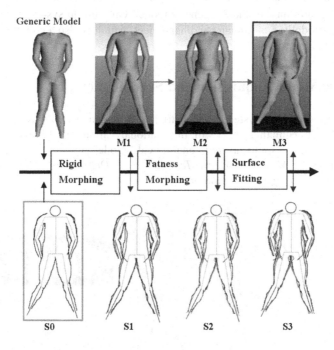

Fig. 2. Transfer a 2D freehand sketch into the 3D body model through an automatic perception and morphing process: Users draw a 2D figure (S0). The system automatically retrieves its 3D pose and body proportion, and performs a rigid morphing on the 3D generic model. The resulting 3D model M1 is projected into 2D (blue lines in S1) and compared with the original sketch (black lines) to evaluate its body fat distribution. M1 is then deformed through fatness morphing into M2, which is projected (green lines in S2) and compared again with the 2D sketch to get the fitting measurements. The final 3D model (M3) is delivered to users, after an automatic surface fitting and beautification process (on M2). Users can incrementally refine their 2D sketches; a similar perception process is performed to update the 3D model.

We investigated a "Creative Model-based Method", which can perceive the size and shape of a sketched figure and transfer it into a plausible 3D counterpart model, through continuous graphical comparisons and template morphing (see Fig. 2). Our

3-layered generic model is digitised from the anatomical male cross-section images of The Visible Human Project® [13]. Although only one template model is employed in the current system, our generic model acquisition technique can be easily replicated on the CT cross-section images generated from whole body CT scanning equipment [15], to create a population of layered generic models of males, females, children, and elderly people for modelling purposes. Since each model is morphable in both geometric and physical senses, it can generate a variety of new body shapes on its own to further expand the template database and enrich virtual human population. After obtaining an initial 3D model from the 2D sketch, incremental modification can be made to change the global body shape. Since a "Stick Figure → Fleshing out" routine is followed, this sketch-generated model is readily animatable. It inherits the skin binding conditions[1] of the 3D generic model. Our current system cannot support sketch-based modelling of human head/hands/feet, which is also a common challenge for other related approaches.

4   Generic Model Acquisition and Specification

The generic model in our system is reconstructed from cadaveric cross-section images from the Visible Human Project® of the National Library of Medicine [13]. The preparation of this multi-layered anatomical model entails: *Virtual Skeleton Registration, Skin Mesh Recovery, Template Fat Distribution Digitisation,* and *Template Fat Percentage Manipulation.*

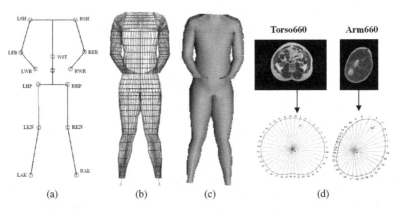

(a)   (b)   (c)   (d)

Fig. 3. (a) The template skeleton (joint -red circle, body root-blue circle). (b) The wireframe 3D generic model. (c) The rendered 3D generic model (d) Ray casting the cross section images for each body part (torso-40 rays, limbs-36 rays) to digitise the 3D template from the human cadaveric images. The ray centre O is the estimated sectional bone position. The image index indicates the corresponding body part and the distance from the head top to the give cross-section slice.

---

[1] In the multi-layered generic model, the skin is bound to the underlying skeleton through assigning the affecting bones and corresponding weights for each mesh vertex.

4.1   Virtual Skeleton Recovery and Skin Mesh Recovery

To apply our simplified skeleton model [10] to the anatomical human body, we used a semi-automatic image registration method. After the skeleton adaptation, the extracted bone/joint measurements are further normalised to achieve the template skeleton, which conforms to the system's pre-stored reference skeletons. To digitise the skin mesh, we divide the overall body into individual parts, and perform "ray casting" (see Fig. 3(d)) for each body part on their indexed/calibrated cross-section images. The ray centres here are acquired from linear interpolation of the neighbouring template joints. The 3D template mesh is constructed by connecting all 3D casting points horizontally and vertically, which results in a wire frame model with 3136 vertices (see Fig. 3(b)). This quadpatch grid structure enables easy feature extraction from raw figure sketches, and the piecewise affine transformation of the 3D template.

4.2   Template Fat Distribution Digitisation

Instead of a general fat distribution [6] describing typical body shapes (i.e. apple, pear), we developed a comprehensive distribution map (see Fig. 4), comprising the fat accumulating condition for each body part, each cross section, and each skin point.

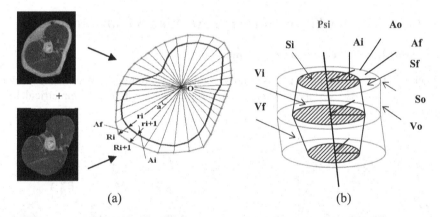

(a)   (b)

Fig. 4. (a) Ray casting each pair of cross section images (with and without fat layer) to retrieve the inner and outer radii for each sectional ray. (b) Digitise the template fat distribution.

As illustrated in Fig. 4, we firstly execute "ray-casting" for each pair of cross section images (with and without the fat layer). Secondly, given the extracted inner and outer radii, the value of A_i and A_o (angular inner and outer area) and S_i and S_o (sectional inner and overall area) is computed. Thirdly, given the vertical distance in-between each pair of cross-sections, the inner and overall volume (V_i and V_o) for each body part is calculated. Correspondingly, the fat value A_f, S_f and V_f is obtained. Next, to digitise the template fat distribution, we first use $P_b = V_f/V_o$ and $P_s = S_f/S_o$ to compute the fat percentages for each body part (P_b) and its sample cross-sections ($P_{s1},...P_{sn}$). We then encode the sectional fat distribution features as: $D_{si} = P_{si}/P_b$ (i=1, 2,...n), where n is equal to the number of cross sections for a certain body part. Given the sectional fat area (S_f) and angular fat area ($A_{f1},...A_{fm}$), the angular fat distribution is encoded as $D_{ai} = A_{fi}/S_f$ (i=1, 2,...m), where m is equal to 36 and 40 for the limb and torso respectively. Next, to morph this anatomical model with new body part fat percentages, we assume that the new fat accumulates proportionally according to the original template fat distribution (preserving D_{si} and D_{ai} unchanged). Then, the corresponding skin vertex positions can be updated through this fattening scheme.

4.3 Template Fat Percentage Manipulation

On the completion of *template fat distribution* digitisation, we investigated a *body-fattening scheme*, through which the 3D generic model can be 'physically' morphed when given a set of new fat percentage values of individual body parts. These new body part fat percentages are deduced from a user's figure sketch (see Section 5). We assume that the fat is distributed according to the original *template fat distribution* (D_{si} and D_{ai} unchanged)[2], whilst the inner body stays relatively invariable (S_i and A_i unchanged). Thus, given a new body part fat percentage P_b, the new sectional fat percentages P_{si} (i=1, 2, ... n) and angular fat areas A_{fi} (i=1, 2, ... m) can be calculated. Then, preserving the inner radii (r_i) value, the corresponding skin vertex positions can be updated when outer radii (R_i) change.

5   From 2D Raw Figure Sketch to 3D Human Body Model

5.1   On-Line Curve Stroke Processing

Freehand figure sketching is essentially rough and imprecise. It contains various "noises" – wiggly/overlapping strokes, missing figure contours, asymmetrical body parts, as shown in Fig. 5(a).

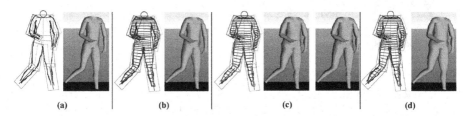

(a)   (b)   (c)   (d)

Fig. 5. (a) The input 2D freehand sketch and the 3D model after rigid morphing. (b) Graphical comparison to get the fat distribution measurements and the fatness morphed model (c) Graphical comparison to get the surface fitting measurements; the model with and without auto-beautification (d) Over-tracing body contour (right lower torso, left lower leg, and right leg) to modify an existing 3D surface model.

In this on-line drawing system, each curve stroke is processed (through stroke identification/segmentation) to identify its locating bone, given the pre-defined bone

---

[2] Everyone has a specific body fat distribution pattern, which is generally preserved when a body fattens or slims. In brief, the area with more fat is more likely to accumulate new fat, and vice versa.

bounding boxes (see Fig. 6(a)). The default bounding box sizes are determined heuristically based on the generic model proportion and a general body physique. Users can interactively adjust the bounding box sizes (e.g. when drawing a large human) and choose to show or hide the bounding boxes according to their needs. Then, this stroke is labeled (according to its assigned bone) and stored for later feature extraction use.

5.2 Rigid Morphing and Body Feature Point Extraction

Once the user completes a figure sketch and chooses to reconstruct the 3D model, a system automatic process starts for *rigid morphing*, *fatness morphing* and *surface fitting*. Rigid morphing is to deform the 3D generic model against the new body proportion and posture of the sketched figure. In our system, a "multi-layered back-front ambiguity clarifier" [10] is developed to recover the 3D pose from the 2D figure sketch. A skeleton-driven skin deformation technique [16] is applied for rigid morphing. After rigid morphing, the updated 3D template is projected onto 2D (Fig. 5(b)) to obtain the body silhouette and 2D cross lines (projected from template cross-section slices). Then, indexed intersection points (template feature points) are found between 2D cross lines and the parsed template silhouette. We use Tf [Lf_{ij}, Rf_{ij}] to save this *template feature point* set, where Lf_{ij} and Rf_{ij} represent the feature point lists on the left and right side of each body part. (i - body part index, j - cross section index). Similarly, intersection points (*sketch feature point* set Sf [Lf_{ij}', Rf_{ij}']) are found between the saved sketch strokes and the template cross lines. Here, an average left/right feature point is taken if there are more than one intersection points extracted on either side of a body part (for each section) because of multiple rendering stokes.

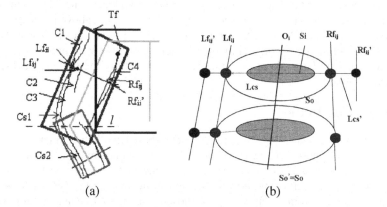

(a)   (b)

Fig. 6. (a) 2D raw sketch processing. For multi-strokes C1, C2 and C3, an average point Lf_{ij}' is computed among the corresponding sectional intersection points. The stroke C4 is located in both the upper torso and upper arm bounding area. After "stroke identification", it is assigned to the upper arm due to a minimum in-between angle with the upper arm than the upper torso. A long stroke C3 is first segmented into stroke Cs1 and Cs2 (through "stroke segmentation"), which are further checked upon the locating bones. (b) Fat distribution estimation.

5.3 Fat Distribution Estimation and Fatness Morphing

The rigid-morphed 3D template model (see Fig. 5(a)) is used to estimate the body part fat percentages of the 2D sketched figure. Here, we assume that when a body fattens/slims, its inner volume stays relatively unchanged compared with the fat volume. That is, for each body cross-section, only its overall area enlarges when new fat accumulates whilst its inner area stays invariant. In this sense, the fat percentage of each body part on a 2D figure drawing can be estimated through graphical comparison. As shown in Fig. 6(b), since the template inner area S_i and outer area S_o are known for each cross-section, a new outer area $S_o{}'$ can be calculated for the given cross section through $S_o{}' = S_o * (L_{cs}{}' / L_{cs})$ (whilst $S_i{}' = S_i$). $L_{cs}{}'$ and L_{cs} here stand for the corresponding cross line lengths on the 2D template and sketched figure, which can be obtained by computing the distance between the previously extracted sketch feature points ($Lf_{ij}{}'$, $Rf_{ij}{}'$) and the template feature points (Lf_{ij}, Rf_{ij}). For some cross-sections that have missing sketch points, $L_{cs}{}'$ is set to be equal to L_{cs}. After getting the $S_i{}'$ and $S_o{}'$ for each cross section, a new body part fat percentage $P_b{}'$ can be obtained as described in Section 4.2, given a set of known cross section in-between distances. Through this graphical comparison process, body part fat percentages across the whole body can be estimated for the 2D sketched figure. A fatness-morphed model (see Fig. 5(b)) can be achieved through deforming the rigid-morphed generic model according to the pre-defined body-fattening scheme (Section 4.3), given a set of new fat percentage input. As illustrated, after fatness morphing, 3D body is "biologically" transformed with fattened belly and thighs.

5.4 Surface Fitting and Interactive 3D Model Modification

After that, surface fitting is performed to match the 3D template with the 2D sketch. Here, an auto-beautification option is provided to regularise the 3D asymmetrical body from users' drawing imperfections (Fig. 5(c)). After the above processing, users are given a realistic 3D character model from their freehand sketch. Then, they can interactively refine this 3D model by over-sketching its 2D figure profiles (Fig. 5(d)). Modifications can be made at any time and on any key frame sketch to achieve the updated 3D model.

5.5 Results and Discussion

As shown in Fig. 7 and Fig 9(top), our sketch-based modelling interface transfers users' freehand figure sketches into plausible 3D human models of various body proportions, shapes, and postures. After illustrating a stick figure posture, users can flesh it out in flexible drawing sequences with natural and artistic contour strokes, like drawing on an electronic canvas. Fig. 7 shows a series of freehand figure sketches (featured by multiple/overlapping strokes, body part foreshortening/occlusion, and drawing imperfections) and their 3D counterpart models in a mixture of figure postures (e.g. Fig. 7a/e – kneeling, Fig. 7b – picking, Fig. 7c – dancing, and Fig. 7d – sitting), drawing views (e.g. Fig. 7a/d – side views, Fig. 7b/c/e – front views), and body shapes (varied body proportions and fat distribution). Our system can handle figure sketches with large overlying areas as shown in Fig. 7a, 7b, 7c, and 7e. Here, the occlusion order of the overlying body parts is solved by identifying the orientation of foreshortened body parts. The problem of missing body contours is handled by labeling the unfilled sketch feature points and processing them specifically during template morphing. Fig. 9(top) shows a range of human body shapes (e.g. apple, pear, hourglass, etc, with distinct body sizes and fat distributions) and even a super human model (S8) generated by different users in a formal user test of our system.

Although our current human models are not as realistic as those generated from [1][5][6] for commercial use, we aimed to provide an intuitive and low-cost tool to enable non-professional users (2D artists and ordinary users) to sketch-out virtual humans and animation for design and entertaining purposes. Since people draw differently with varied drawing skills, the resulting 3D model should primarily match the original sketch as well as showing reasonably plausible effects to meet users' expectation. Therefore, a realistic 3D body model from a rough figure sketch may appear unnatural and may inhibit creativity. Moreover, our system is meant to be a fast prototyping machine for the early stage of virtual human modelling and animation. Therefore, the sketch-generated 3D characters and motions from our system can be exported to and refined by commercial tools to meet practical needs.

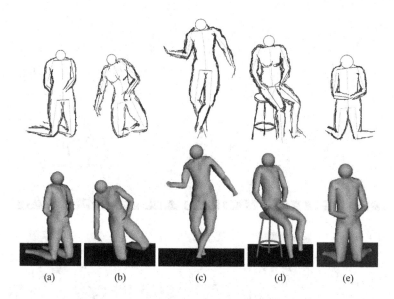

(a)   (b)   (c)   (d)   (e)

Fig. 7. Freehand 2D figure sketches and the reconstructed 3D human body models; the inner contours on some sketches (b, d) were added after 3D model generation, which shows the needs of depicting detailed surface shape through more rendering forms (e.g. suggestive contours).

6   Creating 2D and 3D Virtual Human Animation

Following the "Stick Figure→Fleshing-out→Skin Mapping" pipeline, a 3D virtual human animation is accomplished by wrapping the sketch-generated skin surface onto a series of posed stick figures, which can be further interpolated via VRML. Our system generates 2D silhouette/NPR animation by successively interpolating the extracted key figure contours (with the mapped fleshing-out contours) and playing

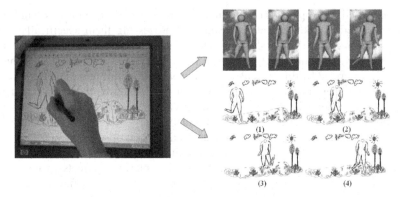

Fig. 8. (Left) The user is sketching-out a virtual human and its motion on a Tablet PC; (Top right) A sketch-generated 3D dancing character; (Bottom right) A 2D NPR animation played on the sketching interface in a doodled countryside view

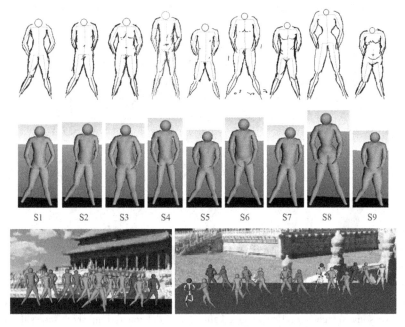

Fig. 9. (Top) A variety of 3D virtual humans and the original drawings created from different users: an artist (S3), a designer (S4), an animator (S6, S7), graduate students (S1, S2, S5, and S9), and a child (S8). (Bottom left) A population of user-created 3D virtual humans (skin colours varied by authors) are playing Chinese Kungfu together in a vivid 3D world with music (the pink ball on the ground is a music trigger). (Bottom right) A crowd of virtual humans and stick figures are fighting with each other in a 3D virtual world. Two of them (the 5th from the left, and the furthest right figures) are performing different actions. It shows individuality among the collective behaviour.

their in-betweens on sketching interface. Fig. 8 shows the snapshots of a 2D NPR animation in a doodled countryside view. Beside the single character animation, our system offers the opportunity to create group animation of a population of virtual humans and to storyboard intercommunications between virtual humans [17] (Fig 9).

7 Implementation and User Experiences

Our prototype modelling and animation system is implemented by Microsoft Visual C++, MATLAB, and VRML. This system has been tested by various users (including artists, an animator, undergraduates and postgraduates, and a 12-year-old boy) through performance tests, sketching observation, and user interviews. After a short tutorial, users rapidly learned the modelling process, and began to sketch-out their own virtual human animation (on Tablet PC) within minutes (6.27 and 6.75 minutes on average for a three-frame stick figure and full figure animation respectively). More details on our user tests and user-centred design approaches have been presented in [18]. Fig. 9 (Top) shows the sketches and various human bodies created by users, which have been integrated into two group animations, shown in Fig. 9 (Bottom).

8 Conclusions and Future Work

In this paper, we have presented our new method and a fast/novel interface for sketching out 3D virtual humans and animation. We investigated a "creative model-based method", which performs a human perception process to transfer 2D freehand sketches into 3D human bodies with various body sizes, shapes, and fat distributions. We created an anatomical three-layered model, which can be morphed against the "perceived" features of the original figure sketch. Our system is well designed for tolerating the abstraction, ambiguity, and imprecision of natural sketches. In the future, we are going to extend our generic template database to allow the generation of a wider range of virtual humans. We plan to improve our current 2D-to-3D modelling techniques to handle more complicated figure poses (e.g. lying) and views (e.g. back view), and to enhance the complexity of the body surface. We propose to adopt more rendering forms including suggestive contours [18], shading, etc, to depict subtle surface features. Moreover, we intend to implement sketch-based modelling of human heads/hands/feet and clothes to deliver a more sophisticated character model.

References

1. Turner, R., Gobbetti, E.: Interactive Construction and Aanimation of Layered Elastically Deformable Characters, Computer Graphics Forum, vol. 17(2) , pp. 135–152 (1998)
2. Choi, J.J.: MAYA Character Animation. 2nd edition, San Francisco, Calif.: London: SYBEX (2004)
3. Fua, P.: Human Modelling from Video Sequence. Geometric Info. Magazine 13(7), 63–65 (1999)

4. Lee, W., Gu, J., Magnenat-Thalmann, N.: Generating Animatable 3D Virtual Humans from Photographs, Computer Graphics Forum. In: Proc. Eurographics '2000 19(3), 1–10 (2000)
5. Anguelov, D., Srinivasan, P., Koller, D., Thrun, S., Rodgers, J.: SCAPE: Shape Completion and Animation of People. In: Proc. SIGGRAPH 05, pp. 408–416 (2005)
6. Seo, H., Magnenat-Thalmann, N.: An Example-based Approach to Human Body Manipulation. Graphical Models 66(1), 1–23 (2004)
7. Igarashi, T., Matsuoka, S., Tanaka, H.: Teddy: A Sketching Interface for 3D Freeform Design. In: Proc. SIGGRAPH '99, pp. 409–416 (1999)
8. Karpenko, O., Hughes, J.F., Raskar, R.: Free-form Sketching with Variational Implicit Surfaces. In: Proc. Eurographics 2002, vol. 21(3) (2002)
9. Davis, J., Agrawala, M., Chuang, E., Popović, Z., Salesin, D.: A Sketching Interface for Articulated Figure Animation. In: Proc. Eurographics/ SIGGRAPH Symposium on Computer Animation, pp. 320–328 (2003)
10. Mao, C., Qin, S.F., Wright, D.K.: A Sketch-based Gesture Interface for Rough 3D Stick Figure Animation. In: Proc. of Eurographics Workshop on Sketch Based Interfaces and Modeling, pp. 175–183 (2005)
11. Thorne, M., Burke, D., van de Panne, M.: Motion Doodles: An Interface for Sketching Character Animation. ACM Transactions on Graphics (TOG) 23(3), 424–431 (2004)
12. Hoshino, J., Hoshino, Y.: Intelligent Storyboard for Prototyping Animation. In: Proc. IEEE Int. Conf. On Multimedia and Expo (2001)
13. National Library of Medicine: The Virtual Human Project, http://www.nlm.nih.gov/research/visible/visiblehuman.html
14. Lipson, H., Shpitalni, M.: Correlation-based Reconstruction of a 3D Object from a Single Freehand Sketch. In: Proc. AAAI Spring Symposium Series - Sketch Understanding (2002)
15. EPA: Information on Whole Body Scanning, http://www.epa.nsw.gov.au/radiation/ctbodyscans.htm
16. Weber, J.: Run-time Skin Deformation, Intel Architecture Labs, http://www.intel.com/ial/3dsoftware/index.htm
17. Mao, C., Qin, S.F., Wright, D.K.: Sketching-out Virtual Humans: from 2D Storyboarding to Immediate 3D Character Animation. In: Proc.of ACM SIGCHI International Conference on Advances in Computer Entertainment Technology, Hollywood, Los Angeles (2006)
18. Mao, C., Qin, S.F., Wright, D.K., Peng, J.: Applying Scenarios in User-Centred Design to Develop A Sketching Interface for Human Modelling and Animation. In: Proc. of Eurographics Workshop on Sketch Based Interfaces and Modeling, pp. 147–156 (2006)
19. DeCarlo, D., Finkelstein, A., Rusinkiewics, S., Santella, A.: Suggestive Contours for Conveying Shape. ACM Transaction on Graphics 22(3), 848–855 (2003)

A Novel Human Computer Interaction Paradigm for Volume Visualization in Projection-Based Virtual Environments

Changming He, Andrew Lewis, and Jun Jo

Griffith University, School of Information and Communication, Australia
{c.he,a.lewis,j.jo}@griffith.edu.au

Abstract. We propose a novel Human Computer Interaction (HCI) paradigm for volume visualization in projection-based immersive virtual environments (VEs). This paradigm is intuitive, highly efficient and allows accurate control over the virtual objects. A *fine control mode* for direct manipulation is proposed to address the low accuracy problem of virtual object manipulation in VEs. An *agent object* interaction method is proposed to provide more flexibility in manipulating the volume objects. A *two-handed scaling* method is proposed to conveniently scale the volume object along one, two, or three axes. Finally, a *ghost object paradigm* is proposed to address the motion constraint problem for virtual objects. An implementation using a 3-state tracked glove setup as the input interface is discussed. How basic functionality for volume visualization can be transferred from the 2D WIMP (Window, Icon, Menu, and Pointer) interface to a 3D VR interface is also systematically discussed.

Keywords: human computer interaction, virtual reality, volume visualization.

1 Introduction

Volume visualization, which allows users to see and explore the internal structure of 3D data sets, is one of the most important forms of scientific visualization. However, the nature of volumetric data makes it a great challenge to display all hidden 3D patterns within the data. Researchers have proposed different volume rendering algorithms, such as iso-surface extraction [1] and direct volume rendering [2], to display these patterns. Various types of transfer function specification methods [3] have been proposed to highlight regions of interest and filter out extraneous details. Virtual Reality (VR) technology has been used to enhance the depth perception of the volume data [4, 5].

Compared with conventional 2D computer displays, virtual environments (VEs) provide two additional depth cues: stereoscopic vision and motion parallax. VEs have been proven to be better media to convey 3D structure to users [6]. VEs provide users with environments that are much closer to the real world, so the interaction paradigms for VEs are fundamentally different from those designed for 2D environments. Interaction in 3D virtual environments requires control over 6 degrees-of-freedom (DoF), in contrast with 2 DoF for 2D environments. More degrees of freedom provide

A. Butz et al. (Eds.): SG 2007, LNCS 4569, pp. 49–60, 2007.

many more possibilities for advanced interaction methods that can improve communication between human and computer, but simultaneously require much more effort in designing the 3D interface.

Researchers have proposed various HCI paradigms [7-11] for general virtual object interaction. Some other researchers proposed different volume visualization systems in VEs (see, for example, [5, 12, 13]). However, few have systematically addressed how to transfer all the basic functionality for volume visualization from 2D interfaces to VR interfaces. This paper addresses this problem by proposing a HCI paradigm for volume visualization in projection-based VR.

2   Interaction Design

The proposed HCI paradigm was implemented in the Complex Active Visualization Laboratory in Griffith University. A 5 x 2 metre polarizing screen and 4 rear projectors equipped with polarizing filters enable stereoscopic capability. A Polhemus FASTRACK system is used to facilitate the 6 DoF motion tracking requirements for VEs. The design of the HCI paradigm is part of the Virtual Reality Volume Visualization (VRVolVis) project, which is attempting to develop an intuitive volume visualization VE with several, novel, volume data exploration tools.

Projection-based VEs have a greater Field of View (FOV) and Field of Regard (FOR) than desktop-based VEs and can provide users with life-size perception of the virtual objects. Compared with Head Mounted Display-based (HMD-based) VEs, projection-based VEs have lower end-to-end delay requirements of the systems, and generate less VR sickness. For these reasons we believe that projection-based VEs are well suited for frequent use for volume visualization purposes. It should be noted, however, that though the proposed HCI paradigm is for projection-based VEs, it can be adapted easily to HMD-based VEs.

2.1   The Basic Interaction Tasks for Volume Visualization

After analyzing a number of visualization systems, such as Volview [14] and Simian [15], four types of basic interaction tasks needed for volume visualization were identified. These are:

- volume object transformation,
- volume exploration,
- transfer function specification, and
- system control.

Volume object transformation includes translation, rotation and scaling of the volume data. Volume exploration is the task of using virtual tools such as a clipping plane to study the internal structure of the volume data. These two types of interaction tasks involve 6 DoF control over the virtual objects, which is naturally provided by immersive VEs. VEs potentially provide a much better interface for these tasks.

Many different methods for transfer function specification have been proposed [3]; all of them use 2D WIMP interfaces. Trial-and-error is one of the most popular methods, and is used by commercial software such as Volview[14]. Volview provides three separable TF settings, which map voxel values to opacity, voxel values to color, and voxel gradient magnitudes to opacity. This interaction to adjust the TF is essentially moving multiple control points on a plane. System controls for volume visualization include loading or saving a volume to the system, configuring simple states, setting simple parameter values, etc. Both TF setting and system controls have worked very well in the WIMP interface. In this work we propose a paradigm that can transfer most 2D WIMP interface functions into a 3D immersive environment.

2.2   The Input Interface and Its Visual Feedback

Guiard proposed a framework for classification of interaction tasks [16], which is well summarized by Haan *et al* [17]. Various types of hand-involved interaction tasks can be grouped into three categories:

1) One-handed task (only one hand performs a task);
2) Double one-handed task (each hand performs a separate one-handed task);
3) Two-handed task (both hands cooperate to perform a single task). The category of two-handed task includes two subclasses:
   a.   symmetric two-handed task (both hands perform the same actions), and
   b.   asymmetric two-handed task (each hand performs different actions involving complex coordinate between hands). Asymmetric two-handed task is the most common form of two-handed task.

An effective interface for VEs should allow users to interact with the virtual world the way they interact with the real world. Therefore, it should support all of the interaction methods mentioned above and have the following features. Firstly, the interface should allow users to use either left or right hand to manipulate objects (support one-handed tasks). Although almost all users do have hand preference (handedness), for many simple tasks either left or right hand would be used, depending merely on which hand is closer to an object. Secondly, the interface should allow users to simultaneously manipulate two different objects (support double one-handed tasks). Finally, the interface should support two-handed tasks in which users employ two-hand interaction to achieve a goal. For some tasks, such as resizing a volume object, using two-handed interaction is much more natural than using one-handed interaction.

Several researchers have used the "pen and pad" metaphor to interact with projection-based VEs [17, 18]. A physical, transparent pad is held by the non-dominant hand to provide a frame for the interactions, and a pen-shaped stylus is held by the dominant hand to perform fine interactions. One of the advantages for this interaction paradigm is that passive, haptic feedback is provided to the users. However, this interaction paradigm has a few disadvantages:

1) The mismatch of the focal depth of the virtual and real panels will cause discomfort; and
2) The hands' activities are limited by the physical tools, so the possible interaction methods are also limited.

Instead of interacting with virtual environments via hand-held physical objects the proposed interaction paradigm projects the users' hands into the virtual world and allows the users to directly manipulate various virtual objects.

To manipulate small objects in real environments, the thumb and index finger are usually sufficient. Most purely-visual virtual environments are mass-less (without inertial effect) and agravic (zero-gravity), so thumb and index finger are considered sufficient for manipulating virtual objects. The input device proposed is a pair of tracked gloves. The right hand setup is shown in Fig. 1. Six DoF motion trackers are attached to the thumb and index finger to track their positions and orientation. A switch is attached to the thumb, and this is used for the "apply" status for some of the tools. This approach provides three unambiguous states for the fingers: open (fingers separated), closed (fingers just touch each other), and apply (when force is exert to close the switch). For many tools, such as the clipping widget, two states (open and closed) are sufficient, because the fingers can be closed to grab the tool, applying it to the volume, then opening the fingers releases the tool. Adding the "apply" state enlarges the vocabulary for interaction. For example, a function "cross-section snapshot" could be added: once a user presses the switch while using the clipping widget, a cross-section of the volume can be taken out for detailed study.

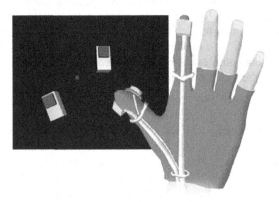

Fig. 1. The tracked glove setup and its visual feedback

When a user wears these gloves, the 6 DoF of the thumb and index finger are continuously updated, and two virtual hands are shown in the virtual space. The user can manipulate virtual objects via these virtual hands. A simple and unambiguous representation of the virtual hands is advocated: instead of rendering the whole hand, just the thumb and index finger are drawn. There are a few reasons for this:

1) To render the whole hand, more tracking and more graphical calculation would be needed;
2) It is not necessary to show the whole hand because just thumb and index finger are used to manipulate virtual objects; and
3) Drawing only thumb and index finger can minimize problems with occlusion.

Two cuboids are used to represent each finger, as shown in Fig. 1. The larger cuboid indicates the position and orientation of the finger, and the smaller cuboid is used to indicate two things: the nail's position (the sensor position) and the finger state. Showing the nail's position further clarifies the fingers' orientation. The status of the fingers is indicated by the color of the nail box: green indicates that the fingers are opened; yellow indicates that the fingers are closed; and red indicates the "apply" state. A tiny cube is drawn at the midpoint between the thumb and index finger. The position of this cube is the position that the fingers will grab when the fingers are closed, so this cube can provide subtle occlusion depth cues to the users and inform them whether the grab point is within, or outside of, a virtual object.

2.3 Basic Interaction

Bowman [19] classified VR interaction into four categories: viewpoint control; object selection; object manipulation; and system control. Following this classification, this section discusses the basic interaction methods proposed for volume visualization in projection-based VEs.

Viewpoint Control. Researchers have proposed various techniques or metaphors for viewpoint control for VEs. For example, Ware [7] proposed the *viewpoint at hand, scene at hand* and *flying vehicle* metaphors, and Stoakley [8] proposed the WIM (*worlds in miniature*) interaction metaphor. Unlike some VE applications that have large virtual spatial extents (such as a virtual theme park), the extents for volume visualization applications are usually not too large, so large scale viewpoint translation is not necessary. VRVolVis generates a virtual space that extends about one meter in front of and a few meters behind the projection screen. View point control is achieved through walking and head movement, which is actually a key component of VR technologies. A user can freely change the viewpoint this way to exploit the active motion parallax depth cue, which has been proved to be an important depth cue for people to understand 3D structures [6].

Object Selection and Manipulation. Researchers have proposed various metaphors or techniques for object selection and manipulation in VEs. Mine [11] believed the direct manipulation metaphor is better than *arm-extension* techniques because direct manipulation allows the user to exploit proprioception in interaction. However, since direct manipulation has a reachable range limited by arm length, he proposed the *scale-world-grab* techniques. Some researchers believe that the scale of the virtual scene should remain stable, otherwise it might confuse the user [20]. Arm-extension techniques like the *Go-Go* interaction technique [9] extend the reachable range of a user. For a large-scale virtual scene, ray-casting [21] or image-plane selection techniques [10] can be used.

Since volume visualization is generally of limited range, it is believed that direct manipulation is suitable. In HMD-based VEs, where the real-world is totally blocked, the virtual hand can overlap with the real hand and thus proprioception can be exploited, but in projection-based VEs, overlapping real and virtual hands causes problems. When a virtual object is closer to the eyes than the virtual hand, the virtual object should occlude the virtual hand, but in projection-based VE the screen is actually behind the real hand, so correct occlusion effects cannot be achieved. This visual conflict between two major depth cues – occlusion and convergence (a strong depth cue when the scene is close to the user) – will destroy the perception of immersion, and produce significant discomfort. Fixed z-axis offset techniques can help to solve these problems by placing the virtual hands in the space, where x and y coordinates follow the real hands while the z coordinate has a fixed offset (from 0.5 to 1.0 metres).

To select and manipulate a virtual object, the user moves the virtual hand to the object, and then closes the thumb and index finger to select the object. Once the object is selected, the object will follow the virtual hand (which means that the relative position and orientation remain constant, as if the virtual object is firmly held by the virtual hand). When rotating a virtual object in space, normally one motion is not enough. In this case the ratchet rotation method can be used. Just like using a ratchet motion to rotate a knob around its axis in the real world, a user can open the fingers, return the hand to a start position, close the fingers and repeat the rotation and the rotation will be accumulated. To achieve a certain spatial angle for a virtual object, a few ratchet motions may be needed, but since manipulation is very similar to real world object manipulation, users need little time to learn to use this method.

Mine [11] pointed out that one of the limitations of VEs is that precise manipulation of virtual objects is difficult. There are a few reasons for this. Firstly, the tracking system is not accurate and stable enough. Most of the motion tracking systems that are based on ultrasonic, optical or electromagnetic tracking have limited precision and show appreciable jitter. Secondly, humans depend on haptic feedback and physical constraints for precise interaction in the real world. In virtual environments, usually there is no physical constraint to guide the interaction.

To address the accuracy problem for virtual object manipulation in projection-based VEs, a *fine control mode* is proposed (in contrast with the direct manipulation mode) to provide finer translation and rotation control over the virtual objects. When a user translates a virtual object in the direct manipulation mode, the virtual object's displacement will be equal to the virtual hand's displacement. When translating a virtual object in the *fine control mode*, the displacement of the object will be a fraction of the displacement of the virtual hand's. In the same manner, in the *fine control mode* angular displacement of the volume object will be a fraction of the angular displacement of the virtual hand's. When interacting in 3D space, unsteady hand movement is unavoidable but the *fine control mode* will reduce its effect and enable a more accurate object manipulation method to the users.

System Control. System control itself is not part of volume visualization, but it is a part of the visualization system, performing tasks like volume loading and setting system parameters. The interaction method should be consistent with that of the virtual object manipulation so that once the program is started the same interface can be used to perform all tasks, instead of having to use mouse and keyboard for system control. Section 2.5 discusses how to map a 2D interface to the 3D environment. Using the method described, most system control can be performed in VEs.

2.4 Volume Object Interaction

In volume visualization, there is only one focused virtual object – the volume object – and several other less focused virtual objects such as tools and setting widgets. Therefore, the use of more resources to manipulate the volume object is affordable. Besides the standard transformations discussed above, the volume object needs to be scaled universally or along individual axes. To study the volume, frequent rotation of the volume is required, so comfortable control is needed. Redundant control is also an advantage, so that a user can manipulate the volume object in the most convenient way. This section discusses methods to address the above problems.

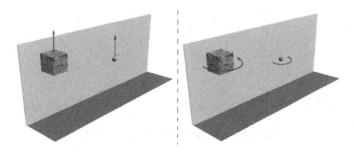

Fig. 2. The concept of the *agent object*

An *agent object* is proposed to manipulate the volume object. Besides directly manipulating the volume object, its translation and rotation can be controlled via the *agent object*. The *agent object* floats in a fixed position in space where it may be reached easily and manipulated by the user in a normal operating position. Fig. 2 illustrates this concept. A cuboid representing the volume object is shown in the projection screen above the floor, and the small sphere to the right is the *agent object*. When the user grabs the *agent object* and moves it, the volume object will move accordingly with the same direction and displacement. When the user releases the *agent object*, it will return to its default position, but the volume object will remain in its new position. This mechanism can be used to achieve cumulative translation (by ratchet translation). In the same manner, when the user rotates the *agent object*, the volume object will rotate accordingly around its own center; ratchet rotation can be achieved in the same way. Using the *agent object*, the user can always manipulate the volume object in a comfortable position, and is able to translate the volume object to a position not directly reachable (e.g. far behind the screen, or high above the head) if needed.

When visualizing volume data, users usually need to change the displayed size of the volume, for example shrinking the volume to have an overall view and enlarging the volume to observe local detail. In virtual environments, users have the option to do this by walking closer to enlarge the volume. (To be precise, the size of the volume object isn't changed, but the visual angle occupied by the volume is increased.) Similarly, walking further away shrinks the apparent volume (the visual angle is decreased). This is a very natural way to explore the volume object, just as in the real world. VRVolVis supports another way of changing the size of the volume object – changing its actual size, either universally or along one axis. Using two virtual hands to grasp one of the cube edges bounding the volume object, the user can lengthen or shorten the cube along that axis by increasing or decreasing the inter-hand distance. If two adjacent edges are held, increasing or decreasing the inter-hands distance will scale the cube proportionally on the plane in which the two edges lie. If two non-adjacent edges are held, increasing or decreasing the inter-hand distance will scale the cube universally along all three axes. Fig. 3 illustrates the concept of two-handed scaling. The crosses represent the grabbed points on the edges of the volume object; the arrows show the directions of hand movements.

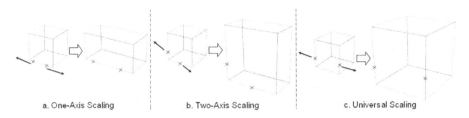

a. One-Axis Scaling   b. Two-Axis Scaling   c. Universal Scaling

Fig. 3. The concept of two-handed scaling

2.5   Transforming a 2D Interface from a 2D to 3D Environment

For daily computer use, the WIMP interface is currently irreplaceable. Mouse and keyboard skills, for most people, are over-learned skills and most are quite adept at them. Furthermore, many concepts are developed and presented in 2D form - for example, the transfer function settings. For these reasons, the 2D interface can't be abandoned (at least immediately), so research on how to transform the 2D interface to the 3D environment is important.

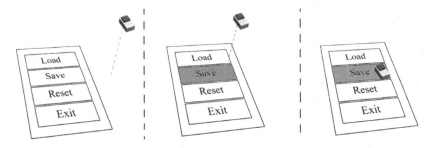

Fig. 4. The concept of transforming a 2D interface to a 3D environment

Schulze [22] suggested a method of transforming a 2D interface into 3D. The 2D interface elements, such as the menus and selectable items, are drawn on a 2D plane in 3D space; the user employs a handheld virtual laser pointer to operate the interface. However, the instability of the tracking system and human hand will be exaggerated using this method, and make accurate item selection very difficult. For VRVolVis, where the virtual scene is within reach, a ray-casting method is not necessary. To maintain consistency with other interaction paradigms, a design somewhat different to Schulze's is proposed, particularly in relation to item selection and operation methods. The menu can be handheld or float in space. When a virtual hand is close to the menu a light dotted line is shown, connecting the virtual index finger to the menu plane; the line is perpendicular to the plane. When the line intersects with a selectable item, the item will be highlighted. To select the item, the virtual hand is used to "press" the item (either by moving the virtual index finger to intersect the item or by pressing the switch attached to the thumb). Fig. 4 illustrates the concept.

For object moving tasks in a WIMP interface, such as moving a slider or moving an icon on a plane, usually a *drag and drop* metaphor is used. A basic object manipulation paradigm in VRVolVis is the *grab and release* metaphor, which can be seen as a 3D extension of drag and drop.

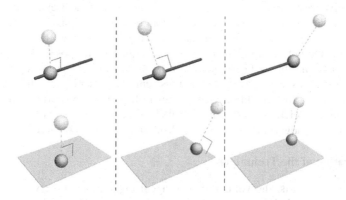

Fig. 5. The *Ghost Object Paradigm* for axial and 2D constraint

In VRVolVis, any movable item on a 2D widget (such as a menu) is represented by a 3D geometric object. To move it, the user can just grab it and move it. However, a motion constraint problem occurs in this situation. There is no physical constraint to limit hand movement in space, but there are many motion constraints in the VEs. For example, movable objects on a 2D widget should be constrained on the menu plane; sub-objects on a virtual tool should be constrained on the appropriate axis. Without proper visual feedback, the user may become confused about the interaction status. To solve this problem, a *ghost object paradigm* is proposed. When the object is within allowed range, the *ghost object* will not appear; when the user tries to move the object outside the allowed range, a *ghost object* (the same size as the controlled object, but shown with lower opacity) will follow the hand, providing visual feedback. The movable object's position is based on the projection of the *ghost object* position onto the menu plane. A dotted line connects the *ghost object* to the movable object. This line is normally perpendicular to the menu plane, but one end is clamped to stay within the menu plane so that the line stops being perpendicular if the hand is moved to a distant position. Once the user opens the fingers, the *ghost object* disappears. Fig. 5 illustrates the concept of the *ghost object*. The solid sphere represents the movable object; the axis and the plane represent the motion constraints; the faint sphere is the *ghost object*; and the rectangular marks denote perpendicular status.

2.6 Some Interaction Conventions

A good interface should inform users what functions of the system are available, instead of requiring them to remember all the commands. However, adding a few interaction conventions can improve the efficiency of the interface. A good example in a WIMP interface is the "right click" convention, which will bring forward a context-sensitive list related to the item that was clicked. Mine [11] proposed a few interaction conventions in VR, including the use of pull-down menus and over-the-shoulder deletion. He stated that three invisible menus can be placed over the user's head (left-top, top and right-top), and when a menu is needed, the user can just pull it down. The core of this idea is that the menus move with the user, having a fixed position relative to the user. Thus, the physical mnemonics of the user can be exploited. Over-the-shoulder deletion is used when a virtual object is no longer needed: the user can make it invisible using a motion like throwing it away over the shoulder. For VRVolVis, related but modified interaction conventions are proposed. An item-related menu is located in the right-behind position. A system menu is located in the left-behind position. We put the menu positions behind the user because this can further clarify the intention of grabbing a menu instead of, perhaps, a nearby virtual object. Over-the-shoulder deletion is used in VRVolVis also. This action will make a virtual object (a tool or a widget) invisible or put it back in its default position.

2.7 Integration of the Techniques

When the system starts, the volume object, agent object, and some virtual tools are floating in their default 3D positions. The user can then manipulate the volume object directly or via the agent object. To scale the volume object, the user uses the virtual hands to grasp two points on its edges to stretch or shrink it (as describe in Section 2.4). Fine control mode can be toggle on or off by touching a virtual box located in the VE space. A ghost object will appear whenever the user tries to move an object outside its allowed range. To use the exploration tools, the user can just take a tool and apply it to the volume object directly. System or object related menus can be brought out at anytime by grabbing in the left-behind or right-behind position, and the changes will be applied to the system immediately after an item is pressed. All the proposed interaction techniques are thus integrated into one, unified system.

3 Evaluations

Formal user studies will be performed to evaluate this interaction paradigm in our future research, but a pilot user study has already shown very positive results.

Eight subjects, all students or staff from Griffith University, were invited individually to the lab to use the prototype VRVolVis system to visualize some volumetric data sets. They all experienced 3 conditions: 1) Fixed-offset enabled; 2) Fixed - offset disabled; and 3) *Agent object* disabled.

After using the system, they were encouraged to talk about their experience and reactions. The following are some observations and subjective evaluations by these users. All considered the interaction paradigm very intuitive to learn and use. They all preferred the fixed-offset mode to the non-offset mode. Most, in fact, refused to use the non-offset mode after a few trials, stating they felt uncomfortable about the confused depth cues. When the *agent object* was enabled, most subjects preferred to use it rather han directly manipulating the volume object. All subjects were able to use the 2D menu in the VE to select desired items. Fig. 6 shows some of the many interaction tasks that the subjects were required to perform.

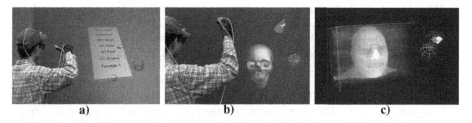

Fig. 6. Some of the interaction tasks for the subjects: a) use the 3D menu to load different volume data sets; b) manipulate virtual objects using fixed-offset or non-offset direct manipulation; c) manipulate the volume object using the *agent object*

4 Conclusions

A Human Computer Interaction paradigm for volume visualization in projection-based immersive virtual environments has been proposed. The paradigm included a number of novel interaction methodologies. A 3-state tracked glove proved to be a simple but powerful input device for VEs. A fixed-offset, direct manipulation method provided an effective method to overcome the problem of real hands occluding the closer-to-eye virtual objects in projection-based VEs. A *fine control mode* interaction method for direct manipulation was proposed to address the low accuracy problem of virtual object manipulation in VEs. An *agent object* interaction method was shown to be readily adopted by users, providing more flexibility and comfort in manipulating volume objects. A two-handed scaling method was proposed to conveniently scale volume objects along one, two, or three axes. A *ghost object paradigm* was proposed to address the motion constraint problem for the virtual objects. The interaction paradigm featured intuitiveness, high efficiency and accurate control for volume visualization in projection-based VEs, as demonstrated in early usability trials.

Acknowledgments. Many thanks to Dr. Mike Jones for his guidance, sharing of ideas and help with development of the proposed HCI paradigm while he was a member of academic staff at Griffith University.

References

1. Lorensen, W.E., Cline, H.E.: Marching cubes: a high resolution 3D surface construction algorithm. In: International Conference on Computer Graphics and Interactive Techniques, ACM Press, New York (1987)
2. Meissner, M., et al.: A Practical Evaluation of Popular Volume Rendering Algorithms. In: Volume Visualization Symposium. Salt Lake City (2000)
3. Pfister, H., et al.: The Transfer Function Bake-Off. Computer Graphics and Applications. IEEE 21(3), 16–22 (2001)
4. Zhrang, S., et al.: An Immersive Virtual Environment for DT-MRI Volume Visualization Applications: a Case Study. In: IEEE Visualization , San Diego (2001)

5. Souza, I., et al.: Direct Volume Rendering of the Visible Human Dataset on a Distributed Multiprojection Immersive Environment. In: Symposium on Virtual Reality. São Paulo (2004)
6. Ware, C., Franck, G.: Evaluating stereo and motion cues for visualizing information nets in three dimensions. ACM Transaction on Graphics 15(2), 121–140 (1996)
7. Ware, C., Osborne, S.: Exploration and virtual camera control in virtual three dimensional environments. ACM SIGGRAPH Computer Graphics 24(2), 175–183 (1990)
8. Stoakley, R., Conway, M.J., Pausch, R.: Virtual reality on a WIM: interactive worlds in miniature. In: The SIGCHI conference on Human factors in computing systems, Denver, Colorado, United States, ACM Press/Addison-Wesley Publishing Co. (1995)
9. Poupyrev, I., et al.: The go-go interaction technique: non-linear mapping for direct manipulation in VR. In: Symposium on User Interface Software and Technology. ACM Press: Seattle, 1996, Washington, United States (1996)
10. Pierce, J.S., Pausch, R.: Comparing voodoo dolls and HOMER: exploring the importance of feedback in virtual environments. In: The SIGCHI Conference on Human Factors in Computing Systems. Minneapolis, Minnesota, USA: ACM Press (2002)
11. Mine, M.R., Frederick, J., Brooks, P.,Sequin, C.H.: Moving objects in space: exploiting proprioception in virtual-environment interaction. In: International Conference on Computer Graphics and Interactive Techniques. ACM Press/Addison-Wesley Publishing Co (1997)
12. Koutek, M.: Scientific Visualization in Virtual Reality: Interaction Techniques and Application Development. In: Faculty of Electrical Engineering, Mathematics and Computer Science. Delft University of Technology: Delft, The Netherlands, p. 251 (2003)
13. Schulze, J.P., et al.: Volume Rendering in a Virtual Environment. In: the 5th IPTW and Eurographics Virtual Environments, Springer, Heidelberg (2001)
14. Kitware Volview 2.0 http://www.kitware.com/products/volview.html
15. Kniss, J., et al.: Interactive texture-based volume rendering for large data sets. In: IEEE Computer Graphics and Applications 21(4), 52–61 (2001)
16. Guiard, Y.: Asymmetric Division of Labor in Human Skilled Bimanual Action: The Kinematic Chain as a Model. The Journal of Motor Behaviors 19(4), 486–517 (1987)
17. Haan, G., Koutek, M., Post, F.H.: Towards intuitive exploration tools for data visualization in VR. In: The ACM symposium on Virtual reality software and technology, Hong Kong, China, ACM Press, New York (2002)
18. Stephenson, P., et al.: Studydesk: Semi-Immersive Volumetric Data Analysis. In: the 1st international conference on Computer graphics and interactive techniques in Australasia and South East Asia, ACM Press, Melbourne, Australia (2003)
19. Bowman, D.A., Hodges, L.F.: Formalizing the Design, Evaluation, and Application of Interaction Techniques for Immersive Virtual Environments. Journal of Visual Languages and Computing 10(1), 37–53 (1999)
20. Bowman, D.A.: Interaction Techniques for Common Tasks in Immersive Virtual Environments. In: Department of Computer Science,Georgia Institute of Technology: Atlanta, Georgia, p. 132 (1999)
21. Bowman, D.A., Hodges, L.F.: An evaluation of techniques for grabbing and manipulating remote objects in immersive virtual environments. In: Symposium on Interactive 3D Graphics. Providence, Rhode Island, United States: ACM Press (1997)
22. Schulze-Döbold, J.: Interactive Volume Rendering in Virtual Environments, in Institute for Visualization and Interactive System. 2003, University of Stuttgart: Stuttgart, Germany. p. 157 (2003)

Intelligent Third-Person Control of 3D Avatar Motion

Chun-Chieh Chen and Tsai-Yen Li

Computer Science Department, National Chengchi University,
64, Sec. 2, Zhi-nan Rd., Wenshan, Taipei 116, Taiwan, R.O.C.
g9425@cs.nccu.edu.tw, li@nccu.edu.tw

Abstract. Interactive control of 3D avatar motions has important applications in computer games and animations. Most of the current games directly map the inputs of a user into canned motions of the 3D character under control. However, an ideal user interface should be more like a human moving in the real life where appropriate motions are chosen according to the environment in the front. In this paper, we have developed an intelligent control interface that helps the user to look ahead a few steps and search a motion library organized in a motion graph for the most appropriate motion for execution. The search is conducted incrementally with the best effort in each frame according to a given available time budget. We have developed a best-first strategy to maintain the search tree in a way that the number of useful nodes is kept as large as possible. Experiments on several example scenes have been conducted to illustrate how this mechanism can enhance the usability of 3D avatar control from a third-person view.

Keywords: Interactive Motion Control, Intelligent Avatar Motion, Intelligent Interface, Third-Person View.

1 Introduction

The ability to control 3D avatars interactively is crucial for many applications such as 3D computer game and virtual environment. It is especially important for the control with a third-person view (such as the one shown in Fig. 1), where the whole body motion is visible and controlled by the user. However, it has never been easy to control a 3D character with many degrees of freedom (DOF) by the use of simple low-DOF devices such as mouse and keyboard [13][1]. Most computer games today map user inputs into canned motions, which are usually triggered according to some finite-state machine. The quality of these motions is good because they acquired from real performers by motion capture techniques. The way of selecting a good motion may be hard-coded in the program for a specific environment or selected by the user interactively. However, these mechanisms all create some burdens at the design or the run-time stage.

We think an ideal user interface for interactive control of 3D avatar motions should be more like a human moving in the real environment, where he/she always looks ahead a few step to plan for a feasible motion that can achieve his/her high-level goal while avoiding obstacles. An avatar control program with an intelligent user interface

A. Butz et al. (Eds.): SG 2007, LNCS 4569, pp. 61–72, 2007.

Fig. 1. Interactive avatar control from a third-person view

should release the burden of the game designer as well as the user in handling envi-ronmental constraints such as collision avoidance and automatically resolve these motion selection problems, which are less related to the game logics. In this paper, we propose an intelligent control mechanism that considers a few steps beyond the cur-rent position of the avatar and automatically selects the most appropriate motion clip from a motion library for the user. The system maintains a dynamic tree of feasible motions in real time while the user is controlling the movement. A best-first strategy has been developed to explore and maintain the most promising and useful portion of the exploration tree for a given time budget in each frame update.

We organize the rest of the paper as follows. We will review the work pertaining to our research in the next section. In Section 3, we will model the user interface problem formally. Then, we will propose our real-time search algorithm to maintain the search tree incrementally and select the best action for the next time frame. In Section 5, we will show some experimental results obtained with our system. Then the paper will be concluded with future research directions.

2   Related Work

In the literature of computer animation, animation of human figure can be generated with three categories of approaches: key-framed, dynamics, and example-based.

The key-frame based approaches use interactive authoring software or procedures, or rules to create key-frames and appropriate interpolation between key-frames [2][15]. It is tedious to generate animation of human figures with key-frames even with the sophisticated animation software available today. If the key-frames are gen-erated in a procedural manner, then the generated animation could be made adaptive to environmental constraints such as moving on an uneven terrain.

The dynamics approaches model the dynamics properties of a human character and use simulation and control to create animations [6][14]. An advantage of this type of approaches is that the generated animations could be realistic and flexible if the physics model is correctly constructed. However, a physically sound model is not easy to build, and the performance of simulation is not real-time in general.

The example-based animation is the most popular approach in recent years. It usually refers to the animations acquired by the technique of motion capture. The advantage of this technique is that the captured motions are reproductions of real human motions and thus are the most realistic. However, the captured motions lack flexibility in situations where the human model or the environment is different from the time when the motions were captured.

Recent work in the computer animation literature strives to solve the above problems to make captured motions more reusable for different characters and environments. For example, a common approach is to use spacetime constraints or optimal control strategies to retarget the motion for the model of a new character [4][5]. Synthesizing a new sequence of motions from a motion library is also a common objective. Kim et al. used signal processing techniques to segment motions into elementary clips that can be used to synthesize new motions [8]. Gleicher organizes elementary motion clips into a motion graph that connect nodes (motion clips) with similar connection frames and use motion wrapping and blending techniques to generate smooth transition between two motion clips [9]. Lee et al. [10] organized the motion clips in a two-level graph, where the higher level organizes the type of motions into groups and the lower level selects a motion clip in the chosen group.

Due to the limited degrees of freedom available on common input devices of a desktop computer, several intelligent user interfaces have been proposed to make the task of 3D navigation or character motion control easier. For example, in [12] and [11], motion planning techniques and virtual force field have been used to improve navigation efficiency. In [7], a real-time motion planning algorithm was used to generate compliant motions for an animated character to avoid obstacles. The motions were generated at run time but limited to the upper-body motions generated procedurally. In [10], Lee et al. used three types of interfaces (menu, sketching, and images) to help a user select appropriate motion clips from a motion library. The menu interface prompts the user with a list of candidate motions at the end of a clip while our approach constantly looks ahead a few steps in every frame and selects the most appropriate motion automatically.

3 Problem Modeling

In this section, we will first review how the third-person view is used to control the animated avatar in common computer games. Then we will introduce the concept of motion graph, which is used to organize the motion library for synthesis purpose.

3.1 User Inputs

The third-person view is a common control interface for many 3D games such as Bio Hazard and Final Fantasy. For a given virtual scene, the designer usually place several cameras at appropriate locations of the scene to cover all regions that may be visited, as shown in Fig. 2. A typical game with the third-person control switches between these cameras automatically when the avatar moves. The user uses simple control

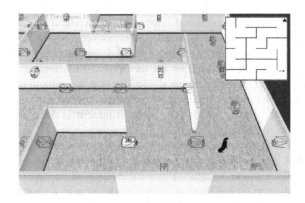

Fig. 2. Automatic transition of cameras from a third-person view

devices such as keyboard (arrow keys) or mouse (dragging) to specify the desired direction for the animated character to follow. Since the direction is specified with respect to the virtual cameras instead of the avatar, this type of control is usually called the *third-person control*. The direction for movement specified in the camera coordinate system is transformed into the avatar's local coordinate system in order to determine the next motion to take.

Most games adopt a finite state machine to map the user's inputs into the avatar's motions according to the current location and state of the avatar. If the game allows the avatar to move in an unconstrained manner, some real-time collision detection mechanism usually needs to be employed to prevent the avatar from running into obstacles. When a collision is detected, some special motion sequence is used to avoid the situation or the user needs to back up the avatar by taking some awkward maneuvers. It is awkward because in our daily life, while moving in a cluttered environment, we usually look ahead a few steps in the front to select an appropriate motion to avoid bumping into obstacles. We believe that an intelligent interface for 3D avatar control also needs to support this feature to make navigation easier.

3.2 Motion Graph

Usually after the game logic is finalized, the desired motions of the avatar are then generated by 3D animation software or motion capture devices. These generated motions are only good for this game. As mentioned in the previous section, much work in the literature of computer animation strives to develop technologies that can reuse a large library of motion data. Motion graph is one way to organize the motions in the library for motion synthesis. Each node in a motion graph represents a motion clip in the library while the edge between two nodes means that a smooth transition between the two motion clips is feasible.

A common way to make use of the motion graph is to develop an interface that allows animation designers to specify high-level constraints (such as a rough path trace) and let the system synthesize a sequence of motions from the motion library that can satisfy the given constraints. Most of the previous work makes use of motion graph in an off-line manner. In our work, we hope to develop an intelligent interactive

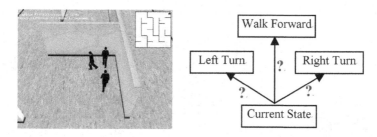

Fig. 3. Problem of selecting an appropriate motion clip with a third-person control

interface that can incorporate real-time planning into the control loop of the user interface in order to facilitate the navigation of a 3D avatar. The system should be able to look ahead a few steps and choose the most appropriate motion for the avatar according to the inputs from the user, the available motion clips in the motion library, and the obstacles in the virtual environment. For example, in the scenario of Fig. 3, the avatar is at a decision point of moving forward, turning left or turning right. For a smooth motion control, the system should be able to look ahead a few steps and select the motion clip that obeys the command of the user in principle while avoiding running into obstacles. In this case, making a left turn is the only feasible choice.

4   Feasible Motion Tree (FMT)

The system is given a motion library that is suitable for an avatar to perform the required tasks in a game. The user specifies the desired movement for the avatar from a third-person view. The main problem, as described in the previous section, is how to select a good motion clip from the library according to the user input and the environmental constraints. In the following subsections, we will first describe how we incrementally maintain a feasible motion tree in real time and then the best-first strategy that has been developed to keep the motion tree as useful as possible over time.

4.1   Maintaining Motion Tree in Real Time

As the computer hardware becomes more powerful, extra CPU cycles can be used to increase fidelity or ease of use of an application. It is generally accepted that the minimal frame rate for a 3D game is 15 frames per second (fps). If the frame rate of the game in a computer is higher than this value, the extra CPU cycles can be exploited to assist navigation. We define *feasible motion tree* as an exploration tree of the motion graph. A node, denoted as $N_k=(Mi,Pj)$, in a feasible motion tree contains the candidate motion clips and the positions (3D coordinates) of the avatar's skeleton root for executing the clips. The root of the tree is the current motion and the nodes below it are the motions that may be selected from the current motion clip in the next few steps.

For example, in Fig. 4(a), assume that we are given a motion graph consisting of six nodes. A directed arc between two nodes represents a feasible transition from the source to the sink. For example, in Fig. 4(b), M2, M3, and M4 are the possible next

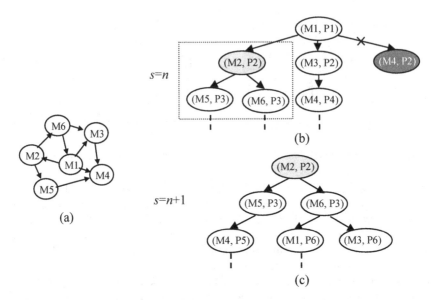

Fig. 4. For the given motion graph in (a), maintaining feasible motion tree at steps (b) *s=n* and (c) *s=n+1*

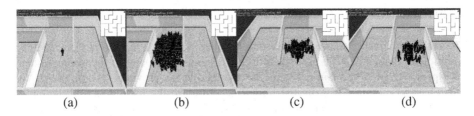

(a)   (b)   (c)   (d)

Fig. 5. Feasible motion trees maintained at different stages (a) initial state (b) after several frames of idle (c) starting moving (d) maintaining tree while moving

motion clips according to the motion graph in Fig. 4(a). However, assume that executing M4 from location P2 results in a collision and makes (M4, P2) infeasible. M2 and M3 are two feasible motions that can be used for the next step. When the time is allowed in every frame, the tree will continue to grow as more motions are tested for feasibility for the subsequent steps. As the motion clip for the current step is finished, the most appropriate next motion clip in the feasible motion tree is selected according to some criteria described in the next subsection. When the next motion clip starts, the root node of the tree moves downward and the sibling subtrees are pruned accordingly, as shown in Fig. 4(c).

An example of feasible motion tree in our experiments is shown in Fig. 5. The avatar started at a position shown in Fig. 5(a) where the feasible motion tree contains only the root node. The tree grew incrementally by using the spare time of each frame after finishing graphical rendering at a user-specified minimal frame rate. Since the user did not issue commands to move the avatar for a while, the tree grew to a significant size after a couple of frames as shown in Fig. 5(b). Sampled frames in the motion

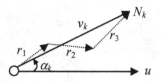

Fig. 6. The command matching method for computing the priority of a node N_k

clips maintained in the tree were overlaid on the screen to show the size of the tree. As the avatar started to move in Fig. 5(c), the tree was pruned accordingly as the root of the tree moved down. Once a new motion clip was chosen for execution in the next step, only the selected branch of the tree remained and new leaves continued to grow on this branch, as shown in Fig. 5(d).

4.2 Exploration Strategies

Given a limited amount of time for exploration in each frame, the quality of the selected motion depends on the strategy of exploration in the motion graph. A straightforward strategy is a breadth-first approach that explores the motion graph in a breadth-first fashion. However, we think a good exploration strategy should be able to grow the most useful branch of the feasible motion tree. For example, the criteria for selecting the best node for growing should consider the depth of the node in the tree as well as how the motion fits the current input of the user. There are many possible ways to design the criteria of goodness. In this paper, we have designed a best-first strategy as described below.

We assume that each node is associated a base priority p_b, where $0 < p_b < 1$. This priority reflects the likelihood of this node being used in the future movement of the avatar according to the input command of the user. We first transform the input command, specified as a vector, u, in the camera space into the coordinate system of the avatar. For each motion clip, we compute the vector of relative movement, r, by taking the difference of the avatar positions before and after executing the motion clip. As illustrated in Fig. 6, for a given node N_k, in the feasible motion tree, the movement (v_k) relative to the current position can be computed by taking the sum of r of the nodes along the path, denoted by σ_k, backtracked to the root node. That is, $v_k = \sum_{\sigma_k} r_i$.

The angle α_k between u and v_k indicates how the resulting motion matches the current input of the user. We then use a function g to map α_k to p_{bk} in [0, 1]. That is, $p_{bk} = g(\angle(u, v_k))$. We call this way of computing the priority the *command matching method*. In the spare time of each frame, we select the leaf node with the highest priority for exploration. The priority, p_k, of a leaf node, N_k, is computed by multiplying p_{bk} of all nodes along the path σ_k to the root (That is, $p_k = \prod_{Ni \in \sigma_k} p_{bi}$). Therefore, the

lower the nodes in the tree or the less they matched the input command, the lower priority a leaf node will get.

Fig. 7. Bounding box model used for collision detection

4.3 Selection Criteria for the Next Motion

When the current motion clip comes to the end, the system selects a most appropriate clip for the next step. The criteria for selecting the next motion clip in our system is based on the information collected in the current feasible motion tree as well as the input command from the user. We assume that a good choice of motion for the next step should be able to guarantee that the next few steps ahead are feasible according to the current input. Since the priority value of each node in the tree reflects how the resulting motion matches the user command and we have grown the tree according to the feasibility and priority of the leaf nodes, the structure of the feasible motion tree is a good indicator for selection. We compute the weighted sum of the priorities values for all the nodes in a branch and select the child with the highest sum among all children of the root. The weights of the priorities are smaller at lower levels of the tree, and their values are determined empirically for now.

5 Experiments

5.1 Implementation and Experimental Settings

We have implemented the intelligent interface for avatar control in a 3D navigation program based on the Direct3D library on the Windows platform. Keyboard is the input device used in the experiments. The motion clips used in our experiments are modified from the motions in the motion capture database provided by the CMU graphics laboratory [3]. The collisions between the avatar and the environment are detected by using the method based on the axis-aligned bounding boxes (AABB) [16] of the geometric models of the objects in the scene, as shown in Fig. 7. The avatar is checked for collisions in every frame of a motion clip, and a motion clip is valid only if all of the frames in it are collision-free. The 3D scenes used in our current experiments are maze-like virtual environments such as the one shown in Fig. 8.

We have conducted extensive experiments to study the effects of the proposed intelligent control interface. However, it is difficult to evaluate the system through repetitive experiments since the commands used by a user to move from one point to another may be different at different times. The learning effects are also difficult to avoid as the user gets familiar with the environment through practice. According to the experiments of using an intelligent user interface from the first-person control

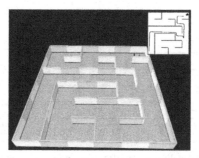

Fig. 8. An example scene used in the experiments

reported in [12], we assume that adopting a look-ahead mechanism with the spare CPU cycles in a frame update is helpful for navigation control from a third-person view. Therefore, instead of measuring the efficiency of navigation (total time to accomplish a navigation task) or the subjective experience of the user, we measure the average size of the feasible motion tree along a recorded path for different exploration strategies. The problem of effectiveness becomes how good the look-ahead information can be maintained to support a good navigation decision.

In the experiments, we first asked the user to navigate through the scene from an initial position to a designated goal position. The user commands and the trajectory were recorded for replay in future experiments. An example trajectory is shown at the upper-right corner of Fig. 8. In each of the subsequent experiments, we use the same input commands to reproduce the same navigation path. The number of nodes in the feasible motion tree in each frame is recorded in each experiment, and the average tree size is computed at the end. Although the input commands and navigation path are the same, the average size of the feasible motion tree is different because of different exploration strategies.

5.2 Experimental Results

In our experiments, we have tested five different strategies for exploration of the motion graph, and the result is shown in Fig. 9. The horizontal axis is the interval between two frames, which is the inverse of frame rate. The larger the interval, the more the spare CPU cycles are used to grow the feasible motion tree. The vertical axis is the average number of nodes that are maintained in the tree during the course of the navigation. The first exploration strategy (Type 0) is the breadth-first strategy. The second and the third strategies (Type 1 and 2) use the command matching method with and without re-sorting the priorities of the leaf nodes in each frame, respectively. Type 3 uses user-defined priorities based on the statistic data of how the children of a node are chosen in a navigation task conducted in the given environment. Type 4 uses a hybrid approach by combining the priorities of Type 1 and Type 3.

The results in Fig. 9 reveal that the size of the tree grows linearly with the available time in each frame update. This means that on slower machines, one can expect that the size of the tree will be smaller and the effect of looking ahead for motion selection can degrade gracefully. For these five types, Type 0 has the smallest average tree size

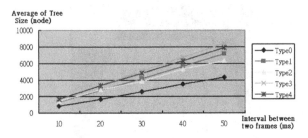

Fig. 9. Evaluation of different exploration strategies

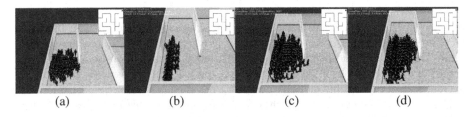

(a)   (b)   (c)   (d)

Fig. 10. Visited avatar positions in the feasible motion trees with different exploration strategies: (a) breadth-first (b) command-matching (c) user-defined (statistic) (d) hybrid

as expected because of its breadth-first strategy. Type 1 and Type 2 (command matching) all perform better than Type 0, and re-sorting the priority list in every frame is important for maintaining a good shape of the tree since the user inputs may change from time to time. Type 3, the user-defined method, has the best performance since the priorities were computed according to statistic data from the history. However, the setting is specific to the given scene and may not work well for other scenes. Type 4 is the hybrid approach combining Type 1 and Type 3 and the effect of this type also falls between these two types as expected.

In Fig. 10, for a given current position of the avatar, we show all the future positions that have been maintained in the feasible motion tree with various strategies. In Fig. 10(a), the shape of the visited region is more evenly distributed because the breadth-first approach is used. In Fig. 10(b), the adopted command-matching method prefers growing in a specific direction because of the consistent commands of walking forward in the past few steps. In Fig. 10(c), the user-defined priorities are used and the size of the tree is the largest. Finally, the tree of using the hybrid approach combining 10(b) and 10(c) is depicted in Fig. 10(d).

In Fig. 11, we show another example scene where obstacles were placed at various locations of the maze to make the movement of the avatar more difficult. In order to facilitate the movement of the avatar through the space, we enrich the motion graph by adding a "crouch-moving" motion and its transition motions to other motions. In Fig. 11(a), the system had chosen a crouch-moving motion for the avatar to pass the obstructive obstacle. In Fig. 11(b), the obstructive obstacle was lower and the avatar chose to make a turn to pass through the region. Finally, the avatar used the crouch-moving motion again to pass underneath the table placed in his way, as shown in Fig. 11(c).

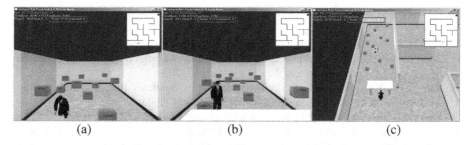

(a)   (b)   (c)

Fig. 11. Examples of versatile motions generated for the avatar to overcome environmental constraints (a) crouch moving (b) left turning (c) crouching underneath the table

6 Conclusions

It has been a long-time research goal to allow a 3D avatar to be commanded interactively with high-level inputs under the constraints of the environment. In this paper, we have developed an intelligent 3D control interface that looks ahead a few steps in order to make a better selection of the next motion clip from the given motion library. The system exploits the spare CPU cycles between two frames to maintain the feasible motion tree incrementally. We also have developed various strategies and conducted experiments to demonstrate the effectiveness of the strategies and compared the tradeoffs of these strategies.

In the current work, we assume that the interface with the look-ahead mechanism should work better than the one without this feature since similar claims have been made before. In the future, we would like to conduct further experiments to measure the improvement of the navigation efficiency more precisely. In addition, we will conduct more experiments to study how to select a good cut-off depth for tree growing such that a good balance between frame rate and tree size can be obtained.

Acknowledgments

This research was funded in part by the National Science Council (NSC) of Taiwan under contract no. NSC 95-2221-E-004-015.

References

1. Bowman, D., Kruijff, E., LaViola, J., Poupyrev, I.: 3D User Interfaces: Theory and Practice. Addison-Wesley, Boston (2004)
2. Bruderlin, A., Calvert, T.W.: Goal-Directed Dynamic Animation of Human Walking. In: Computer Graphics (Proc. of SIGGRAPH 89) vol. 23, pp. 233–242 (1989)
3. CMU Graphics Lab Motion Capture Database. http://mocap.cs.cmu.edu/
4. Gleicher, M.: Motion Editing with Spacetime Constraints. In: Proc. of the 1997 Symposium on Interactive 3D Graphics (1997)
5. Gleicher, M.: Retargeting Motion to New Characters. In: Computer Graphics (SIGGRAPH 98 Proceedings) pp. 33–42 (July 1998)

6. Hodgins, J.K., Wooten, W.L., Brogan, D.C., O'Brien, J.F.: Animating Human Athletics. In: Proc. of SIGGRAPH 95, pp. 71–78 (1995)
7. Hsu, H.W., Li, T.Y.: Third-Person Interactive Control of Humanoid with Real-Time Motion Planning Algorithm. In: Proc. of IEEE International Conf. on Intelligent Robots and Systems, IEEE Computer Society Press, Los Alamitos (2006)
8. Kim, T.H., Park, S.I., Shin, S.Y.: Rhythmic-Motion Synthesis Based on Motion-Beat Analysis. ACM Transactions on Graphics 22(3), 392–401 (2003)
9. Kover, L., Gleicher, M., Pighin, F.: Motion Graphs. In: Proc. of SIGGRAPH 2002 (2002)
10. Lee, J., Chai, J., Reitsma, P., Hodgins, J.K., Pollard, N.: Interactive Control of Avatars Animated with Human Motion Data. In: Proc. of SIGGRAPH 2002 (2002)
11. Li, T.Y., Hsu, S.W.: An Intelligent 3D User Interface Adapting to User Control Behaviors. In: Proc. of International Conf. on Intelligent User Interfaces (IUI'04) (2004)
12. Li, T.Y., Ting, H.K.: An Intelligent User Interface with Motion Planning for 3D Navigation. In: Proc. of the IEEE Virtual Reality 2000 Conf, pp. 177–184. IEEE Computer Society Press, Los Alamitos (2000)
13. Nielson, G.M., Olsen, D.R.: Direct Manipulation Techniques for 3D Objects Using 2D Locator Devices. In: Proc. of the 1986 Workshop on Interactive 3D Graphics, pp. 175–182 (1987)
14. Paloutsos, P., van de Panne, M., Terzopoulos, D.: Composable Controllers for Physics-Based Character Animation. In: Proc. of SIGGPRAH2001, pp. 251–260 (2001)
15. Perlin, K., Goldberg, A.: Improv: A System for Scripting Interactive Actors in Virtual Worlds. In: Proc. of SIGGRAPH 96, pp. 205–216 (1996)
16. van den Bergen, G.: Efficient Collision Detection of Complex Deformable Models Using AABB Trees. Journal of Graphics Tools 2(4), 1–14 (1997)

Highly Realistic 3D Presentation Agents with Visual Attention Capability

Arjen Hoekstra[1,2], Helmut Prendinger[1], Nikolaus Bee[3],
Dirk Heylen[2], and Mitsuru Ishizuka[4]

[1] National Institute of Informatics
2-1-2 Hitotsubashi, Chiyoda-ku, Tokyo 101-8430, Japan
helmut@nii.ac.jp
[2] Computer Science, Human Media Interaction
University of Twente, PO Box 217, 7500 AE Enschede The Netherlands
a.h.hoekstra@student.utwente.nl, heylen@cs.utwente.nl
[3] Institute of Computer Science, University of Augsburg
Eichleitnerstr. 30, D-86135 Augsburg, Germany
[4] Graduate School of Information Science and Technology, University of Tokyo
7-3-1 Hongo, Bunkyo-ku, Tokyo 113-8656, Japan
ishizuka@i.u-tokyo.ac.jp

Abstract. This research proposes 3D graphical agents in the role of virtual presenters with a new type of functionality – the capability to process and respond to visual attention of users communicated by their eye movements. Eye gaze is an excellent clue to users' attention, visual interest, and visual preference. Using state-of-the-art non-contact eye tracking technology, eye movements can be assessed in a unobtrusive way. By analyzing and interpreting eye behavior in real-time, our proposed system can adapt to the current (visual) interest state of the user, and thus provide a more personalized, context-aware, and 'attentive' experience of the presentation. The system implements a virtual presentation room, where research content of our institute is presented by a team of two highly realistic 3D agents in a dynamic and interactive way. A small preliminary study was conducted to investigate users' gaze behavior with a non-interactive version of the system. A demo video based on our system was awarded as the best application of life-like agents at the GALA event in 2006.[1]

1 Introduction

The challenge of giving a good presentation is to provide relevant and interesting content in an easily accessible way while keeping the attention of the audience during the entire presentation time. Human presenters often obtain feedback from listeners regarding their level of attention by simply looking at their behavior, specifically whether they are looking at the currently presented material, typically visualized on slides, at the presenter, or somewhere else. If a presenter,

---

[1] http://hmi.ewi.utwente.nl/gala/

A. Butz et al. (Eds.): SG 2007, LNCS 4569, pp. 73–84, 2007.
© Springer-Verlag Berlin Heidelberg 2007

e.g. a museum guide, observes that the attention of the spectators is diverted by other objects, he or she will try to adapt the presentation by taking the interest shift of the audience into account.

Although speech conveys the richest information in human-computer inter-action, it is not the preferred input modality for scenarios such as presentation settings, which, as monologues, typically do not assume verbal expressions of in-terest from the audience. To determine the user's current focus of attention and interest, we therefore propose a system that is based on human eye movements. As an input modality, eye gaze has the advantage of being an involuntary signal that reflects the user's visual interest [16], and its signal is robust and can be assessed accurately [5].

As an interactive system, our proposed setup can be conceived as reviving the 'self-disclosing display' concept introduced in [21], where eye gaze is utilized as an input modality to recognize and respond to a user's interest. Their system would zoom in to areas of user interest and provide explanations via synthesized speech. Our work extends this concept by detecting both user interest and preference between two (visual) alternatives to continue the presentation, and by embodied life-like characters rather than a disembodied voice.

The remainder of this paper is structured as follows. Section 2 discusses related work. Section 3 describes our methods to assess (visual) interest and (visual) preference. Section 4 provides details about the application scenario and the gaze-contingent responses of the agents. In Section 5, we report on the main findings of our preliminary study based on a non-interactive version of the agent application. Section 6 discusses and Section 7 concludes the paper.

2   Related Work

Life-like characters or virtual animated agents are intended to provide the il-lusion of life or 'suspend disbelief' [3], such that users interacting with those agents will apply social interaction protocols and respond to them as they would to other humans, e.g. by listening to their story and attending to their face and gestures through eye gaze [15]. Life-like characters have been shown to serve multiple purposes successfully; besides presenters, they can act as tutors, ac-tors, personal communication partners, or information experts [14]. An excellent overview of the evolution of virtual presenters – starting from a non-interactive single presenter to multiple presenters with the capability of processing natural input from users – can be found in [18].

Eyes are an intriguing part of the human face, and are sometimes even seen as 'windows to the soul'. In verbal communication, the major functions of eye gaze include paying and signaling attention, conversation regulation, and demonstra-tion of intimacy [1,8]. In dyadic communication, two types of core functions of gaze direction can be distinguished [10]: (1) *Monitoring functions*. The speaker observes the interlocutor to gather information about the listener's attending behavior (e.g. at the end of long utterances) or about signals indicating that the listener will 'take floor'. (2) *Regulatory and expressive functions*. The speaker manages turn taking, e.g. by looking away from the listener to signal that he or she is going to speak. The speaker may also express an emotion of embarrassment or high arousal by averting the eyes from the listener. An investigation of gaze direction among multiple conversational partners can be found in [22]. It should be noted that the usage of our system differs from the interaction situation described above in that users cannot converse with agents verbally. In our case, the agents will monitor a user's state of visual interest (or lack of interest) in the presentation, and react accordingly.

Recent attempts to integrate eye behavior into interactive systems are reported in [23,19], who discuss the use of eye tracking in various applications - so-called 'attentive user interfaces' or 'visual attentive interfaces'. *Magic Pointing* is based on the user's conscious eye behavior in order to improve the positioning of a mouse pointer [23]. An eye-pointer approach is implemented in our augmented reality videoconferencing system called *iPick* [2]. *InVision* exploits involuntary gaze movements to estimate a user's plan or needs [19]. Similar *InVision*, our system exploits the non-conscious nature of eye movements in a non-command fashion.

Approaches that rely on eye gaze as input and life-like characters as communication media are currently rare. In the context of computer mediated communication, [6] conducted a study where different conditions (video, audio-only, avatar with random gaze, avatar with informed gaze) are compared for their effectiveness. Here, the virtual avatar based on a gaze model derived from [10] scored highest in terms of naturalness and involvement (experience) except for the video condition. Another study assessed the level of engagement and attentiveness in a situation where two humans converse with a virtual agents [17]. The authors were able to confirm findings from human communication, e.g. that persons look more at their conversational partners as listeners than as speakers. An agent-specific (and possibly surprising) result is that users attend more to an agent talking to them than to the human speaker.

3   Interest Estimation

The focus of interest is determined by a modified version of the algorithm described in [16]. These authors implemented an intelligent virtual tourist information environment (*iTourist*), for which they propose a new interest algorithm based on eye gaze. Two interest metrics were developed: (1) the Interest Score (IScore) and (2) the Focus of Interest Score (FIScore). IScore refers to the object 'arousal' level, i.e. the likelihood that the user is interested in a (visual) object. When the IScore metric passes a certain threshold, the object is said to become 'active'. The FIScore calculates the amount of interest in an active object over time. Since we were mainly interested in whether a user's attention is currently on a particular object, a simplified version of the IScore metric was sufficient for our purpose. The basic component for IScore is $p = T_{ISon}/T_{IS}$, where T_{ISon} refers to the accumulated gaze duration within a time window of size T_{IS} (in our application, 1000 milliseconds). In order to account for factors that may enhance or inhibit interest, [16] characterize the IScore as $p_{is} = p(1 + \alpha(1 - p))$. Here, α encodes a set of parameters that increase the accuracy of interest estimation.

The modification factors are modelled as follows [16]:

$$\alpha = \frac{c_f \alpha_f + c_c \alpha_c + c_s \alpha_s + c_a \alpha_a}{c_f + c_c + c_s + c_a}$$

The terms in this formula are defined as:

- α_f is the frequency of the user's eye gaze 'entering' and 'leaving' the object ($0 \leq \alpha_f \leq 1$),
- α_c is the categorical relationship with the previous active object ($\alpha_c = -1|0|1$),
- α_s is the average size of all possible interest objects compared to the size of the currently computed object ($-1 \leq \alpha_s \leq 1$),
- α_a encodes whether the object was previously activated ($\alpha_a = -1|0$), and
- c_0, c_f, c_c, c_s, and c_a represent empirically derived constant values of the corresponding factors. Some of these factors are domain dependent and are thus not applicable in all contexts.

The factors α_c and α_a were not (yet) integrated to our system. α_c concerns (semantic) relations between objects; α_a can be used to make the system respond in a different way when an object is activated multiple times.

We continue by explaining α_f and α_s, the two remaining factors. α_f is represented as $\alpha_f = \frac{N_{sw}}{N_f}$, where N_{sw} denotes the number of times eye gaze enters and leaves the object and N_f denotes the maximum possible N_{sw} in the preset time window. When the user's gaze switches to some object many times, the value of the modification factor will increase and hence there will be a higher chance on excitation. α_s is represented by $\alpha_s = \frac{S_b - S}{S}$, whereby S_b represents the average size of all objects, S denotes the size of the currently computed object, and the smallest object is never more than twice as small as the average object. This modification is intended to compensate for the differences between the size of the potential interest objects. Due to some noise in the eye movement signal, larger objects could have a higher chance of being 'hit' than smaller ones, which should be avoided.

In order to determine the user's preference in situations involving a two-alternative forced choice (2AFC), i.e. "how the presentation should continue", we exploited the so-called 'gaze cascade' effect. This effect was discovered in a study where users had to choose the more attractive face from two faces [20]. It could be demonstrated that there was a distinct gaze bias towards the chosen stimulus in the last one and a half seconds before the decision was made.

Our system integrates a recently developed real-time component for automatic visual preference detection, the *AutoSelect* system, which is based on the gaze cascade phenomenon [4]. *AutoSelect* was tested in a study where users were instructed to choose their preferred necktie from two presented neckties, i.e. in a 2AFC setting. There was no input modality available except the subjects' eye gaze. After the decision of *AutoSelect*, subjects were asked to confirm (or reject) the result of the system. Starting from an initial set of thirty-two pairs of neckties, subjects repeatedly indicated their preference, amounting to sixty-two decisions. The system achieved an accuracy of 81%. In order to avoid 'polite' answers from subjects, we conducted a follow-up study, where system and subject decisions were assessed independently. The accuracy of the re-designed system was slightly lower (72%).

Examples of the exploitation of the gaze cascade effect and of the use of the interest algorithm will be given in the next section.

4 Responding to User Interest and Preference

Our implemented system involves a team of two presentation agents that introduce the user to research at the National Institute of Informatics (NII), Tokyo (see Fig. 1 and video clip[2]).

The two agents were designed based on the appearance of two famous Japanese actors. In order to support their life-likeness, the agents are highly realistic and expressive. They can perform various gestures, such as greeting and counting, or 'beat' and deictic gestures. In addition to body gestures, mimics for "joy", "surprise", and "sadness" are available. High-quality synthesized speech using the Text-to-Speech (TTS) engine from Loquendo[3] is combined with proper lip synchronization, and the head of the agents can be adjusted to any (natural) direction, e.g. to the direction of the other agent when giving turn, or to the virtual slide. (When listening to a presentation, paying attention to its visualized content is of key importance. However, the audience will also focus on the presenter's face to increase comprehension via perception of lip movements in addition to speech, especially when listeners are not native speakers of English, as in our case.) A discussion about the animation techniques employed for our agents can be found in [12].

Both the agents and the environment are controlled by MPML3D [13], a reactive framework that supports anytime interaction, such as real-time interpreted input from the eye tracker. The agents will adapt their performance based on user eye gaze in two ways:

- If the user shows interest in a particular interface object (an 'interest object') not currently discussed (e.g. the view), or non-interest in a currently discussed object (e.g. a presentation slide), the agents will interrupt their presentation and react accordingly.
- At decision points in the presentation flow, the user's preference determines the subsequent topic.

4.1 Adapting to User Interest

In the system, the following interest objects are defined (see Fig. 1; from left to right): (a) NII logo; (b) male agent; (c) left part of the slide; (d) right part of

---

[2] A demo video can be found at http://research.nii.ac.jp/~prendinger/GALA2006/

[3] http://www.loquendo.com/

Fig. 1. Interest objects in the virtual environment

the slide; (e) female agent; (f) the view out of the window to the right. For each interest object, the IScore is calculated every second. When the score exceeds the threshold, the object becomes 'activated' and the agent(s) will react (if a reaction is defined). Agent responses (or non-responses) are defined for three types of situations:

1. *Continuation of presentation*: If the user attends to the currently explained (part of a) presentation slide (which is desired), the agent will continue with the presentation. Fig. 2 depicts a situation where the user attends to the explanation of the male agent by gazing at the slide content.
2. *Interruption of presentation*: If the user is detected to be interested in an interface object that is not currently discussed, the system chooses between two responses:
   (a) Suspension: If e.g. the user looks out of the virtual window (at the "View" object) rather than attending to the presentation content explained by the male agent, the female co-presenter agent asks her colleague to suspend the research presentation and continues with a description of the view (see Fig. 3).
   (b) Redirecting user attention: Here, the presenter agents do not suspend the presentation to comply with the user's interest. Instead, the co-presenter alerts the user to focus on the presentation content.

The existing implementation of our presentation system handles interruptions in a simple way. If a user's interest object is not the currently explained object (typically a slide) the presentation will be suspended at first by providing information about that object, and subsequently, the co-presenter agent will try to redirect the user to the presentation content.

Fig. 2. User is interested in slide content. The corresponding gaze trail is visualized by 'heat trails'.

Ken:	The transductive learning makes up for the smallness of user feedback. The transducer assigns labels from which the relevance is unknown with the same label as neighboring terms with known relevance.
User:	*[IScore exceeds threshold of the "View" object and gets activated.]*
Yuuki:	Ken, hold on a second... I couldn't help noticing that you are admiring the view we have from NII at the city. You can see our building is very close to the Imperial Palace. All the greenery belongs to the park of the palace. Well, so much about our neighborhood. Let's go back to our presentation, but please concentrate this time.

Fig. 3. Sample agent dialogue when the user is interested in the outside view

4.2 Following User Preference

At predefined points during the presentation, the agents ask the user to choose the next presentation topic, while a slide depicting two options is displayed. The gaze cascade phenomenon will occur naturally in this situation. Users alternately look at the left part and the right part of the slide, and eventually exhibit a bias for one part. The decision process occurs within seven seconds. Thereafter, the presentation continues with the selected topic.

5   Exploratory Study

A small study was conducted to assess users' eye behavior when watching a non-interactive version of the research presentation by the agent team, i.e., although eye gaze was recorded, the agents did not adapt to user interest or preference.

Fig. 4. Experimental setup

This approach seemed justified as a first step, given the lack of experience with attentive behavior of human spectators of a presentation performed by two animated agents. Hence, the aim of the study was to assess likely types of gaze behaviors. This information can then be used to refine the functionality of the interactive system, which will be followed by an extensive study.

5.1   Method

Subjects: The data of four subjects (average 30 years) were analyzed. Subjects received a monetary compensation for participation (1,000 Yen).

Apparatus and Procedure: Subjects were seated in front of a 30 inch screen (distance 80 cm) and stereo cameras of the faceLAB eye tracker from Seeing Machines.[4] The cameras and speakers were located below the screen. Two infrared pods were attached at the upper part of the display for illumination of the eyes (see Fig. 4). Then calibration of each subject was performed. Subjects were given no instruction other than watching the presentation.

In the presentation prepared for the study, the agents first introduce themselves, and then explain the researches of three professors of NII. The total length of the presentation is 14:49 min.

Data Analysis: The faceLAB software allowed us to extract the coordinates of gaze points on the screen. The recorded data was then processed and analyzed with MATLAB. 'Heat trails' were used for visualization, as they present the amount of fixations over time as a continuous movie. The heat trails were made transparent with the chroma key (Bluescreen) effect and merged with the

---

[4] http://www.seeingmachines.com/

captured video of the presentation. Animations and (virtual) environment changes were analyzed with the ANVIL annotation tool [11].

5.2 Results

The most distinctive result of the study could be found for situations where the agents ask the subject to select the subsequent topic. All of the subjects showed the gaze pattern characteristic of the 'gaze cascade' effect in both occurrences of a decision situation. This outcome generalizes the results of [20,4] to a setting featuring two agents referring to slide content depicting two choices (displayed left and right on the slide). It indicates that the cascade phenomenon can be reliably used to let users select the continuation of the presentation in a non-command fashion.[5]. It should be noted, however, that in the non-interactive presentation shown in the study, the subjects' preference had no effect on the continuation of the presentation.

Deictic arm gestures of embodied agents and agents' head-turning to slide content are an effective way to redirect the attention of users to the (virtual) slides [15]. We were interested in differences in the effect of deictic gestures depending on whether a new slide is shown, or some textual content of a displayed slide is changed, e.g. a new item is added to a given slide content. In the study, every subject had noticed a new slide within 2 sec (19 new slides presented). On the other hand, changes on slides (18 occurrences) were noticed with some delay, with 97% redirected attention within 3 sec. Although we expected more occasions where an attentive agent would have to alert the user, a 15 min presentation is probably too short to observe a user's diminishing attention.

The functionality of the interactive system also provides for the possibility that users attend to interface objects not related to the presentation content, such as the NII logo or the view outside the building (see Fig. 1). In the study, however, subjects spent 99% of the total time on the agents or slides. Since the actual view of the subjects was essentially limited to those interface objects (see Fig. 4), there was little room for attending to anything else. Other results regarding cumulative gaze distribution include attention to speaking agent (53%), attention to presented slides (43%), and attention to non-speaking agent (3%).

6   Discussion

While gaze-contingent interfaces are getting increasingly popular [5], it remains an open question how 'responsive' an interface that relies on eye gaze as an input modality should be. The problem of distinguishing between eye movements that are just explorative and those that are meant as an input is known as the 'Midas Touch' problem: "Everywhere you look, another command is activated; you cannot look anywhere without issuing a command." [9, p. 156]. Our presentation system avoids the Midas touch problem by (i) strictly confining the

---

[5] Given the small sample size, our results should always be seen as preliminary.

screen areas that could yield an agent response (the interest objects), and (ii) calculating user interest based on a well-established metric [16].

While we can determine visual interest and preference with high accuracy, the system is not perfect and might misinterpret the user's intention. The current implementation does not allow the user to 'undo' incorrect system decisions. Conceivable remedies include: (1) the user explicitly confirms a decision of the system, e.g. by simple verbal input ("Yes", "No"), and (2) the system detects the user's acknowledgement (head nodding) or negative signal (head shaking).

Another question concerns the manner in which an interface should be manipulated by gaze behavior. [7] propose the following types of interactivity:

1. *Change in information.* Objects of user interest are explained in more detail.
2. *Change in point-of-view.* The camera position changes to the interest object of the user.
3. *Change in storyline.* The sequence of story events is dependent on where the user attends to.

Our current system supports all of those possibilities (to some extent). For instance, when the user is interested in the virtual outside view, the agent provides additional explanation of the view and the (virtual) camera shifts to show a full screen image of the view. Interest objects can also be conceived as 'hyper-links' to particular scenes of a story. Our gaze cascade based selection method can be seen as a (restricted) implementation to decide the progress of the presentation.

7   Conclusions

The use of eye gaze offers a powerful method to adapt a presentation to the current interest of a user, i.e. make the presentation contingent to user interest. Eye gaze as an input modality is particularly beneficial when verbal feedback is either not assumed or difficult to provide. Most presentations given by lecturers or museum guides are one-way communications that can nevertheless be adaptive to the audience if a presenter is sensitive to the behavior of the audience, such as their exhibition of visual interest or non-interest. Furthermore, while the audience certainly has interest in specific presentation topics or parts of the presentation, it is unusual (or at least impolite) to verbally point out objects of interest repeatedly during the presentation. The online analysis of eye behavior thus provides an unobtrusive method to estimate user interest continuously.

In this paper, we describe a presentation system that features two virtual 3D presentation agents capable of responding to a user's focus of attention and interest in a natural way. The agent system [13] supports synchronized speech and lip movements, timed gestures, mimics, and head movements. In order to estimate user interest, the presentation system uses a previously developed algorithm [16], and has the presentation agents respond in an appropriate way. The gaze cascade effect [20,4] is exploited at decision points in the presentation in order to determine with which presentation topic the user would like to continue.

In our future work, we will proceed along two research avenues. First, we plan to extend the interest estimation algorithm to cover relationships between interest objects in order to unveil e.g. a user's interest in comparing visual objects rather than choosing between them. Second, we intend to improve the presentation system by integrating narrative principles. This is important since currently, agent response to user input (visual interest) mostly 'interrupts' the presentation flow, which is thereafter simply resumed following the pre-defined storyline. It would be desirable to utilize user attention as a means to control the presentation in a natural and non-conscious way while preserving the narrative cohesion and persuasiveness of the presentation flow.

Acknowledgements

The research was supported by the Research Grant (FY1999–FY2003) for the Future Program of the Japan Society for the Promotion of Science (JSPS), by a JSPS Encouragement of Young Scientists Grant (FY2005–FY2007), and an NII Joint Research Grant with the Univ. of Tokyo (FY2006). The first author was supported by the JSPS Encouragement Grant. The third author was supported by an International Internship Grant from NII under a Memorandum of Understanding with the Faculty of Applied Informatics at the Univ. of Augsburg. We are also indebted to Dr. Ulrich Apel (NII) for scripting the dialogues.

References

1. Argyle, M., Cook, M.: Gaze and Mutual Gaze. Cambridge University Press, Cambridge (1976)
2. Barakonyi, I., Prendinger, H., Schmalstieg, D., Ishizuka, M.: Cascading hand and eye movement for augmented reality videoconferencing. In: Proceedings 2nd IEEE Symposium on 3D User Interfaces 2007 (3DUI-07), pp. 71–78. IEEE Computer Society Press, Los Alamitos (2007)
3. Bates, J.: The role of emotion in believable agents. Communications of the ACM 37(7), 122–125 (1994)
4. Bee, N., Prendinger, H., Nakasone, A., André, E., Ishizuka, M.: AutoSelect: What You Want Is What You Get. Real-time processing of visual attention and affect. In: Tutorial and Research Workshop on Perception and Interactive Technologies (PIT-06) LNCS (LNAI), vol. 4021, pp. 40–52. Springer, Heidelberg (2006)
5. Duchowski, A.T.: Eye Tracking Methodology: Theory and Practice. Springer, London, UK (2003)
6. Garau, M., Slater, M., Bee, S., Sasse, M.A.: The impact of eye gaze on communication using humanoid avatars. In: Proceedings of the SIGCHI Conference on Human Factors in Computing Systems (CHI-01), pp. 309–316. ACM Press, New York (2001)
7. Hansen, J.P.,Engell.-Nielson, T., Glenstrup, A.J.: Eye-gaze interaction: A new media – not just a fast mouse. In: The Second Swedish Symposium on Multimodal Communication (1998)
8. Heylen, D.: Head gestures, gaze and the principles of conversational structure. International Journal of Humanoid Robotics 3(3), 241–267 (2006)

9. Jacob, R.J.K.: The use of eye movements in human-computer interaction techniques: What You Look At is What You Get. ACM Transactions on Information Systems 9(3) 152–169 (1991)
10. Kendon, A.: Some functions of gaze-direction in social interaction. Acta Psychologica 26, 22–63 (1967)
11. Kipp, M.: Gesture Generation by Immitation – From Human Behavior to Computer Character Animation. PhD thesis, Saarland University, Disseration.com, Boca Raton, Florida (2004)
12. Nischt, M., Prendinger, H., André, E., Ishizuka, M.: Creating three-dimensional animated characters: An experience report and recommendations of good practice. Upgrade. The European Journal for the Informatics Professional VII(2), 36–41 (2006)
13. Nischt, M., Prendinger, H., André, E., Ishizuka, M.: MPML3D: a reactive framework for the Multimodal Presentation Markup Language. In: Gratch, J., Young, M., Aylett, R., Ballin, D., Olivier, P. (eds.) IVA 2006. LNCS (LNAI), vol. 4133, pp. 218–229. Springer, Heidelberg (2006)
14. Prendinger, H., Ishizuka, M.: Life-Like Characters. Tools, Affective Functions, and Applications. In: Cognitive Technologies, Springer, Heidelberg (2004)
15. Prendinger, H., Ma, C., Ishizuka, M.: Eye movements as indices for the utility of life-like interface agents: A pilot study. Interacting with Computers 19(2), 281–292 (2007)
16. Qvarfordt, P., Zhai, S.: Conversing with the user based on eye-gaze patterns. In: Proceedings of the SIGCHI Conference on Human Factors in Computing Systems (CHI-05), pp. 221–230. ACM Press, New York (2005)
17. Rehm, M., André, E.: Where do they look? Gaze behaviors of multiple users interacting with an embodied conversational agent. In: Proceedings of International Conference on Intelligent Agents (IVA-05), LNCS (LNAI), vol. 3661, pp. 241–252. Springer, Heidelberg (2005)
18. Rist, T., André, E., Baldes, S., Gebhard, P., Klesen, M., Kipp, M., Rist, P., Schmitt, M.: A review of the development of embodied presentation agents and their appication fields. In: Prendinger and Ishizuka [14] pp. 377–404
19. Selker, T.: Visual attentive interfaces. BT Technology Journal 22(4), 146–150 (2004)
20. Shimojo, S., Simion, C., Shimojo, E., Scheier, C.: Gaze bias both reflects and influences preference. Nature Neuroscience 6(12), 1317–1322 (2003)
21. Starker, I., Bolt, R.A.: A gaze-responsive self-disclosing display. In: Proceedings CHI-90, pp. 3–9. ACM Press, New York (1990)
22. Vertegaal, R., Slagter, R., van der Veer, G., Nijholt, A.: Eye gaze patterns in conversations: There is more to conversational agents than meets the eyes. In: Proceedings of CHI-01, pp. 301–308. ACM Press, New York (2001)
23. Zhai, S.: What's in the eyes for attentive input. Communications of the ACM 46(3), 34–39 (2003)

Adaptation of Graphics and Gameplay in Fitness Games by Exploiting Motion and Physiological Sensors

Fabio Buttussi, Luca Chittaro, Roberto Ranon, and Alessandro Verona

HCI Lab, Dept. of Math and Computer Science, University of Udine
Via delle Scienze 206, 33100 Udine, Italy
{buttussi,chittaro,ranon}@dimi.uniud.it
http://hcilab.uniud.it

Abstract. Obesity and lack of physical fitness are increasingly common in adults as well as children and can negatively affect health. Regular physical activity, such as jogging or training in a fitness center, is recommended by physiologists to fight obesity and improve one's fitness, but usually requires considerable motivation. Recently, researchers as well as companies have proposed a few *fitness games*, i.e. videogames where users play by performing physical exercises, in which game elements (such as graphics and gameplay) are used to encourage people to exercise regularly. This paper proposes a fitness game system which aims at combining arcade-style game graphics, physiological sensors (e.g. heart rate monitor, 3D accelerometer), and an adaptation engine. The adaptation engine considers personal information provided by the user (e.g., age and gender), her current heart rate and movements, and information collected during previous game sessions to adjust the required intensity of physical exercises through context-aware and user-adaptive dynamic adaptations of graphics and gameplay. Besides describing the general system, the paper presents two implemented games and a preliminary user evaluation, which also led us to introduce in the system a 3D virtual human.

Keywords: Fitness games, user-adaptive systems, context-awareness, physiological parameters.

1 Introduction

Obesity and lack of physical fitness due to inappropriate eating habits and insufficient physical activity are increasingly common in adults as well as children. This is detrimental to people's wellness and productivity, can negatively affect health, and increase the need for medical assistance. Regular physical activity, such as jogging or training in a fitness center, is recommended by physiologists to fight obesity and improve one's fitness, but usually requires considerable motivation. Since videogames are attractive and may easily engage people (especially youngsters), a solution recently proposed by some researchers (e.g., [1,2,5,6])

A. Butz et al. (Eds.): SG 2007, LNCS 4569, pp. 85–96, 2007.

and companies (e.g., [7]) consists in videogames that users play by performing physical exercises. While some of these videogames (e.g., [1,2]) are entertainment systems that may have a positive effect on users' fitness, others (e.g., [5,7]) have been specifically thought as fitness applications and are called *fitness games*.

While the idea of providing motivation to perform physical activity by exploiting videogame elements (such as attractive graphics and gameplay) has shown to be promising [1,2], there is still the risk that the user will exercise irregularly or in a wrong way (e.g., because she does not performs the right movements or she exercises at too high intensity), thus wasting potential benefits and even risking injuries. To ensure that the user will exercise at the right intensity, Masuko and Hoshino [5] have recently proposed to continuously monitor the heart rate of the user and use the measured value to dynamically adjust the behavior of the game.

In this paper, we extend Masuko and Hoshino's idea, and propose a fitness game system which aims at combining the attractive graphics and gameplay of arcade games, physiological and motion sensors, and an adaptation engine. In our system, the user provides input to arcade-style videogames by performing physical exercises which were recommended by a sport physiologist and a professional trainer. The adaptation engine of the system considers personal information provided by the user (e.g., age and gender), information collected during previous game sessions (e.g., score), and sensor readings (to detect the user's current physiological parameters and movements) to suggest the proper exercise intensity through context-aware and user-adaptive dynamic adaptations of graphics and gameplay.

The paper is organized as follows. Section 2 surveys related work. Section 3 introduces our fitness game system by describing its architecture, sensed context, the adaptive engine, and two implemented games. Section 4 describes the results of a preliminary user evaluation. In Section 5, we describe how the evaluation led us to introduce a 3D virtual human to provide in-game movement demonstrations and advice. Section 6 concludes the paper.

2   Related Work

Computer applications that support fitness activities by exploiting videogame graphics and gameplay have been explored by some research projects [1,2,5,4], as well as by a few commercial products (e.g., [7]). For example, in the Shadow Boxer [2] game, user's movements control an avatar that has to hit the objects which are displayed on the screen. The user plays by performing the basic movements of fitness boxing, which are detected by a camera. Another example is Kick Ass Kung-Fu [1], a martial arts game in which the user fights against virtual opponents with punches, kicks and acrobatic moves. In this game, the video image of the user (acquired through a camera) is embedded into a 3D world projected on two screens. To add fun, the game can exaggerate user's jumps and use slow motion for players' acrobatic moves.

The potential benefits of Shadow Boxer and Kick Ass Kung-Fu on user's fitness have been investigated by carrying out evaluations, in which both games were able to significantly increase users' heart rate. For example, the evaluation of Kick Ass Kung-Fu on 46 users showed that the game could be used as a fitness activity, since the median of users' heart rate after fighting an opponent was at 90% of their maximum heart rate. However, as suggested in [5], in these games people might not exercise efficiently, since exercise intensity is not adjusted individually based on heart rate (as it is recommended also by sport physiologists). The proposed solution is to monitor the user's heart rate during the game, and adjust the game behavior so that the user exercises at the right level of intensity. This approach was experimented in a boxing-like videogame [5], where the user's arms movements were detected by a camera, and the behavior of computer-controlled opponents was dynamically adjusted so that the user could reach and maintain a target optimal heart rate.

Other fitness games and fitness applications provide a user interface based on a virtual human that motivates the user to exercise or even acts as a virtual trainer. For example, the Philips Virtual Coach [4] system employs a stationary exercise bike, heart rate sensors, and a 2D virtual coach projected on a screen, which also displays a virtual environment representing an open-air landscape. The virtual coach appears every minute to give feedback to the user, based on her heart-rate information. A study on 24 users found that the virtual coach lowered perceived pressure and tension, while the virtual environment was perceived as fun and had a beneficial effect on motivation. The application EyeToy: Kinetic [7] is an example of commercial fitness game. It exploits a webcam to capture the user's body image and visualize it on the screen together with synthetic game elements, which the user has to hit by making specific movements. The game allows the user to choose between a male or female 3D virtual trainer, and creates an individual 12-weeks training plan, taking into account user's height, weight, age, physical fitness and familiarity with EyeToy games (information is acquired through a questionnaire). During the game, the virtual trainer gives suggestions on how to correctly perform the exercises. Moreover, the virtual trainer comments on the user's performance, giving her marks and congratulations for the results or encouraging her to keep training and further improve. Finally, it is interesting to note that EyeToy: Kinetic motivates the user also by giving purely graphic rewards, e.g. it draws a shining aura around the user's image on the screen if she correctly performs the required sequences of movements.

3   A Context-Aware and User-Adaptive Fitness Game System

To bring together the benefits of videogame graphics and gameplay on motivation and those of physical exercises performed at correct intensity on one's fitness, we propose a context-aware and user-adaptive fitness game system. Our approach differs from the fitness games mentioned in the previous section in the sense that we aim at mapping fitness exercises into control actions for any kind of videogame and graphical environment. Therefore, while most of the solutions proposed in the literature are restricted to specific sports games (e.g., boxing, fighting) and exercises (e.g., punches, kicks), our system has been designed to be more general, e.g. allowing us to implement a space game where the user controls the position of her spaceship by performing an exercise based on knee bends.

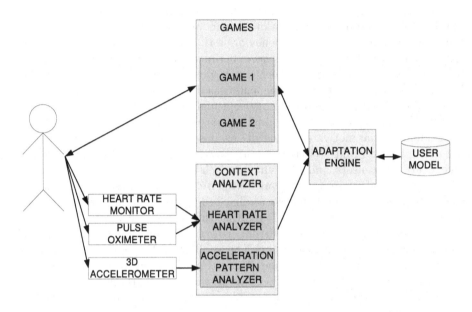

Fig. 1. The architecture of the proposed fitness game system

The architecture of our system is illustrated in Figure 1:

- The *Context Analyzer* subsystem acquires raw data from available physiological and motion sensors and analyzes it to derive higher level information on the user's physiological state and movements. In particular, the *Heart Rate Analyzer* module processes ECG data provided by an heart rate monitor or pulse data provided by a pulse oximeter to derive the user's current heart rate. The *Acceleration Pattern Analyzer* processes acceleration data provided by 3D accelerometers and recognizes patterns that correspond to specific user's movements. The Context Analyzer then sends the derived information, such as current heart rate and user's movements, to the Adaptation Engine.
- The *User Model* database stores personal information provided by the user (i.e., nickname, age, gender, weight, height) as well as information acquired during game sessions which are related with the user's physiological state.
- The *Adaptation Engine* subsystem considers the information provided by the Context Analyzer as well as the information contained in the User Model

database, and applies fitness training rules to decide if (and which) game adaptations, such as an increase in difficulty, are needed. Moreover, it analyzes user's movements and converts them into more conventional input (e.g., up, down, fire actions) for the Games subsystem. Finally, the Adaptation Engine analyzes the personal information provided by the user as well as game events (e.g., current score) to update the User Model database.

– The *Games* subsystem provides the Adaptation Engine with a unified way to give input commands and requests for adaptations to the currently played game (possibly chosen from a set of available ones). The subsystem also handles other user's inputs (e.g., mouse events) and widgets that are reused among games (e.g., graphical representation of user's heart rate), while each particular game is implemented by a dedicated module.

All the subsystems and modules have been implemented in Java. The following subsections analyze in detail each of the three subsystems.

3.1 The Context Analyzer

In the proposed approach, the term "context" refers to all the information about the user and the environment currently acquired or derived from sensors. Each type of sensor is managed by a different module of the Context Analyzer. Current modules handle heart rate sensors and 3D accelerometer, but one could extend the Context Analyzer with additional modules that handle other types of sensors, e.g. to recognize user's movements through a camera as in some of the systems discussed in Section 2.

Considering the Heart Rate Analyzer module, we support two different wireless sensors: heart rate monitor and pulse oximeter. The considered heart rate monitor (Figure 2a) provides electrocardiographic (ECG) data, which the Heart Rate Analyzer examines to count the local maximum values in a time interval and derive user's heart rate in beats per minute. The considered sensor has some drawbacks though: it is not easy to wear, since the user has to attach two electrodes to her chest, a misplacement of the electrodes may prevent the sensor from retrieving data, and electrodes tend to detach during intensive exercise.

The pulse oximeter (Figure 2b) is clipped to the ear of the user and measures the amount of oxygen in the blood. Since the monitored signal bounces in synch with the heartbeat, the pulse oximeter can be conveniently used to acquire user's heart rate, provided that the user does not suffer from cardiovascular pathologies (in this case, the sensor provides a less accurate value). In our experience, this sensor was easier to wear, did not detach during exercises, and had the additional advantage of not requiring users to take off clothes to wear it.

To recognize some movements of the user, we employed a wireless 3D accelerometer. The 3D accelerometer is attached to a strip worn by the user and measures accelerations along the X,Y and Z axes. This sensor allows us to detect user's movements in any point within the range of the wireless network (in our case, a Bluetooth one), therefore the user has considerable freedom in choosing the preferred position where the physical exercises will be performed.

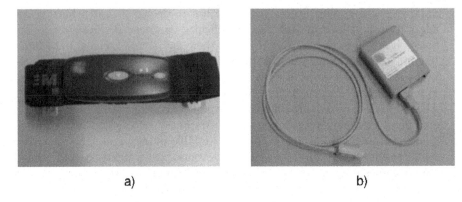

a)   b)

Fig. 2. Sensors currently managed by the Context Analyzer. a) heart rate monitor with integrated 3D accelerometer b) pulse oximeter.

The games we implemented exploit two patterns of acceleration:

– knee bends, characterized by variations of the acceleration along the y axis;
– left-to-right and right-to-left jumps, characterized by an acceleration along the y axis followed by accelerations along the x axis;

In our tests, the Acceleration Pattern Analyzer was able to recognize such patterns with an accuracy close to 95%. 3D acceleration data from a single accelerometer could also be exploited to recognize bends and twists of the spine by considering how gravity acceleration is distributed among the three axes: for example, when the user is standing erect, gravity acceleration is detected on the Y axis. When the user bends the spine 45 degrees to the right or to the left, half of the gravity acceleration is detected on the Y axis, and half on the X axis. More complex movements could be detected by using more accelerometers or by moving to (more expensive) motion sensors.

Finally, sensors can be combined with other game controls. For example, the heart rate monitor and 3D accelerometer in Figure 2a is equipped with an event button that we use to start the game, so that the user does not need to use the mouse or the keyboard during a game session.

3.2 The Adaptation Engine

The Adaptation Engine contains rules to:

– decide, on the basis of the user model and current context, if the user should put less or more physical effort in the game;
– consequently, during game sessions, request the Games subsystem to change graphics and gameplay to motivate the user to exercise at the optimal intensity; more specifically, each game offers three possible game modes: *keep*, to keep the user in the current heart rate range, *relax*, to reduce user's heart rate, and *exert*, to increase user's heart rate;

- at the beginning of each game session and for the chosen game, request the Games subsystem to set the difficulty level associated with each game mode; the difficulty level is a set of game specific parameters (e.g., speed of game elements, number of new opponents per minute) that ultimately determine the intensity of physical effort required to the user;
- update the user model to keep track of the relation between the performance in game sessions and the physical fitness of the user.

The user model consists of a set of personal information provided by the user on the first game session (i.e., nickname, age, gender, weight, height) and data that automatically is acquired and updated during game sessions (i.e., amount of time elapsed in each of the three above mentioned modes, maximum score reached for each game).

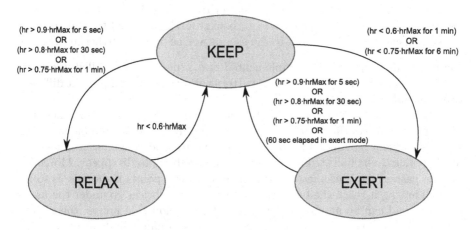

Fig. 3. Finite state automata to switch among game modes during a game session (*hrMax* is the user's maximum heart rate, determined by her age and gender)

The Adaptation Engine can prescribe within-game as well as between-games (long-term) adaptations. By considering personal information provided by the user, it can determine her maximum heart rate (*hrMax*). During interviews we carried out with a professional trainer and a sport physiologist, it was pointed out that the optimal heart rate for fitness practice is in the interval [0.6*hrMax*, 0.75*hrMax*]. Therefore, by comparing *hrMax* with the current heart rate, the Adaptation Engine can detect if the user is exercising at, below, or above the optimal intensity and thus dynamically require the Games subsystem to switch to one of the above mentioned modes. More specifically, the rules that determine transitions between modes are shown in Figure 3, where the formulas associated to the arcs were suggested by the interviewed experts.

Between-games adaptations are meant to better tailor the system to long-term changes in users' physical fitness, e.g., improvements due to regular activity with the system. More specifically, at the beginning of a game session, the Adaptation

Engine considers the information collected during previous sessions, and if it detects that the user is improving (e.g., because the game was often in the exert mode) or worsening, it requires to modify the difficulty level associated with each game mode. In this way, a trained user playing in the keep mode will exercise faster than an untrained user in the same mode, i.e., the difficulty level of the game mode will correspond to the actual fitness of the user.

3.3   The Games Subsystem

The Games subsystem runs the chosen game and changes the graphics and gameplay according to the requests of the Adaptation Engine. In general, changes of mode are mapped into:

- changes in game difficulty (e.g., speed or number of game opponents), that require the user to move faster or slower to progress in the game;
- changes in graphical elements (e.g., background, graphical theme) to make system choices more explicit to the user as well as provide further motivation.

Following this approach, we implemented two fitness games, called *Flareqoor* and *GeoKaos*, which exploit different patterns of movement and present different graphics and gameplay.

GeoKaos (Figure 4) was inspired by the *Arkanoid* [8] arcade game. The user controls a small pad that can be moved horizontally in the bottom of the screen and has to hit a moving white ball, attempting to send it against a number of colored bricks. The ball striking a brick causes the brick to disappear. Moreover, as time passes, the bricks move down. The user loses points if she misses to hit the ball letting it reach the bottom of the screen, or if bricks go under the user's pad. The pad can be moved by performing left or right side jumps: the greater is the jump, the more the pad is moved. Changes in game mode are translated into changes in the ball speed. Moreover, the graphical theme of the game is chosen among three possibilities to make explicit that a game mode change has happened.

Flareqoor (Figure 5) is aspace shoot'emup game. The user moves a continuously firing spaceship (left part of Figure 5) up and down by standing erect or bending knees and has to shoot the enemy spaceships coming from the right. If an enemy spaceship hits the user's spaceship or reaches the left side of the screen, the user loses points, while she gains points by destroying the enemy spaceships. Since the user's spaceship fires continuously, the user has to control only its position by performing knee bends. The speed of enemy spaceships varies with the game mode, and no graphical elements are adapted dynamically.

4   Preliminary Evaluation

We carried out a preliminary evaluation of the system on 8 users (4 male, 4 female; age ranging from 23 to 26, averaging at 24.5). Before the experiment, we acquired personal information (i.e. age, weight and height), and asked users

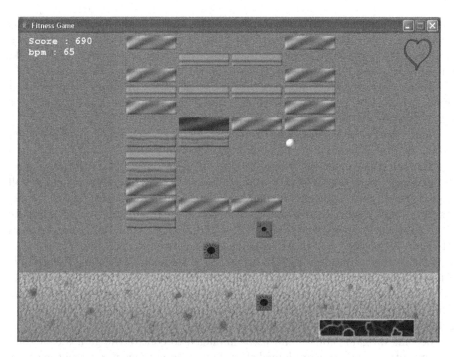

Fig. 4. The GeoKaos game

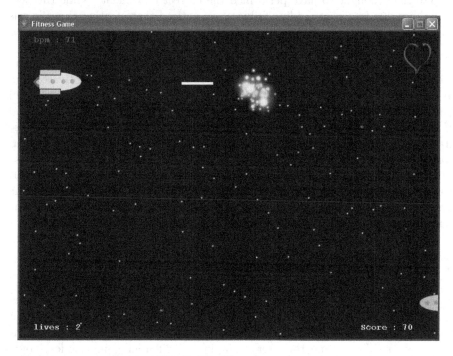

Fig. 5. The Flareqoor game

about their experience with videogames and physical activities. In particular, 2 subjects were very familiar with videogames (owning a console and playing at least once a week), 5 occasionally played PC videogames (not every week, but at least once a month), and one very rarely (a few times a year). Only 3 subjects were regularly involved in fitness activities or sports, 2 performed them occasionally (i.e., they sometimes play sports with friends, but they do not regularly train), while 3 did not perform any fitness activity or sport.

Then, users were asked to wear the sensors and try the two games described above. Before each game, we demonstrated the required body movements.

After the experiment, we asked users about their experience with the system. In particular, we asked them (i) to name a few adjectives to describe their overall experience; (ii) to comment on their experience with game control; (iii) to list strengths and weaknesses of the system; (iv) if such a system could motivate them to perform physical activities; (v) which was the game they preferred and why; (vi) if they had any other comment or suggestion to provide.

Considering the first question, 4 users named the adjective *entertaining*, while 3 thought the system was *engaging* and *nice*, but also *fatiguing*. Positive adjectives employed once were *energetic*, *interesting*, *new*, *outstanding*, and *useful*. The only negative adjective was *frustrating* (used only once), used because the game failed to identify movements a few times.

Focusing on game control, all users managed to control the games to a good extent, but five of them complained that they could not always control the game, despite they thought to have performed the correct movement. While this was sometimes due to sensor reading failures, we noticed that at other times it was due to incorrect movements (e.g., knee bends with incorrect spine position or sidesteps instead of side jumps).

With respect to strengths and weaknesses, users liked the idea of combining fitness activity and videogames, and said that the system could motivate them to perform more physical activity. However, 3 users expected more variety in gameplay and graphics, in particular for Flareqoor, which was the less preferred of the two games (only 2 of the 8 users preferred this game), probably because graphical adaptations were absent and thus the game tended to be perceived as boring.

Users provided us also with suggestions to improve the system. In particular, a user suggested us to calculate and display the calories she burnt during the game to provide further motivation, while another user asked for visual in-game demonstrations of the correct movements.

5   Introducing a 3D Virtual Human

As described in the previous section, the evaluation highlighted that some users had difficulties in understanding the correct movements, so in-game advice about them could be a useful improvement. Moreover, reports on the results of the game sessions (e.g., time the user spent in the different game modes) could provide further motivation and make system choices even more explicit. To satisfy these requirements, we introduced a 3D virtual human (Figure 6). When the Adaptation Engine decides that suggestions or demonstrations are needed, the appropriate 3D virtual human animations and speech are retrieved from a database and played to the user.

The virtual human can:

– show the correct movements that control the game (before the game starts, but also during game, if the system detects that the user is not performing movements that can be translated into inputs to the game);
– encourage and motivate the user when game modes are changed, e.g. telling the user that she needs to relax or exercise faster.

Technically, the virtual human is ISO H-Anim [3] compliant with Level of Articulation 2 and implemented in the X3D language [9]. Therefore, it can rotate 71 joints and is thus suited to show how to correctly perform the exercises required to control the games. Moreover, using a 3D model for the virtual human allows us to display the exercise from multiple points of view and thus improve the understanding of the demonstrated exercise.

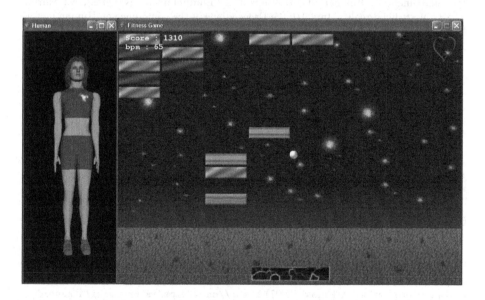

Fig. 6. The GeoKaos game with the 3D virtual human

6   Conclusions and Future Work

In this paper, we proposed a fitness game system which adapts game graphics and gameplay to user's movements and physiological parameters. We implemented two different games with the system and carried out a preliminary evaluation on 8 users, with encouraging outcomes. Since the need for demonstrations of correct movements and in-game advice emerged from the evaluation, we added a 3D virtual human which provides them. However, a more thorough evaluation with users is needed to assess the benefits of the 3D virtual human, and a longitudinal study is required to evaluate long-term effectiveness of the system.

An interesting opportunity for future work is to experiment with more sophisticated adaptations (in graphics and/or gameplay). For example, in more complex games, changes in game mode could be translated into different AI behaviors of opponents, or determine the actions that the user is allowed to perform physically as well as in the game.

Acknowledgments. We are very grateful to Luca Plaino (professional trainer) and Carlo Capelli (sport physiologist) for sharing their expert knowledge with us. Our research has been partially supported by the Italian Ministry of Education, University and Research (MIUR) under a PRIN 2005 grant.

References

1. Hämäläinen, P., Ilmonen, T., Höysniemi, J., Lindholm, M., Nykänen, A.: Martial arts in artificial reality. In: CHI '05: Proceedings of the conference on Human factors in computing systems, pp. 781–790. ACM Press, New York (2005)
2. Höysniemi, J., Aula, A., Auvinen, P., Hännikäinen, J., Hämäläinen, P.: Shadow boxer: a physically interactive fitness game. In: NordiCHI '04: Proceedings of the 3rd Nordic conference on Human-computer interaction, pp. 389–392. ACM Press, New York (2004)
3. Humanoid Animation Working Group. ISO/IEC 19774 Humanoid Animation (H-Anim) (2004) http://h-anim.org
4. IJsselsteijn, W., de Kort, Y., Westerink, J., de Jager, M., Bonants, R.: Fun and sports: Enhancing the home fitness experience. In: Rauterberg, M. (ed.) ICEC 2004. LNCS, vol. 3166, pp. 46–56. Springer, Heidelberg (2004)
5. Masuko, S., Hoshino, J.: A fitness game reflecting heart rate. In: ACE '06: Proceedings of the 2006 ACM SIGCHI international conference on Advances in computer entertainment technology, pp. 53–59. ACM Press, New York (2006)
6. Mueller, F., Agamanolis, S., Picard, R.: Exertion interfaces: sports over a distance for social bonding and fun. In: CHI '03: Proceedings of the SIGCHI conference on Human factors in computing systems, pp. 561–568. ACM Press, New York (2003)
7. Sony Computer Entertainment Europe and Nike Motion Works. Eyetoy: Kinetic (2005) http://www.eyetoykinetic.com/
8. Taito Corporation. Arkanoid (2007) http://en.wikipedia.org/wiki/Arkanoid
9. Web3D Consortium. ISO/IEC 19775:2004 Extensible 3D (X3D) (2004) http://www.web3d.org/x3d/specifications/

Correlating Text and Images: Concept and Evaluation

Timo Götzelmann[1], Pere-Pau Vázquez[3], Knut Hartmann,[1] Andreas Nürnberger[2],
and Thomas Strothotte[1]

[1] Graphics and Interactive Systems Group
[2] Information Retrieval Group
University of Magdeburg / Germany
{timo,knut,tstr}@isg.cs.uni-magdeburg.de,
nuernb@iti.cs.uni-magdeburg.de
[3] Modeling, Visualization, and Graphics Interaction Group
Technical University of Catalonia / Spain
ppau@lsi.upc.edu

Abstract. This paper presents the concept and an evaluation of a novel approach to support students to understand complex spatial relations and to learn unknown terms of a domain-specific terminology with coordinated textual descriptions and illustrations. Our approach transforms user interactions into queries to an information retrieval system. By selecting text segments or by adjusting the view to interesting domain objects, learners can request additional contextual information. Therefore, the system uses pre-computed multi-level representations of the content of explanatory text and of views on 3D models to suggest textual descriptions or views on 3D objects that might support the current learning task.

Our experimental application is evaluated by a user study that analyzes (i) similarity measures that are used by the information retrieval system to coordinate the content of descriptive texts and computer-generated illustrations and (ii) the impact of the individual components of these measures. Our study revealed that the retrieved results match the preferences of the users. Furthermore, the statistical analysis suggests a rough value to cut-off retrieval results according to their relevancy.

1 Introduction

Students of human anatomy, many scientific and technical areas have to learn many technical terms of a domain-specific terminology. As an example, anatomic textbooks focus on descriptions of geometric properties and spatial relations: chapters on *osteology*, for example, contain descriptions of characteristic features of complex-shaped bones, chapters on *myology* employ these bone features as landmarks to describe the course of muscles, the *syndesmology* explains the direction of movements in joints. These examples illustrate the main difficulties for medical students: (i) to learn denotations of many semantic concepts, (ii) to relate information of several sub-disciplines that are spread throughout voluminous documents or even over several documents, and (iii) the need to mentally reconstruct complex spatial configurations.

The ultimate goal of anatomy is to provide a profound knowledge of characteristic features that enables experts to identify objects and knowledge of spatial relationships between objects. As images can efficiently convey visual properties and spatial

A. Butz et al. (Eds.): SG 2007, LNCS 4569, pp. 97–109, 2007.
© Springer-Verlag Berlin Heidelberg 2007

relations, many expressive illustrations complement textual descriptions in anatomic textbooks. However, the printing costs prevent to include illustrations that depict every single spatial configuration. This lack legitimates a specialized class of textbooks—anatomic atlases—*only* containing illustrations. Another characteristic of illustrations in human anatomy is that a large number of mutual overlapping small, thin, or complex-shaped objects have to be depicted. The complexity of these spatial configurations forced human illustrators to develop a large number of abstraction techniques, which are also useful to focus on the attention of the learner.

This paper presents a novel interactive tool where students can interactively explore comprehensive tutoring material that are enhanced with computer-generated illustrations. By selecting text segments or navigations to view directions that show objects of interest, students can initiate queries to an information retrieval system that suggests those sections in text documents or those views on 3D models that best describe or present relevant domain objects in the current context. Moreover, several emphasis techniques on text and graphics are applied (i) to focus the user's attention on the most relevant objects in the presentation and (ii) to refine the relevance of specific terms in the query. Note that we do *not* aim to replace hand-made illustrations, but to complement them with computer-generated renditions. Finally, a dynamic label layout establishes co-referential links between textual and visual elements. In our system, students can use labels to learn those technical terms that are required to understand small text segments.

These explanations demonstrate (i) the relevance of basic learning tasks in human anatomy as well as for almost all scientific or technical domains and (ii) the need to complement textual descriptions with expressive illustrations. Therefore, we implemented an experimental system, which allows medical students to access the entire area of human anatomy. Our corpus comprises an electronic version of Gray's popular textbook on human anatomy [3] and all anatomic models contained in the Viewpoint library of 3D models [2]. Similarity measures between descriptors for the content stored in a database and query terms enabled us to suggest text segments that provide additional information and views on 3D models that might support learning tasks in the current context. We proposed multi-level content descriptors for text documents and 3D visualizations. Based on these pre-computed data structures, students can search for *paragraphs* in voluminous textual documents and for appropriate *views* from sets of 3D models. Technical details about the algorithm, the system's architecture, and our implementation are provided in [4].

The complexity of the spatial relationships presented in illustrations makes it difficult to select 'good' views. In order to determine the quality of views on a 3D model, our system incorporates several metrics to measure the visibility of objects, the relative size of objects on the projection, and the amount of contextual information provided by a view. We designed several tests to evaluate the impact of these factors in a user study. This paper presents the design and the results of this evaluation.

This section motivated the problem statement. Sec. 2 introduces the related work and the problem-related terminology. In the following, Sec. 3 briefly explains the concept to employ information retrieval techniques to correlate views and text, while Sec. 4 evaluates this approach. Finally, Sec. 5 discusses directions of future work.

2   Related Work

Our system proposes formal content descriptors for views on 3D models that enable a uniform treatment of textual and visual elements in *information retrieval techniques*. The second challenging problem of our approach—the definition of criteria to evaluate the quality of views with respect to contextual requirements or *communicative goals*—is also a central problem for *camera planning systems*. In the latter area, many researchers proposed complex mechanisms to maintain user-specified constraints during the course of animations, in guided explorations of dynamic or complex scenes, or to adjust the camera during user interactions.

The characteristics of our application domain—compact arrangements of complex-shaped static objects—allow us to simplify the problem statements. In our system, as in many other anatomic tutoring systems, the navigation is restricted to an orbit which encloses the 3D scenes. Hence, the number of camera parameters is reduced to 2 polar coordinates.

Uninformed methods to determine 'good' views are purely based on topological properties of the geometric object or on evaluations of visible or occluded geometric features. Many researchers propose measures that depend (i) on the projected areas of faces or (ii) on the number of faces visible from (a set of) viewpoints. Some of these measures for 'good views' aim to minimize the number of degenerated faces as seen at orthogonal projection [5] or maximize the amount of details shown in a view [9].

A very influential measure is based on the amount of *geometric* information that can be captured from a certain view. The *viewpoint entropy* proposed by Vázquez et al. [13] is defined as:

$$H_p(X) = - \sum_{i=0}^{N_f} \frac{A_i}{A_t} \log \frac{A_i}{A_t}, \tag{1}$$

where p is a point on an orbit around a scene, N_f refers to the number of faces of the scene, A_i denotes to the projected area of face i, A_t is the total area covered over the sphere, and A_0 represents the projected area of background in open scenes. In a closed scene, or if the point does not see the background, the whole sphere is covered by the projected areas and consequently $A_0 = 0$. The maximum entropy is obtained when a certain point can see all the visible faces with the same relative projected area A_i/A_t.

The viewpoint entropy measure yields a good balance between the number of visible faces and the area covered by them. The measure is sensitive to the geometric level of detail, in the sense that a fine tessellation of a patch may result in a high number of faces. However, this is not a problem as the entropy may be measured in terms of faces instead of patches.

Informed methods are able to assign object-specific quality measures for the components of a 3D scene and consider object-specific relevance values defined by an external application. There a just a few systems which consider object-specific relevance values. Viola et al. [12], for example, used context-depended relevance values to determine appropriate views on volumetric data sets. Recently, Mühler et al. [6] presented a system, which employs an exhaustive amount of pre-processed information to determine several view-dependent quality measures and to weight their influence during run-time.

All these systems as well as ours incorporate the view entropy as one parameter in a complex view metric.

Mühler's system prefers *canonical views* that have been suggested by Palmer and Rosch [8] in **cognitive psychology**. Canonical views ease the identification of visual objects. The exhaustive study of Blanz [1] proved that these views were also preferred in interactive 3D visualizations. To the best of our knowledge, however, the impact of context-dependent relevance values that are assigned to the individual components of a complex object to the quality of views has not been evaluated.

Our new approach combines view-dependent information with manually created textual annotations in the construction of view descriptors that are used in an **information retrieval system**. The *vector space model* [11] allows an efficient storage of the content and a quick access even for very large databases. Moreover, term-specific weights are computed according to (i) their frequency in the document to be represented and (ii) according to their frequency in the database. In order to estimate the relevance of a document with respect to a query often the popular cosine measure [10] to determine the similarity between the document and the query is used. Our work also employs a *boost function* to consider emphasized terms or prominent visual objects.

3   Correlating Views and Text

This section briefly discusses the concept of the interactive approach to determine correlating text and views.[1]

3.1   The Indexing Process

Before search engines can retrieve search results, the source documents have to be indexed. We are using a popular text retrieval engine: LUCENE, which processes text documents. In our approach, we extract textual descriptors for the source documents (text of books and 3D models) which specify them. We break up the documents into a finer granularity—text documents are segmented to paragraphs, and views of 3D models are sampled from a defined number of camera positions on their bounding sphere.

The extraction of the paragraph descriptors is performed as follows (see also Fig. 1): First, a simple text parser (i) breaks up the documents into single paragraphs. Subsequently, each of these paragraphs are (ii) processed by another text parser, which removes unnecessary stop words (e.g., 'a', 'and', 'with') and writes the remaining terms into the paragraph descriptor. Finally, the parser detects emphasized words in the paragraphs and marks these words in the paragraph descriptor with a higher importance value, which is recognized by the text retrieval indexer.

Likewise, 3D models are analyzed in order to extract textual view descriptors (see also Fig. 2). Obviously, the denotations of geometric objects cannot be purely extracted from their shape. But often hierarchical geometric models (e.g., scene graphs) use technical terms to identify their constituting components. Moreover, our system allows to directly add or manipulate textual annotations for geometric objects within the 3D visualization of 3D models. This information is stored in an annotation table that links

---

[1] For a detailed technical descriptions, see [4].

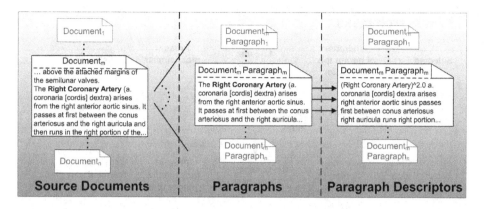

Fig. 1. The extraction of paragraph descriptors

unique color codes for geometric components to technical terms. For a given 3D model, a number of sample views located on an orbit are analyzed with color-coded renditions. We determine the visibility of their components as well as their size and position on the projection. Finally, we construct a view descriptor that contains reference terms for all visible objects, that specifies their relative size and a measure that specifies how centered these objects are located on the projection area.

3.2   The Search Process

Both indices generated in the pre-processing step serve to find corresponding text descriptors ↔ view descriptors. The overview of the search results—a set of paragraphs respectively views—are presented to the user (see Fig. 3). Subsequently, the user is able to select and explore the results.

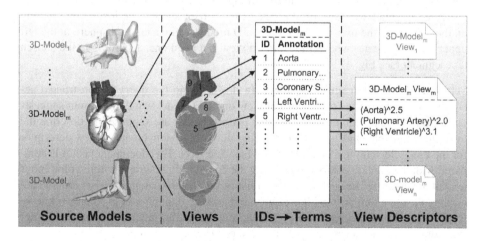

Fig. 2. The extraction of view descriptors

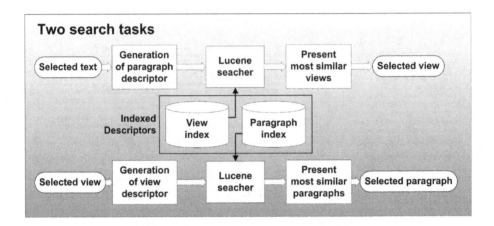

Fig. 3. Both search tasks between text and images

Learners can navigate through the material and interactively adjust the content of the original textbooks and computer-generated 3D visualizations. By selecting a text segment, learners can submit a query to the information retrieval system and initiate a search for views which correspond with the text segment. But those queries can also be initiated by adjusting views on 3D models to object of interest. The aim of the information retrieval system in this scenario is to retrieve paragraphs which correspond with the visible objects of the selected view. The following paragraphs will present examples for both scenarios.

Selected Text ↦ View Query: In order to obtain images for user-selected text segments, the system creates paragraph descriptors for the selected text segment (see Sec. 3.1). This document vector represents the query and is compared with view descriptors of all available 3D models. The best fitting 3D model is loaded and the best view is presented immediately; the remaining good views of different 3D models are presented in small windows on the side of the screen and can be loaded by clicking on them. Finally, the user can explore the 3D model, while a colored sphere in the left upper corner indicates whether the current view is a good one, according to the chosen text segment (see Fig. 4).

Selected View ↦ Paragraph Query: In this scenario the query is constructed according to the properties of the current view on a 3D model while the system suggests corresponding text segments of available textbooks that are supposed to describe the most salient visible objects (see Fig. 5). Therefore, the system creates a view descriptor for the user-selected view on a 3D model (see Sec. 3.1). This document vector is compared with document vectors representing the content of paragraph within voluminous textual documents. The search result—a list of pointers to paragraphs—is ordered according the their similarity with the query and presented to the user in a manner known from common search engines. By clicking on one of the presented results, the user immediately gets to the correct position of the chosen document.

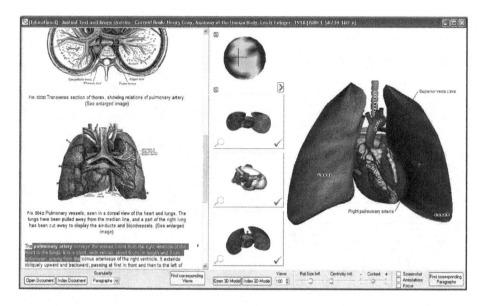

Fig. 4. Text $\mapsto$ Image Query (left) and Results (right)

As an additional feature users can induce combinations of those queries. Hence, the user can type in a text query to determine all corresponding views and similar text segments, as well as a view query can determine all corresponding text segments and similar views.

4   Evaluation

We performed a user study to determine (i) what influence the metrics relative size and centricity have, and (ii) if the algorithms used for the determination of good views to text segments as well as the determination of text segments to specific views are appropriate. To address the first study, we simplified the problem to a set of 8 spheres, which were spatially arranged in a cubical manner. Some of the spheres were important (green colored), whereas the remaining spheres were not important (gray colored). By rotating this 3D arrangement, we were able to derive several configurations, covering visibility and centricity problems. The second study used a well known 3D object (car) and applied our algorithms to derive a set of good views for a specified textual description or good textual descriptions for a specified view.

4.1   Method

Subjects and design. We disigned a test in 3 different languages (Catalan, English, and German); the user study was carried out with 115 subjects. The subjects (47 female, 68 male) were subdivided into one test group g_1 (76 participants) without prior

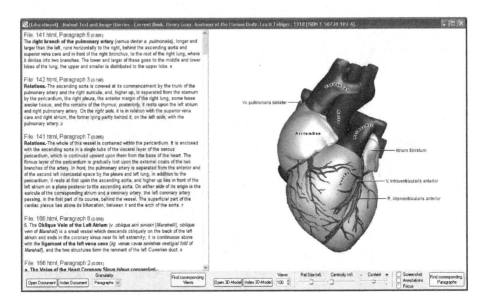

Fig. 5. Image ↦ Text Query (right) and Results (left)

knowledge of 3D software (e.g., 3D games, 3D modeling software), and one test group g_2 (39 participants) with knowledge in that field. Both test groups had to solve the same blind tests.

Materials and apparatus. The user study consisted of 12 single tests, where the subjects had to choose one out of 3 alternatives. The test was presented in a printable document, but could also be performed on a computer monitor. The users were also asked if they had problems in understanding the test or recognizing the images, thus, those results were excluded from the study to remove distortion by uncertainty.

The first part p_1 of the study consisted of 6 single tests (t_1-t_6). In order to avoid distortions the tests were extremely simplified, and presented cubical arranged spheres. It evaluated, which of the criteria (relative size or centricity) humans consider as superior for a 'good view' and to which level. To determine the three alternatives, we used the

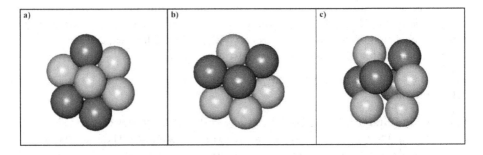

Fig. 6. Select the alternative (a,b,c) where the green spheres are optimally visible

measures of visible relative size and centricity, as described in Sec. 3. The users had to select the view they preferred in terms of visibility (see Fig. 6).

The second part p_2 consisted of 6 tests (t_7-t_{12}) to investigate text↔image correlations with a well known 3D object. Since the approach is designed for tutoring purposes in general (i.e. in the fields of medical, natural science, engineering etc.) we chose a model of a BMW Z3 car, as most subjects know its interior parts by its denomination. The tests (t_7-t_9) assessed, whether our approach algorithmically determines the same views the users would select for a given text (see Fig. 7). In the tests (t_{10}-t_{12}), the users were presented a specific view of the car and they had to select one of 3 alternative textual descriptions in order to find out if the proposed algorithm correlates with the users selections (see Fig. 8).

Procedure. A short preliminary user test with 2 subjects (excluded from the user study), followed by a short interview about their decisions, revealed minor problems in understanding the tests. Their choices of views were distorted by a preference of several spatial arrangements (i.e., canonical views), which negatively influenced the visibility. Thus, for the user study we included a note, remarking that the focus of the test is on the visibility of the important parts.

4.2   Results and Discussion

Scoring. In the tests 1-6, we calculated the value of both measures (visible relative size and centricity). Since the users chose one favored alternative, we were able to determine if the results of both measures corresponded to the preferences of the users.

In the tests 7-9 we indexed 100 views of the car model. Then, the system was queried by 2-3 technical terms of well-known car components (e.g., steering wheel, leather seats). The top scored results, together with two lower scored results, were presented to the user in a random order. In the tests 10-12, we indexed 3 different descriptions (each with 2-3 technical terms of well-known car components) and queried the system with a specific view of the car, in order to find out which of the descriptions optimally fits

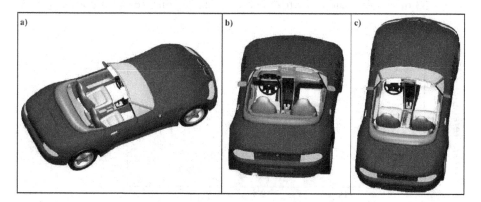

Fig. 7. Which view (a,b,c) shows the optimal visibility of the *steering wheel*, the *gearshift lever*, and the *center console*?

a) Rear lights, Center console, Mirrors	
b) Rear lights, Door, Leather seats	
c) Rear lights, Mirrors, Wind shield	

Fig. 8. Which text (a,b,c) describes the visible parts of the image most appropriate?

to the image. The top scored description, as well as the lower scored descriptions, were presented to the user in random order.

Hypothesis 1: Subjects with knowledge of 3D software select different images than those without

Since the approach copes with 3D objects, we first determined if participants with knowledge of 3D software (3D modeling, 3D games) have different preferences in the selection of 3D views than those without. The majority of the subjects of both groups g_1 and g_2 chose the same alternatives. We also applied *Student's* t-test to get evidence if at least the percentages differ significantly. Statistical significance cannot be considered with a result $\geq 5\%(p \geq 0.05)$. The t-test neither determined a significant difference for p_1 (F=0.062, p=0.808) nor for p_2 (F=0.278, p=0.610). In the following, we merged the groups g_1 and g_2 with group g.

Hypothesis 2: Relative visible size is more important than centricity

Part p_1 aimed at determining the influence of both measures *relative visible size* m_1 and *centricity* m_2 (see Fig. 9). We used the χ^2-test; since 115 subjects contributed to the user study and each of the tests had three alternatives, there was an expected frequency of 38.333 of choosing an alternative. For statistical significance χ^2 has to be ≥ 5.99 ($\alpha = 0.05$).

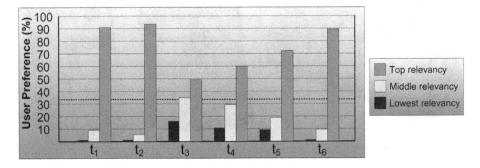

Fig. 9. Test results of the measures relative visible size and centricity

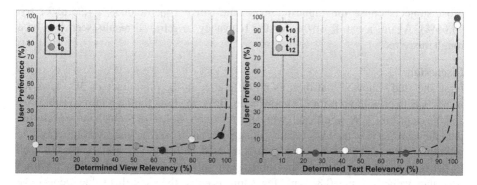

Fig. 10. Text-Image retrieval results (left) and Image-Text retrieval results (right)

In order to test m_1, t_1 and t_2 equalized m_2 of the important objects, while m_1 differed. There was a strong significance for m_1 ($t_1 : \chi^2 = 169.793$ and $t_1 : \chi^2 = 184.976$). In t_1 90.43% chose the alternative with highest value for m_1, while did for t_2 93.04%.

For testing m_2, the tests t_3 and t_4 equalized m_1 of the important objects, while m_2 differed. There was a significance for m_2 ($t_3 : \chi^2 = 17.965$ and $t_4 : \chi^2 = 40.192$). In t_3 only 48.7% chose the alternative with highest value for m_2, while did for t_4 59.13%. Thus, m_2 is significant, but seems to be much less important than m_1.

Finally, the t_5 and t_6 tested m_1 and m_2 against each other. m_1 had a higher support (t_5: 73.04% and t_6:88.70%) than m_2 (t_5: 19.13% and t_6:9.57%), while the remaining subjects chose the alternative, where neither m_1 nor m_2 was maximized (t_5: 7.83% and t_6:1.74%).

As we assumed, relative visible size is clearly more important than centricity. Thus, the following tests were carried out with an unequal weight on both measures m_1 and m_2 (5:1).

Hypothesis 3: The approach presents desired views for a given paragraph
In the tests t_7-t_9 we presented a set of common technical terms of the car and showed three alternative views of the car. The user had to select the one where the named objects were optimally visible. The higher the computed relevance of our algorithm was, the more users preferred the view (see Fig. 10-left). Most subjects chose the highest ranked alternative (t_7:86.09%, t_8:84.35%, t_9:89.57%). At a relevancy of less than 0.8 only a few subjects preferred the view, but with a relevancy greater than 0.8 the preference increased exponentially. Thus, this seems to be a rough measure for a cutoff of retrieval results.

Hypothesis 4: The approach presents desired paragraphs for a given view
In the tests t_{10}-t_{12} we presented an image of a car and showed three alternatives with multiple common technical terms of the car. The subjects had to choose the alternative that optimally describes the image. Like in the previous test, the higher the computed relevance of our algorithm was, the more users preferred the view (see Fig. 10-right).

Most subjects chose the highest ranked alternative (t_{10}:100.00%, t_{11}:95.65%, t_{12}: 95.65%). Again, a cutoff of 0.8 for the relevancy of retrieval results seems to be a rough measure.

Discussion

First, the study showed that there is no difference in the preference of 3D views for subjects with or without prior 3D knowledge. Both, the tests for the relative visible size and the centricity were significant, while the relative visible size is much more preferred than the centricity. In the tests for text-image queries as well as image-text queries, the relevancy determined by our algorithm correlated with the user preferences. In each of the tests more than 80% of the subjects chose the top ranked view. Since with a relevancy value less than 0.8—only few subjects chose the view, this value seems to be a good measure for a cutoff of the retrieval results.

5   Discussion and Future Work

This paper proposes a novel concept to support learners in the interactive exploration of comprehensive multi-modal tutoring material. We implemented an experimental application that facilitates an evaluation of the fundamental assumption underlying our application—the measures and the weights to describe the properties of computer-generated renditions of 3D models. Additional contrastive analyses should evaluate the efficiency of our approach in comparison to traditional scientific textbooks with performance tasks (e.g., seeking time of text-image relations).

Other researchers proposed more measures to evaluate the quality of a view (e.g., [6]). But as no formal comparisons or evaluations of their impact on specific tasks in learning environments have been been done yet, it remains unclear whether these measures improve the quality of the retrieval results. Therefore, additional user studies have to be designed in order to determine the impact of different view descriptors to both search tasks in relating the content presented within multi-modal tutoring systems. Moreover, new measures that extend the idea of view entropy have been recently proposed (e.g., mutual information). Up to now, they have been used to measure the geometric contents of a scene by using faces' projected areas. This paper shows the relevance of perception-based factors. Therefore, we plan to integrate these measures into our application to develop new measures that consider new perception-based features, such as silhouettes, and to run a contrastive analysis of for viewpoint entropy measures.

The experimental application used annotated polygonal models. Frequently, medical tutoring systems also employ annotated volumetric models (e.g., the visible human data set [7]). The view descriptors that are proposed in this work are also applicable to volumetric models. Therefore, our approach could be easily extended with volumetric visualizations.

Acknowledgments

We would like to thank all persons who contributed to our user study. The 2nd author has been supported by the TIN2004-08065-C02-01 project of the Spanish Government.

References

1. Blanz,V., Tarr, M.J., Bülthoff,H.H.:What Object Attributes Determine Canonical Views? Perception, 28:575–599 (1999)
2. Digimation Inc. Viewpoint 3D Library (2007)
3. Gray, H.: Anatomy of the Human Body, 20th edn. Lea & Febiger, Philadelphia (1918)
4. Götzelmann, T., Vázquez, P.-P., Hartmann, K., Germer, T., Nürnberger, A., Strothotte, T.: Mutual Text-Image Queries. Preprint 1/2007, Department of Computer Science, Otto-von-Guericke University of Magdeburg (2007)
5. Kamada, T., Kawai, S.: A Simple Method for Computing General Position in Displaying Three-Dimensional Objects. Computer Vision, Graphics, and Image Processing 41(1), 43–56 (1988)
6. Mühler, K., Neugebauer, M., Tietjen, C., Preim, B.: Viewpoint Selection for Intervention Planning. In: EG/IEEE-VGTC Symp. on Visualization (to appear 2007)
7. National Library of Medicine.Visible Human Project (2007)
8. Palmer, S.E., Rosch, E., Chase, P.: Canonical Perspective and the Perception of Objects. In: Attention and Performance, vol. 9, pp. 135–151. Erlbaum, Hillsdale (1981)
9. Plemenos, D., Benayada, M.: Intelligent Display in Scene Modeling. New Techniques to Automatically Compute Good Views. In: Int. Conf. on Computer Graphics & Vision (GraphiCon'96) (1996)
10. Salton, G., Allan, J., Buckley, C., Singhal, A.: Automatic Analysis, Theme Generation, and Summarization of Machine-Readable Texts. Science 264, 1421–1426 (1994)
11. Salton, G., Wong, A., Yang, C.S.: A Vector Space Model for Automatic Indexing. Communications of the ACM 18(11), 613–620 (1975)
12. Viola, I., Feixas, M., Sbert, M., Gröller, M.E.: Importance-Driven Focus of Attention. IEEE Transactions on Visualization and Computer Graphics 12(5), 933–940 (2006)
13. Vázquez, P.-P., Feixas, M., Sbert, M., Heidrich, W.: Viewpoint selection using viewpoint entropy. In: Vision Modeling and Visualization Conference (VMV-01), pp. 273–280 (2001)

Lighting-by-Example with Wavelets

Hai Nam Ha and Patrick Olivier

Culture Lab
School of Computing Science
Newcastle Univeristy
Newcastle Upon Tyne, NE1 7RU, UK
{h.n.ha,p.l.olivier}@ncl.ac.uk

Abstract. Automatic lighting design aims to provide users with semi-automated approaches, and easy-to-use tools, to configure lighting for 3D scenes. We present LIGHTOPEX the first fully automatic example-based local illumination lighting design system. Utilizing a wavelet-based lighting design framework, by which image quality is modeled using a cognitively inspired objective function, this approach to lighting design both: (1) allows the declarative specification of lighting; and (2) facilitates intuitive and natural specification of scene lighting. LIGHTOPEX enables users to select the desired lighting for a scene using exemplar 2D images and uses the spatial distribution of the luminance in these images as the target values of an optimization step. We demonstrate the utility of LIGHTOPEX through a range of examples, and conduct a preliminary investigation of the performance of a number of different of optimization schemes.

1 Introduction

Lighting design is the problem of finding optimal lighting parameters – positions, directions, colors, and intensities of light sources – to achieve the visual properties required of a 3D scene. The means by which the required visual properties are specified, and the degree of manual intervention by which this can be achieved, is highly application dependent. In the case of visualization it is necessary that lighting design is a fully automatic process in which the perceptual qualities of real-time generated views of 3D objects are maximized.

Effective lighting can help to convey information about a scene and the automatic generation of images with highly discernable visual characteristics is a pressing requirement, as components of a scene and their relative configuration with respect to the viewers cannot be anticipated in advance. By contrast, in the case of conventional design activities, such as game level design and traditional animation, lighting is used to convey both spatial information and a sense of emotion and mood. A lighting design tool is expected to support expert and non-expert users and provide significant reductions in design time within a process in which a designer has fully interactive control.

Insights from studies of visual cognition are increasingly applied to computer graphics. Much research has been carried out aimed at narrowing the gap between

A. Butz et al. (Eds.): SG 2007, LNCS 4569, pp. 110–123, 2007.

perception of real images and computer-generated images [5,11]. Realism in a computer-generated image is not only a matter of physical correctness, but also of perceptual equivalence of the image to the corresponding real world scene. Achieving perceptual equivalence between a computer-generated image and the scene is a significant challenge. Since many perception-based problems must be taken in to consideration. In particular, quantifying the perceptual quality of an image. Much research has been carried out to find efficient perception-based image quality metrics [5,10,11,19].

We present a wavelet-based lighting framework that has been developed as the core function used for optimizing lighting parameters with a set of target values of different components in an objective function, we propose a lighting-by-example approach as an alternative for users to design lighting. The underlying motivation for lighting-by-example is the fact that perceptual optimality is not always the appropriate goal for lighting design.

In almost all narrative films, or static images with a narrative theme, lighting positions and the subsequent spatial distribution of luminance in an image plays an important role in conveying both mood and emotion. In film this is particularly important as the mood a shot evokes plays a crucial role in supporting the narrative goals of the director and used to great effect to influence the subjective judgments of the audience as to the emotional tone of both particular scenes and the work in its entirety. Furthermore, viewers are highly skilled at identifying the emotional tone of an image based on its lighting. Non-expert viewers will have little or no insight into the configuration of lights with which such effects are created. Indeed they are often the result of highly artificial configurations of lights on a studio set (and post production editing). In short, we know what we want when we see it, but have little idea of how to reproduce it. This is the premise on which we base the lighting-by-example approach – that lighting is best configured for 3D scenes on the basis of existing exemplar images and not by through direct manipulation of lighting types, positions and luminance.

2 Previous Work

The traditional approach to lighting design for image synthesis is based on direct design methods. Users interactively specify values of lighting parameters, and iteratively render the scene and modify the parameters until the desired visual properties of the scene are obtained. Despite the fact that this can be a tedious and time-consuming process there have been relatively few attempts either to automate or assist the process of lighting design.

2.1 Inverse Design

Early attempts at lighting design rarely made explicit reference to models of users' perceptual responses to lighting. Kawai et al. [17] optimized light emission, direction and surface reflectance to obtain the desired illumination for an environment rendered using radiosity-based techniques. In this approach, users have to specify the illumination expected in the final image.

Early interactive techniques are typified by the approach of Poulin and Fournier [9,16] who developed a framework for the inverse design of light positions through the specification of shadows and highlights in a 3D scene. Using a sketch-based interface, users are able to sketch desired shadow areas with a mouse pointer. An objective function was defined such that the shadow region for a computed point light (and also some classes of extended light geometries) bounds the sketched regions as tightly as possible. Jolivet et al. [18] presented an approach to optimizing light positions in direct lighting using Monte-Carlo methods as part of a declarative paradigm that help users specify the lighting goal in an intuitive way.

More recently, there has been significant work on the development of approaches to computer graphics based upon explicit models of a viewer's perception. Perceptually adaptive approaches have ranged across the whole scope of graphics algorithm and interaction development, from schemes for polygon simplification and global illumination that take account of limits on visual attention and acuity, to the design of anthropomorphic animations and gaze-contingent displays [10,11].

Perception-based lighting design has included implicit approaches that aim to maximize illumination entropy for a fixed viewpoint. Gumhold [13] describes a perceptual illumination entropy approach in which he uses limited user studies to model user preferences in relation to brightness and curvature. By contrast, the Light Collages framework [12] uses an explicit model of perceptual preferences in which lights are optimized such that the diffuse illumination is proportional to the local curvature and specular highlights are used only for regions of particularly high curvature.

2.2 Example-Based Approaches

Schoeneman et al [2] also address lighting design as an inverse problem. Users were able to configure a set of desired properties that are expected to appear in the final image and the system tries to find out a solution whose properties are closest the set of desired properties. Directly painting on the surfaces of the rendered scene causes a change in surface radiance functions, and these after-painted surface radiance functions are used as target values in the optimization process that follows. Painted surfaces in the rendered image are given more weight, which biases the optimization towards solutions to those with properties that best match the painted surfaces. In this approach, painted surfaces can be considered as examples affecting the target radiance surface functions, though in this approach Schoeneman et al only address the problem for finding matching light intensities and colors for fixed light positions.

2.3 Lighting Scenes

One noticeable exception to the work on optimizing the lighting for individual objects, and inverse lighting design through the manipulation of object properties (such as shadows) is Design Galleries [3]. Marks et al's goal was the design of an interactive system to allow a user to interactively reduce the design space for light configurations through the use of a mapping function between an input vector containing light position, light type, and light direction and an output vector containing a set of values that summarizes the perceptual qualities of the final image.

During the optimization step lights are moved from one predefined position to another. At each position a light type is selected from a set of light types; and a corresponding image is generated. Final images are then arranged in clusters on the basis of the perceptual distance between images. Design Galleries can be considered to be in the spirit of an example-based approach despite the fact that there is no specific target used as the basis for an objective function (to be optimized). Through its generation of a wide range of clustered images as examples, Design Galleries presents sets of exemplars for users to perform selection on as part of an render-selection lop. Thus, there is no information about what effects users want to have in the final images, but the user has the opportunity to select good candidates.

3 Lighting Design Framework

Other than Design Galleries, which utilizes significant user interaction, no fully automatic example-based lighting design method has to date been proposed. Furthermore, existing approach to lighting design have concentrated on the development of metrics for optimizing the distribution of luminance on single objects so as to enhance the salient geometric features such as edges and curvature. In practice, the illumination characteristics of a whole scene are of equal, if not greater, importance.

LIGHTOPEX is a system that uses the principle of lighting-by-example to address the inverse lighting design problem by allowing the user to select an exemplar photograph (or other image), which contains the desired lighting effects, and uses this exemplar as the reference for an objective function based on our perceptual response to lighting.

3.1 Motivations

In LIGHTOPEX, photographs are selected as exemplars, or targets, for lighting 3D scenes. During the optimization process, the system tries to minimize an objective function that captures information in the photograph that is important to human visual system (HVS). A fundamental component of the workings of the HVS, in reconstructing the structure of objects, is the use of rapid relative changes in information from one region of the optic array to another. Thus the HVS filters out low frequency temporal and spatial frequencies – in broad terms, the HVS can be considered as a spatial filter [21].

Thus, given a static image, an image function contains spatially distributed patterns of light intensity, which remain when the image is transformed to the frequency domain. Our basic observation, as to the use of target images in lighting-by-example, is that this spatial frequency information is of primary importance. That is, the final image of a rendered 3D model derived by optimizing lighting parameters relative to a target image must have a spatial frequency distribution close to that of the target. In using an image as an exemplar, we need not only consider the relative distribution of a image function energy among spatial frequencies for the whole image function but also the relative distribution of a image function energy over specific frequencies at specific locations in the image. To achieve this we must convert the images (source and target) into a appropriate representation and for this we use a wavelet transform.

3.2 Wavelet Formulation

Wavelet transforms have been used widely in signal processing. The image function can be considered as a signal with two spatial variables. A wavelet transform of an image function provides us with information about the distribution of energy in the image function over different spatial frequencies and different subspaces in an image. Wavelet transforms aim to represent an image function by a set of basis functions. Thus an image can be represented by a set of basis functions and each basis function is weighted by a coefficient. Therefore, applying the same set of basis functions to different image functions results in different sets of coefficients.

The larger the coefficient of a certain basis function, the more harmonics there are that have spatial frequency similar to the basis function at the location pertaining to that function. Therefore, by analyzing a set of the coefficients, we know which basis functions dominate an image function at a specific location in the image function. In other words, we know the energy spectrum of a image function over basis functions. To achieve this, a set of basis functions used for a wavelet transform must be designed to capture information about both the spatial and frequency properties of a signal.

Basis functions are specific to an application, so for example, in image retrieval, wavelets are widely used to characterize and model a number of image features, including texture features [24] and salient points and corners [25].

We adopt a related approach in which the basis functions are derived by modifying the Haar basis [22,23]. We extend the Haar basis wavelets to create a basis function for the wavelet transform as follows:

$$B_w = \left[\phi_h(x, y) + \phi_v(x, y) \right] \tag{1}$$

Where $\phi_h(x, y)$ is the horizontal basis function for the wavelet transform defined in equation (2).

$$\phi_h(x, y) = \begin{cases} 1 & 0 \le x < 1/2 \quad and \ 0 \le y < 1 \\ -1 & 1/2 \le x < 1 \quad and \ 0 \le y < 1 \\ 0 & otherwise \end{cases} \tag{2}$$

$\phi_v(x, y)$ is the vertical basis function for the transform defined in equation (3).

$$\phi_v(x, y) = \begin{cases} 1 & 0 \le y < 1/2 \quad and \ 0 \le x < 1 \\ -1 & 1/2 \le y < 1 \quad and \ 0 \le x < 1 \\ 0 & otherwise \end{cases} \tag{3}$$

By scaling and shifting (2) and (3) we have a set of basis functions represented in equations (4) and (5).

$$\phi_h^{a,b}(x, y) = \phi_h\left(2^{b_h} x - a_h, 2^{b_v} y - a_v\right) \tag{4}$$

$$\phi_v^{a,b}(x, y) = \phi_v\left(2^{b_h} x - a_h, 2^{b_v} y - a_v\right) \tag{5}$$

b_h, b_v: scaling factors for the horizontal and vertical basis functions, respectively.
a_h, a_v: shifting factors for the horizontal and vertical basis functions, respectively.

We can rewrite (1) as follows:

$$B_w^{a,b} = \phi_h^{a,b}(x, y) + \phi_v^{a,b}(x, y) \tag{6}$$

We can define $_iE^{a,b}$ to be the normalized energy spectrum coefficient of a wavelet transform of the image function $I(x,y)$ corresponding to i^{th} basis function $B_w^{a,b}$ where:

$$_iE^{a,b} = {_i}E_h^{a,b} + {_i}E_v^{a,b} \tag{7}$$

$_rE_h^{a,b}$ and $_iE_v^{a,b}$ are the normalized energy spectrum coefficients of a wavelet transform of the image function $I(x,y)$ respectively corresponding to the horizontal and vertical components of the basis function $B_w^{a,b}$ where:

$$_iE_h^{a,b} = \frac{4}{2^{(b_h+b_v)}} \sum_{x=0}^{W-1} \sum_{y=0}^{H-1} I(x, y)\phi_h^{a,b}(x, y) \tag{8}$$

$$_iE_v^{a,b} = \frac{4}{2^{(b_h+b_v)}} \sum_{x=0}^{W-1} \sum_{y=0}^{H-1} I(x, y)\phi_v^{a,b}(x, y) \tag{9}$$

Where $I(x,y)$ is the intensity image function, W is the width of the image, and H is the height of the image.

Finally, we have a set E of normalized energy spectrum coefficients for a wavelet transform of the image function $I(x,y)$ as follows:

$$E = \{ {_i}E^{a,b} \} \quad i = 0...N\text{-}1 \tag{10}$$

Where N is the number of basis functions.

3.3 Wavelet Transforms and Lighting Design

The goal of *lighting-by-example* is to set up lighting parameters, comprising positions and specular and reflectance intensities of lights, in order to recreate the illumination apparent in a selected exemplar (the target). Lighting effects can be considered as a distribution of different light intensity levels over different locations in images and ratios of average luminance between adjacent locations of different grain sizes.

As described in section 3.2, a wavelet transform captures information about the distribution of energy of image function over different frequencies at different locations in an image function. Each wavelet transform of an image function is characterized by a set of normalized energy spectrum coefficients. The optimization

```
Integer current_depth;
Boolean BuildQuadTree(WLNode *pNode,
                      Window wnd)
Begin
    Window wnd1,wnd2,wnd3,wnd4;
    current_depth = current_depth+1;
    If(current_depth > maxdepth)
            Return TRUE;.
    Calculate wavelettransform with wnd;
    Save energy to pNode->fenergyFreq ;
    Divide wnd into 4 equal squares;
    wnd1 = lower-left square of wnd;
    wnd2 = lower-right square of wnd;
    wnd3 = upper-left square of wnd;
    wnd4 = upper-right square of wnd;
    BuildQuadTree(pNode->child[0],wnd1);
    BuildQuadTree(pNode->child[1],wnd2);
    BuildQuadTree(pNode->child[2],wnd3);
    BuildQuadTree(pNode->child[3],wnd4);
    current_depth = current_depth-1;
    Return TRUE;
End.
```

Fig. 1. Recursive wavelet transform implementation

process tries to make the set of energy spectrum coefficients of the rendered image close to that of the selected exemplar.

The Euclidean distance is used to measure the distance between two sets of energy spectrum coefficients. In other words, the optimization process tries to find a set of lighting parameters such that the distance between two sets of energy spectrum coefficients, those of the rendered image and those of the selected exemplar, is as small as possible. Suppose we have a set of target values derived from the wavelet transform of the target image $T = \{t_i\}$ $i = 0... N-1$. The objective function is given by:

$$F\left(\theta_k, \varphi_k, I^s{}_k, I^d{}_k\right) = \frac{1}{N}\sqrt{\sum_{i=0}^{N-1}\left({}_iE^{a,b} - t_i\right)^2}$$

$F(\theta_k, \varphi_k, I^s{}_k, I^d{}_k, R_k)$ is the objective function
θ_k is the elevation angle of kth light.
φ_k is the azimuth angle of kth light.
$I^d{}_k$ is the diffuse intensity of kth light.
$I^s{}_k$ is the specular intensity of kth light.
R_k is the distance k^{th} light (fixed for directional lights).
N is the number of basis functions.

4   Implementation

4.1   Parameter Selections

The scaling and shifting parameters a_h, b_h, a_v, b_v of the wavelet transform are selected such that at each spatial frequency whole image is scanned without overlapping sections of windows used for each basis function. A full quadtree is used to represent normalized energies derived by a wavelet transform of an intensity image function $I(x,y)$. Nodes at each level of the quadtree represent normalized energy spectrum coefficients at a spatial frequency at different locations in the image specified by the shifting parameters a_h, a_v.

The number of basis functions can be determined by the maximum spatial frequency used for wavelet transform. The highest spatial frequency is calculated at a 2x2 pixel window. The higher the maximum spatial frequency used for wavelet, the greater the computational complexity. Each node of a quadtree is defined as a structure:

```
struct WLNode{
    Real fenergyFreq;
    Window wind;
    WLNode *child[4];
};
```

Where `fenergyFreq` is the normalized energy spectrum coefficient of a wavelet transform of the image function corresponding to a basis function, and `wind` is the location of the basis function. The wavelet transform is implemented as a recursive algorithm (see the pseudo-code is in figure 1). Given an input image, the algorithm will construct a full quadtree, and populate each node of the quadtree with information as to the energy of a specific spatial frequency at a specific location of the image function.

4.2   Optimization Strategy

The function evaluation scheme is used for optimizing the objective function. At each step of the optimization process, the positions and intensities of lights are modified (according to the optimization scheme being used) and the corresponding values of the objective function calculated. A range of optimizations schemes have been implemented including steepest descent, a genetic algorithm (GA), and simulated annealing.

As anticipated (see figure 2) the steepest descent scheme converges fastest, but usually to a local minimum. Figure 2 illustrates the performance characteristics for the three schemes on our first example (figure 3). Each scheme was run 10 times and the average values of the objective function are plotted at each iteration.

The performance of a genetic algorithm strongly depends on selection of the parameters for mutation, crossover and elitism. We experimented with different parameter set-ups and settled on a common configuration for optimization problems of this size: a population size of 30, 10% elitism, and crossover and mutation rates of 80% and 20% respectively. GAs often gives a better (in this case lower) solutions in comparison with steepest descent searches, but with the drawback of relatively long run times.

The performance of simulated annealing depends on the selection of the initial temperature parameter T and the cooling schedule. In our approach, T was empirically determined such that the uphill probability was made equal to downhill probability at a random initial state. Temperature T was repeatedly reduced 10% for each iteration. Simulated annealing often converges to a solution better than that of steepest descent, and has a significantly lower time complexity than a GA (yielding similar, and in this case more optimal solutions).

5   Results and Discussion

We have tested LIGHTOPEX on a range of 3D scenes and in figures 2 3, 4 and 5 present 3 examples lit using LIGHTOPEX, under local illumination, utilizing two lights and exemplars (target images) captured from well known films. In broad terms the results demonstrate that spatial information such as the ratio and positions of bright/dark regions in the exemplar images are replicated in the rendered images. Note that, as in these example, the highest spatial frequency used in the wavelet transform was a 2×2 pixel window, thus the wavelet transform captures information about shading gradients.

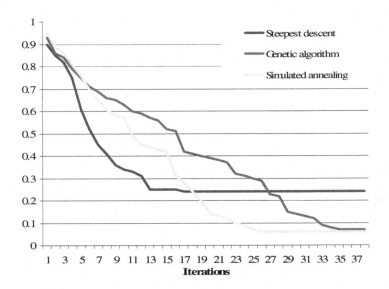

Fig. 2. Plot of the objective function (y-axis) for each iteration of the optimization schemes. Steepest descent converges fastest, but to a local minimum. Simulated annealing converges to the most optimal value in the shortest time.

Fig. 3. Test scene comprising geometric objects and planar walls, ceiling and floor

We have tested different 3D models with target images captured from a range of movies[1] and sample results are shown in figures 3, 4, and 5, using a simulated annealing optimization scheme. In figure 3 the scene to be lit includes smooth untextured objects with planar background polygons, figure 4 contains mostly planar background objects with no foreground features, and figure 5 contains a mixture of foreground and background objects with of mid-range geometric complexity typical of a 3D computer game. The spatial distribution of image function energy over different spatial frequencies in the exemplars is clearly replicated in the optimized results.

---

[1] "Entrapment" (© 20th Century Fox); "Cat Woman" (© Warner Brothers); "SecretWindow" (© Columbia Tristar Films).

Fig. 4. Test scene comprising simple geometric objects and planar walls

In row 3 of figure 3, and row 2 of figure 4, we notice that the upper regions of both the exemplar and the optimized result are significantly darker than lower half. This demonstrates the ability of LIGHTOPEX to capture the distribution of image function energy over low spatial frequencies in the vertical direction. Likewise, a close viewing right hand-side regions of the images in rows 1 and 3 of figure 4, and row 2 of figure 5, reveals a replication of this effect in the horizontal direction, mirroring the low frequency distribution of luminance in the target scenes.

A different effect can be seen in rows 1 and 3 of figure 4 in which small dark and bright regions alternate in both the exemplars and the optimized results. This can be explained by the fact that the distribution of image function energy over higher spatial frequencies in the exemplars is replicated in the optimized result. The examples show that the dark and bright regions of the exemplar are not exactly mapped to the

Fig. 5. Test objects of moderate geometric complexity and non-planar background objects (27706 polygons)

optimized result, in terms of their precise spatial locations, but the relative distribution of dark and bright areas as well as luminance of each area are captured.

The highest spatial frequency used in wavelet transform utilizes 2×2 pixel window. Here the wavelet transform captures information about shading gradients, and, as illustrated by figure 5 (the only scene with a significant number of geometric features), and also figure 3, the shading gradient information of the exemplar images is replicated (particularly in row 1 of figure 3, and row 1 of figure 5).

As the examples demonstrate, both high and low spatial frequency effects (not just overall luminance levels) are important factors in establishing the mood of a scene – and such high level notions have to date been beyond the scope of automated lighting design systems.

6 Conclusion

In this paper, we have presented a *lighting-by-example* approach to lighting design. A wavelet-based objective function was used at the core of the approach to capture the the distribution of spatial frequencies over an image function. A set of basis functions for the wavelet transform has been developed, specifically targeted to this application.

The likely outcome of a program of research into the design of lighting will be a framework for the specification of lighting using example photographs – and tools to allow artists to interactively modify scene lighting through inverse design. Such approaches presume the ability to model target scenes in the form of a perceptually meaningful objective function, and to optimize source scenes using these objectives. We see this declarative approach to lighting design presented here as part of this wider enterprise to build new tools for the specification and design of lighting.

References

[1] Shacked, R., Lischinski, D.: Automatic Lighting Design using a perceptual quality metric. In: Proceedings of EuroGraphics, vol. 20(3) (2001)

[2] Schoeneman, C., Dorsey, J., Smits, B., Arvo, J., Greenburg, D.: Painting with light. In: Proceedings of. SIGGRAPH, pp. 143–146 (1993)

[3] Marks, J., Andalman, B., Beardsley, P.A., Freeman, W., Gibson, S., Hodgins, J., Kang, T., Mirtich, B., Pfister, H., Ruml, W., Ryall, K., Seims, J., Shieber, S.: Design galleries: a general approach to setting parameters for computer graphics and animation. In: Proceedings of. SIGGRAPH, pp. 389–400 (1997)

[4] Gross, M.: Visual Computing. Springer, Heidelberg (1994)

[5] McNamara, A.: Comparing real and synthetic scenes using human judgments of lightness, Ph.D. Thesis, University of Bristol (2000)

[6] Millerson, G.: Lighting for Television and Film. 3rd edn. Focal Press (2005)

[7] Barzel, R.: Lighting Controls for Computer Cinematography. Journal of Graphics Tools 2(1), 1–20 (1997)

[8] Spillmann, L., Werner, J.S.: Visual Perception the Neurophisiological Foundations. Academic, San Diego (1990)

[9] Poulin, P., Fournier, A.: Lights from highlights and shadows. In: SI3D '92. Proceedings of the 1992 Symposium on interactive 3D Graphics (Cambridge, Massachusetts, United States), pp. 31–38. ACM Press, New York, NY (1992)

[10] Reitsma, P.S.A., Pollard, N.S.: Perceptual metrics for character animation: sensitivity to errors in ballistic motion. ACM Transactions on Graph 22(3), 537–542 (2003)

[11] Farugia, J.P., Pollard, B.: A progressive rendering algorithm using an adaptive perceptually based image metric. In: Proceedings of Eurographics (2004)

[12] Lee, C.H., Hao, X., Varshney, A.: Light Collages: Lighting Design for Effective Visualization. In: Proceedings of IEEE Visualization 2004, Austin (October 2004)

[13] Gumhold, S.: Maximum entropy light source placement. In: Proceedings of IEEE Visualization (2002)

[14] Saito, T., Takahashi, T.: Comprehensible rendering of 3-D shapes. In: Proceedings of SIGGRAPH, pp. 197–206 (1990)

[15] Hall, R.: Illumination and Color in Computer Generated Imagery. In: Monographs in Visual Communication, Springer, New York (1993)

[16] Poulin, P., Ratib, K., Jacques, M.: Sketching Shadows and Highlights to Position Lights. In: Proceedings of Computer Graphics International (CGI'97) (1997)

[17] Kawai, J.K., Painter, J.S., Cohen, M.F.: Radioptimization – Goal Based Rendering. In: Proceedings of SIGGRAPH'93, pp. 147–154 (1993)

[18] Jolivet, V., Plemenos, D., Poulingeas, P.: Inverse Direct Lighting with a Monte Carlo Method and Declarative Modelling. CG&GM' (2002)

[19] Farrugia, J.P., Albin, S., Peroche, B.: A Perceptual Adaptive Image Metric for Computer Graphics. In: Proceedings of the International Conference in Central Europe on Computer Graphics, Visualization and Computer Vision (WSCG04) (2004)

[20] Brajovich, V.: Brightness Perception, Dynamic Range and Noise: A Unifying Model for Adaptive Image Sensors. In: Proceedings of IEEE Computer Society Conference on Computer Vision and Pattern Recognition (CVPR '04), vol. 2, pp. 189–196 (June 2004)

[21] Bruce, V., Patrick, R.G., Mark, A.G.: Visual Perception. Psychology Press (1997)

[22] Haar, A. Z.: Theorie der orthogonalen Funktionensysteme. Math. Ann, vol. 69, pp. 331–371 (1910)

[23] Crandall, R.E.: Topics in advanced scientific computation. Springer, Heidelberg (1996)

[24] Do, M.N., Vetterli, M.: Wavelet-Based Texture Retrieval Using Generalized Gaussian Density and Kullback-Leibler Distance. IEEE Trans. Image Processing 11(2), 146–158 (2002)

[25] Tian, Q., Sebe, N., Lew, M.S., Loupias, E., Huang, T.S.: Image retrieval using wavelet-based salient points. Journal of Electronic Imaging 10(4), 835–849 (2001)

Semantic Information and Local Constraints for Parametric Parts in Interactive Virtual Construction

Peter Biermann, Christian Fröhlich, Marc Latoschik, and Ipke Wachsmuth

Laboratory for Artificial Intelligence and Virtual Reality, Faculty of Technology,
University of Bielefeld

Abstract. This paper introduces a semantic representation for virtual proto-typing in interactive virtual construction applications. The representation reflects semantic information about dynamic constraints to define objects' modification and construction behavior as well as knowledge structures supporting multimodal interaction utilizing speech and gesture. It is conveniently defined using XML-based markup for virtual building parts. The semantic information is processed during runtime in two ways: Constraint graphs are mapped to a generalized data-flow network and scene-graph. Interaction knowledge is accessed and matched during multimodal analysis.

1 Introduction

One important task when implementing a virtual construction platform like [3] the definition of new building parts. These part-definitions must cover more than the geometry of the new part. Since the parts are to be employed in virtual construction their definition must include mating geometries, which can be used to connect two parts. If the parts are to be parametrically modifiable, their definition needs to specify such parameters as well as their effect exerted on the geometry of the parts. Such modifications may, e.g., involve scaling, rotation or translation of subparts. More complex modifications should enable to couple different transformations, which can also be used for the simulation of kinematic chains [4].

The interaction with the parts in the virtual environment with speech and gesture requires further semantic information. This information should also be generated from the description of the part. The enrichment of virtual environments with semantic information can be useful in many ways, especially in virtual construction and object manipulation, as we pointed out in [11]. Several research groups have recently made use of such an idea. Lugrin and Cavazza [13]for example use semantic representations to specify certain object behaviors. They have integrated a knowledge layer in an interactive virtual environment, which contains possible processes and actions that can be carried out inside the environment, as well as common sense knowledge for supporting inferences on virtual objects.

Semantic networks are a powerful means to represent data for intelligent virtual reality applications. They allow virtual objects to be enriched by task-specific information, such as physical properties, by way of introducing meaningful semantic

A. Butz et al. (Eds.): SG 2007, LNCS 4569, pp. 124–134, 2007.

relations. Intelligent simulative virtual environments supported by semantic networks are for example presented by Latoschik et al. [12] or Kalogerakis et al. [9]. Semantic information has also been used to design virtual reality applications, as is shown in [10].

One focus in our current research is the interaction via iconic gestures, which is accomplished using a shape description via the IDT model developed by Timo Sowa [15]. The testbed for this interaction is the generation of new parts and interaction for the modification and assembly of building parts with parametric bendable sections.

Fig. 1. A bendable elbow with different base geometries and bend-values

For the definition of new parts and their properties – geometric as well as semantic information – we use the XML-definition for parametric parts – the Variant Part Markup Language (VPML)[2]. While other XML-based markup languages for parametric CAD-models – for example the representation presented by Yang et al. [7] or commercial products like CadXML[1] – concentrate on the exchange between different CAD-Tools, our markup language allows a fast and convenient definition of new parts, their parametric transformations and further semantic information. In the following sections, we describe how VPML is extended by template definitions to create meta-descriptions of parametric building parts. These meta-definitions allow, in addition to the specification of parameters, the usage of predefined properties, such as, e.g., base geometries or common attributes. Figure 1 shows various instances of a bendable part-template with different base geometries and bend-values from 0 to 180 degrees.

2 Definition of New Parts

New building parts are defined using the XML-based markup language VPML. For more complex parts, which are designed as parametrical meta-descriptions, a new extension for VPML was developed to describe part templates. These part templates can be instantiated by using predefined XML-attributes to change e.g. the appearance of the part and including further XML-tags which can be inserted in the resulting description. For this meta-definition of such part templates we use an XSLT script [16], which translates the template to the more general VPML-description. This VPML description is used to build the resulting scene-graph structure for the new building part and its subparts including special constraint engines (see Section 3), which realize the constraint movement of the defined subparts. The example of a part template in Section 2.1 is used to generate bendable elbows for different sweep geometries.

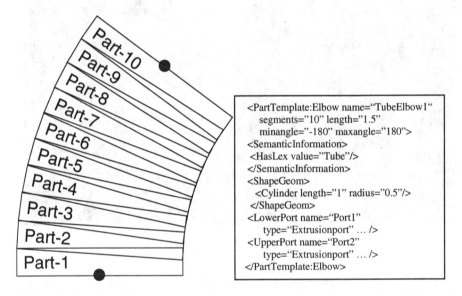

Fig. 2. Illustration of a bendable tube with connection ports (black dots) and its VPML-meta-definition, shown right

Fig. 2 shows an instantiation of this template for a bendable, cylindrical tube with 10 segments and a connection spot at each end. The meta-definition is translated to a description of a part with 10 subparts whose rotation is coupled to a bend-parameter of the main part. The resulting subparts have a cylinder-geometry and are rotated by a fraction of the bend-parameter depending on the amount of segments. Each segment is connected at the center of the upper end as child of it predecessor in a linear scene-graph tree. To realize a continuous surface at the outer edge of the bended structure the subparts are scaled along the sweep direction commensurate to the bend-parameter. This simple scaling causes an internal overlap of the segments at the inner edge, which is acceptable for a real-time visualization, whereas a correct bending simulation requires an inhomogeneous scaling of the segments.

This is planned by means of Vertex-Shaders (see [8]) for real time processing. A real time feedback process is needed for an interactive modification of the parameters to show the user the effect on the geometry of the parts. After adjusting a parameter, a new polygonal representation of the part is computed using CSG-Operations of the ACIS [6] CAD kernel. The problem of the overlapping inner surfaces can also be handled by the CSG-Operations of this process.

2.1 Processing of Part Templates

The part templates for the meta-description of VPML-parts are defined using an XSLT-description. Fig. 3 shows the template description for a bendable elbow which is used in the example before (see Figure 2). The Template defines an additional Parameter (the bend-angle), a number of subparts together with their rotational and scaling constraints and the placement of the two ports at each end of the Tube.

```
<xsl::template match="PartTemplate:Elbow">
<Part name="@name">                                    <!-- Begin main part with a bend parameter-->
<Parameter name="BendAngle" min="0" max="180" init="0">
<SemanticInformation>
 <Attribute name="is-bendable" value="true">
 <xsl:value-of select="SemanticInformation">
</SemanticInformation>
<xsl:value-of select=„LowerPort" >                     <!--insert lower port -->
<xsl:repeat* count=„{@segments}">                      <!-- start the segments -->
<Subpart name=„ElbowPart-{$count-number*}" translation=„{@length div @segments} 0.0 0.0">
 <ParentScaling fixpoint="-{1 div @segments} 0.0 0.0">
  <ScaleMode axes="XYZ" mode="none">
 </ParentScaling>
<ParametricTrf>
  <Rotation name=„ElbowPart-{$count-number*}-Rot" axis=„0 1 0"
    connect=„BendAngle" transmission=„{1 div @segments}"/>
  <Scaling name=„ElbowPart-{$count-number*}-Scl" axis=„1 0 0"
    connect=„BendAngle" transmission=„{(1 div @segments) + 1.0}"/>
</ParametricTrf>
  <Geometry scale=„{@length div @segments } 1 1">
   <xsl:value-of select=„ShapeGeom" >
  </Geometry>
</xsl:repeat*>
<xsl:value-of select=„UpperPort" >                     <!--insert upper port at last segment-->
<xsl:repeat* count=„@segments">                        <!-- finish the segments -->
 </Subpart>
</xsl:repeat>
</Part>
</xsl::template>
```

Fig. 3. VPML-template for a bendable elbow

The template is defined using common XSLT-commands[1], which allows the direct translation of the template instances to the complete VPML-code. At compile time the VPML-Code is generated and translated into a scene-graph structure together with an underlying semantic representation.

3 Generating Scene-Graph Structures with Local Constraints

The virtual parts are automatically generated by translating the VPML-definition to a) a scene-graph structure, b) additional constraint engines and c) semantic information, as will be explained below.

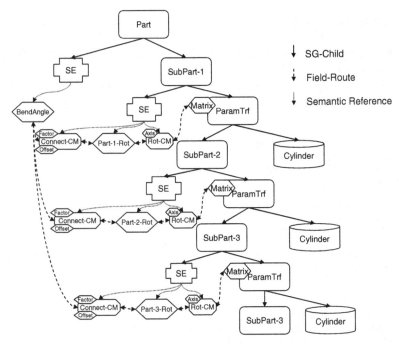

Fig. 4. Scene-Graph with Constraint Mediators

Fig. 4 shows the resulting scene-graph for the part defined in section 2. The Parameters of the part template can define the number of the subparts and their geometry. The parameters of the Connect-Constraint-Mediators, which implement the coupling of the BendAngle-parameter and the Rotation-parameter of the subparts, are derived from the number of instantiated subparts for the elbow. Fig. 4 shows three different levels of graph structures for the building part:

---

[1] An exception is the xsl:repeat* command which is not part of the regular XSLT 1.0 reference. It is assumed that this command loops for "count"-times, while '$count-number*' is increased in each loop. Simple repeat-loops like this have to be realised, for example by using recursive structures in XSLT. It is simplified here for better readability of the code.

- a common Scene-Graph structure, which encodes geometric shapes and their hierarchy and relative positions. In this example the SG simply consists of group- or transform-nodes, basic geometry-nodes and parent-child relations
- an application graph, which consists of the parameter-fields of the part and subparts respectively, the Constraint-Mediators and the field routes between them
- a semantic structure, which binds the semantic properties of a part/ subpart to its Semantic Entity

A Semantic Entity (SE) is a special scene-graph node, that can reference objects which belong to the definition of the part but are not located in the scene-graph structure. In the example above these objects are the fields, which hold the parameter of each subpart and the constraint engines, which implement the local constraints for these parameters. Instead of adding these objects directly to the scene-graph, as e.g. done in VRML/X3D [5], the Semantic Entities can store different types of objects as key-value pairs for easy referencing. The Semantic Entity also acts as the link between the scene-graph and the underlying semantic structure. This semantic structure reflects all aspects of the previously presented graphs and structures. It is described in the next section.

4 The Knowledge Representation Layer

The virtual as well as the interaction-relevant parts of the real world (in general, simplified user representations of, e.g. the hands) are defined by a knowledge representation layer (KRL). The KRL provides a net of interconnected entity definitions on top of a semantic net base formalism which ties possibly distributed world representations together. The KRL's primary purpose is to provide a common application layer for *semantic reflection*. By this we mean, that the relevant aspects of a given simulation as a whole are mapped on the KRL and made accessible to participating software modules on a unified basis. This approach enables software designers to develop portable and extendable tools since the KRL effectively decouples application design from utilized software modules.

For example, Figure 5 illustrates a snippet of the knowledge base which represents a virtual part that can be bent by user interaction. Both, the actual bending functionality of the part itself as well as the user's interaction can be implemented in a variety of ways, e.g., the part's morphological changes can be implemented using tailored scene graph metaphors, hardware accelerated shading routines, or volumetric rendering approaches. Each of these methods requires its own software module to gain control over the manipulated part during the interaction. An example for a scene graph based approach is illustrated in Figures 5 and 6.

From a user's point of view the actual simulation method utilized for a required object or part related functionality is of minor importance. The same is true for the simulation system itself. It just has to provide (e.g., link to) and activate the software module responsible for the actual function implementation. The KRL semantically

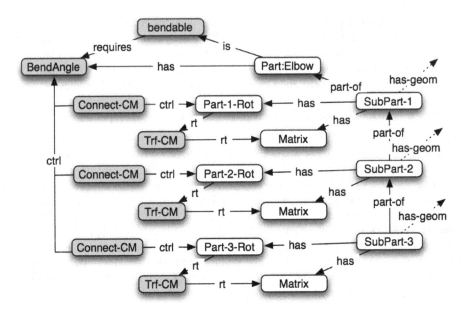

Fig. 5. A snippet of the KRL which describes a bendable virtual part. The overall knowledge structure defines parts, subparts, their attributes and relations which are a generalization of a possible scene graph oriented representation. The grey boxes depict the required concepts which may implement bending as a function of the main part using a specific field-route based simulation module.

reflects the required object-related function specification, the specific implementation module's capabilities and features as well as the interaction specification. An interaction is established by automatically matching a user action with a possible object function. This requires both sides to be linked to a common concept which represents the object feature to be changed as illustrated in Figure 5 by the bendable concept. For the sake of clarity, Figure 5 only depicts the functional decomposition for the virtual part which we will further illustrate here. With respect to the interaction representation, the bendable concept in Figure 5 has additional links to an interaction representation which defines interactions and their required parameters for multimodal interactions which is out of scope for this paper.

4.1 Transformation to Scene-Graph Structures

The chosen semantic decomposition of the virtual part in Figure 5 already depicts a hierarchical object structure which can be easily mapped and transformed to a concrete scene graph for a running simulation. The grey-colored nodes define a more specific application design which requires additional functionality by the interpreting module. Figure 6 illustrates a partial transformation of the knowledge structure in Figure 5. The part-of relations naturally map to a scene graph's child-of relation. The

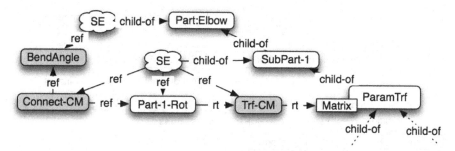

Fig. 6. Transformation of the KRL structure from Figure 1 into an enhanced scene graph structure (see text). Additional Semantic Entity (SE) nodes allow KRL access during scene graph traversal.

has relation for matrices transform to a new node (ParamTrf) with a matrix attribute which now is inserted in-between the Sub-Part nodes and their geometry as depicted in Figure 6 for SubPart-1.

The specific grey structures map their control (ctrl) and routing (rt) to object references and field routing in Figure 6. Semantic Entity nodes grant KRL access during scene graph traversal. They enable the development of portable methods since information of the required object-structures can automatically be accessed via the SE. This target structure requires an enhanced scene graph library which supports field-routing as well as referential access between nodes. Even if this example in Figure 5 still shows some module specific structures in the grey nodes, it illustrates the basic idea: While the structures in Figure 5 somehow depend on a specific scene graph based tool, the concept shown in Figure 6 is an important step toward a complete decoupling of the parts' functional, graphical and other simulation related aspects using the KRL. Linked by a common ontology, multiple substructures can be provided which represent a specific implementation for a required function and interaction for specific application provided modules, e.g., for certain graphic, physics or interaction libraries whose basic capabilities will additionally be semantically reflected on the KRL. The KRL's base formalism is already tailored for this approach and it is the central structure of a new simulation core currently under development [12].

4.2 Semantic Information for Multimodal Interaction with Parametric Parts

Multimodal interaction is an integral feature provided by the developed object representation and simulation system. Successful analysis of user input requires knowledge structures that reflect conceptual, lexical, and gesture relevant information about the virtual parts. Possible interactions range from direct interactions to simultaneous speech and gesture utterances. The latter are used to

a) *reference* parts, objects, and places (deictic gestures),
b) *modify* parts' and objects' attributes (mimetic gestures), and
c) describe parts and objects' shapes (iconic gestures), either to *reference* them or to *modify* their appearance.

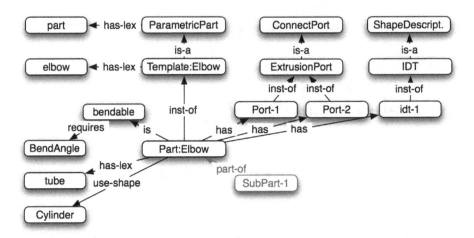

Fig. 7. A different view on the KRL-structure for the Part:Elbow part. The part's concept is augmented with lexical information required for speech-based disambiguation of the part itself using **has-lex** relations. The **bendable** concept allows a functional mapping of the interaction. The **IDT** concept provides the necessary links to a graph-based representation of the part's shape that is matched with a similar representation as generated by gesture analysis.

The VPML-description of the building parts is the source to build up the underlying KRL, which is accessible from the scene-graph via the Semantic Entities. This semantic information is used while interpreting the user's instructions. Figure 7 illustrates a part of the KRL-structure generated from the VPML-meta-description. The semantic information for the new building parts allows to reference the parts in natural language descriptions such as: "the tube", "the elbow" or "that part", etc. by following the **has-lex** relations during the multimodal analysis phase.

This information is integrated with deictic information generated by the gesture analysis process directly from the user-centric spatial arrangement of the graphical scene. For example, a close temporal relation between articles or nouns of nominal phrases and the climax of an accompanying pointing gesture will sort the set of all objects matching the noun phrase w.r.t. the main pointing direction. Interaction mapping is provided by attribute assignments as depicted for the **bendable** concept of part **Part:Elbow**. That is, required user actions are matched to the part's features to identify possible interactions, e.g., adjustment of a given bending parameter is matched to the semantic analysis of the sentence "Change the bend angle of the elbow to 90 degrees".

In addition, the KRL also includes links to Imagistic Description Trees (IDTs) as shape descriptions specially designed for interaction with iconic gestures. They contain abstract information about the described movement of the user's body. For example, IDTs are used to represent linear path movements, their possibly varying relative length, angles between these linear segments, or symmetry aspects. For detailed information about the IDT-model see [14].

The same base formalism is used to describe a given object's form and extent. During reference resolution, the IDTs generated from the user's gestures are compared with the IDTs of existing parts. Since both are represented in the same graph based formalism, this is done using a graph match approach. For artificially generated man-made objects like the building parts, the IDTs complexity can be assumed to be rather low, hence graph matching causes no performance impacts.

The IDTs of the user's expression is also enhanced with information from the speech channel. Where the vocal instruction contains words, describing the shape of an object – such as "round", "long" or "cylindrical" – this information is translated and also coded in the resulting IDT.

A visual programming system provides an intuitive rapid prototyping approach for the development of dataflow programs. This system is the core module of the gesture analysis process. It includes various gesture analysis and detection networks required by the application. These dataflow networks receive their input from sensor data recorded from 6DOF markers and the user's hands and detect significant movement features.

5 Conclusion

We have presented a convenient way of defining new building parts and their properties for interactions in virtual construction. The XML-based description format allows the translation into different structures which are needed for multimodal interaction and virtual construction simulation. The direct translation to scene-graph structures enhanced with field routes and local constraint engines enables the simulation of restricted or coupled movements and connections.

The underlying Knowledge Representation Layer provides semantic information for the multimodal interaction, whereas the Imagistic Description Trees allow the comparison of the shapes of different parts or iconic gestures. Altogether this forms a powerful model for various interactions within virtual construction environments.

Acknowledgement

This work is partially supported by the Deutsche Forschungsgemeinschaft (DFG) under grant Wa 815/2.

References

[1] AfterCAD Software Inc. CadXML: vendor Neutral File Format for CAD Data Exchange. fromhttp://www.aftercad.com/cadxml.html
[2] Biermann, P., Jung, B.: Variant Design in Immersive Virtual Reality: A Markup Language for Scalable CSG Parts. In: Perales, F.J., Draper, B.A. (eds.), AMDO 2004. LNCS, vol. 3179, pp. 123–133. Springer, Heidelberg (2004)
[3] Biermann, P., Jung, B., Latoschik, M., Wachsmuth, I.: Virtuelle Werkstatt: A Platform for Multimodal Assembly in VR. In: Proceedings Fourth Virtual Reality International Conference (VRIC 2002), pp. 53–62. Laval, France (2002)
[4] Biermann, P., Wachsmuth, I.: Non-Physical Simulation of Gears and Modifiable Connections in Virtual Reality. In: Proceedings of Sixth Virtual Reality International Conference (VRIC 2004), Laval, France (2004)

[5] Carey, R., Bell, G.: The Annotated VRML 2.0 Reference Manual. Addison-Wesley, Reading (1997)

[6] Corney, J.: Theodore Lin. 3D Modeling with ACIS. Paul & Co Pub, Consortium (2002)

[7] Yang, J., Han, S., Cho, J., Kim, B., Lee, H.: An XML-Based Macro Data Representation for a Parametric CAD Model Exchange. Computer-Aided Design and Applications (CADA) 1, 153–162 (2004)

[8] NVIDIA Corp.: Cg Toolkit, a Developer's Guide to Programmable Graphics. Santa Clara, CA (2002)

[9] Kalogerakis, E., Moumoutzis, N., Christodoulakis, S.: Coupling ontologies with graphics content for Knowledge Driven Visualization. In: Proceedings of the IEEE Virtual Reality Conference 2006 (IEEE VR '06), pp. 43–50. Virginia, USA (2006)

[10] Kleinermann, F., De Troyer, O., Mansouri, H., Romero, R., Pellens, B., Bille, W.: Designing Semantic Virtual Reality Applications. In: Proceedings of the 2nd INTUITION International Workshop, Senlis, France (2005)

[11] Latoschik, M.E., Biermann, P., Wachsmuth, I.: Knowledge in the loop: Semantics representation for multimodal simulative environments. In: SG 2005. LNCS, vol. 3638, pp. 25–39. Springer, Heidelberg (2005)

[12] Latoschik, M.E., Fröhlich, C., Wendler, A.: Scene synchronization in close coupled world representations using SCIVE. In: International Journal of Virtual Reality, IJVR, vol. 5(3), pp. 47–52 (2006)

[13] Lugrin, J., Cavazza, M.: Making sense of virtual environments: action representation, grounding and common sense. In: Proceedings of the 12th international Conference on intelligent User interfaces (Honolulu, Hawaii, USA, January 28 - 31, 2007). IUI '07, pp. 225–234. ACM Press, New York, NY (2007)

[14] Sowa, T.: Towards the integration of shape-related information in 3-D gestures and speech. In: Proceedings of the Eighth International Conference on Multimodal Interfaces, pp. 92–99. ACM Press, New York (2006)

[15] Sowa, T., Wachsmuth, I.: Coverbal Iconic Gestures for Object Descriptions in Virtual Environments: An Empirical Study. In: Rector, M., Poggi, I., Trigo, N. (eds.) Proceedings of the Conference Gestures. Meaning and Use, Porto: Edições Fernando Pessoa, pp. 365–376 (2003)

[16] W3 Consortium. XSL transformations (XSLT) W3C Recommendation (1999) http://www.w3c.org/TR/xslt

Artistic 3D Object Creation Using Artificial Life Paradigms

Iver Bailly-Salins and Herve Luga

IRIT-UT1 (UMR 5505)
2 rue du doyen Gabriel Marty - 31042 Toulouse Cedex
iver.baillysalins@gmail.com,luga@univ-tlse1.fr

Abstract. This article describes a new interaction model for artistic shape generation. Instead of using a metaphor of the classical sculpting tools we propose a new approach based on a two level editing which both uses genetic programming methods: objects are created by means of subjective selection and generative evolution. We develop a new way to define these objects combining algebraic definition of implicit surfaces and CSG-like composition of these shapes. Along with these we propose a software tool that implements a simple way to manage this new approach in three dimensional objects design.

1 Introduction

Artificial life paradigms[Lan89], have been used in various fields of computer graphics like behavioral animation[SLD06], artificial creatures generation [Sim94] [LLD06] or constrained modelling [LDPB95] [SLRLG03]. Some of these are creative fields, where those technologies are applied to artistic purposes [Kaw05] [Bre00]. This paper focuses on the field of artistic virtual objects creation but is not related with our previous studies [ABGC05] [LG06]. In this domain, artificial life methods provides with an original way to settle a creation process. Usual tools give a user the means to create an object as close as possible to a preconceived idea of what it should look like, through a process that is as precise as possible and perfectly repeatable. They often use a metaphor of real sculpting tools like knives or bumps. This process does leave room for experimentation, through trial and error. However it often requires the user to have a precise idea of what he wishes to create and a good knowledge of each individual operation that will lead him to the desired result. This approach is close to virtual prototyping used in industrial applications. With the use of artificial life methods, the creation process includes random, unrepeatable elements. We propose here a new model where the user doesn't need to know precisely the mechanisms underlying each operation, he only needs to judge intuitively whether an object pleases him or not. This process can resemble a sort of dialogue with the machine, out of which something may come that the creator hadn't previously explicitly conceived, but which satisfies its purpose. Although such tools do not aim to replace the commonly used deterministic methods, we do believe they can play an

A. Butz et al. (Eds.): SG 2007, LNCS 4569, pp. 135–145, 2007.

interesting role in an artistic creation process [Whi04]. This article presents our model which offers genetic programming methods [Koz92b] [Koz92a] to sculpt implicit surfaces and create 3D objects. In section 2, we show how similar methods have been used in different ways [JKW01] [BE98] [Jon99]. Then we present how we extended, combined and further developed some aspects of the latter to provide with a new interaction model. We will briefly present aspects of these works and others in the domain of artistic creation [Sim91][TL94]. We will then describe our own work and analyze some results.

2   State of the Art of Related Subjects

2.1   Evolutionary Design Systems: Different Goals

Peter Bentley [Ben99] distinguishes 4 categories of computer designs applications using artificial life: Evolutionary optimization of design, Creative evolutionary design, Evolutionary artificial life forms, Evolutionary art. The boundaries between these categories are not always very strict. The goal of this categorization is to distinguish motives and methods used to obtain a shape or design. Shapes can evolve from a parameterized model (optimization of design) or from nothing (creative design). Shapes evolve to satisfy criteria that can vary from the objective suitability to perform a perfectly defined task, to a more subjective way of simply looking good, which necessitates a user's judgement. We will see our model combines elements from both ends of these spectrums.

2.2   Evolutionary Design Systems: Similar Methods

Although artificial life methods may be used in these different contexts, they share a set of similarities. We must define what we will consider as an individual. Each individual is a solution to a specific problem. The problem is defined by the user, as well as the means to evaluate each individual's suitability to solve that problem. Having decided of some criteria on the quality of a solution, successive algorithm's propositions and recombinations generate a dialogue-like process. In our work, individuals are shapes. These shapes need to support two levels of representation: One, *genotypical*, on which evolutionary operators such as crossings and mutations will be defined. Another, *phenotypical*, on which the individuals will be evaluated. Artificial evolutionary systems, in a manner similar to the Darwinian evolution [Dar59], organize the amelioration of a population of individuals in relation to a defined criteria. An exploration of the genotype space around the genotypes of the best individuals is conducted by iterative crossings and mutations. Shapes can be defined by several methods on the genotype level. For example Bentley in GADES [Ben98] represents shapes by a conglomerate of elementary polyhedral blocks, which are themselves explicitly defined in the genotype. A genotype can also be defined by a set of numerical parameters modulating a parameterized shape. Yet another way to represent the genotype of a shape is by using implicit surfaces [BBB+97].

2.3   Implicit Surfaces

Blobby implicit surfaces are usually defined by
a mathematical function known as potential func-
tion $f_p : \mathbb{R} \to \mathbb{R}$, as well as a set of explicitly
defined geometrical primitives known as the skele-
ton. Typically the skeleton is a set of points or a
segment, and the potential function is a decreasing
function that is null for every value over a threshold. Each point of a three dimensional bounded
space is associated a value, which is the evaluation of the potential function on the distance between the particular point and the skeletal primitive. The values define a potential field. The shape

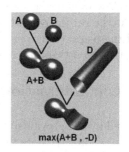

Fig. 1.

is then defined by an isosurface of the potential field. The shapes defined are
usually smooth envelopes around the skeleton, and are often known as blobby
objects. These surfaces present advantages in the artificial life context:

Their genotype representation is light and easy to manipulate, usually consisting of a particular potential function and a small set of a lines and points.
They offer a wide variety of possible shapes while maintaining similar properties,
like smoothness and natural, soft appearances. Several simple shapes defined in
this manner can be used in a CSG tree (a tree structure representing a hierar-
chized construction, where leaves are elementary shapes and nodes are operators on these shapes such as unions, intersections and blendings) to define more
complex shapes.

A CSG tree representation of a complex
shape (Fig.1) can then be admitted as this particular shape's genotype, and genetic programming methods of crossing and mutating applied
to this tree and the skeletal elements composing it can be used in an evolution mechanism
on a population of shapes. Jacob, Kwong and
Wyvill [JKW01] have tested this idea with some
success. One of the evaluation functions used in
their tool was to assess the capacity of a given
shape to hold falling particles. The result of evo-
lutions gave shapes resembling those of pots and
plates. In this case the genetic algorithm was ap-

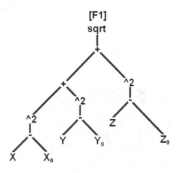

Fig. 2.

plied to the shapes independently of a user's subjective judgment on the result.

Algebraic implicit surfaces are defined by a more complex potential function which is not associated to any explicit structural information such as the
skeleton used in previously defined blobby implicit functions. In this case it is
the evaluation of a more complex mathematical function $f_p : \mathbb{R}^3 \to \mathbb{R}$ on a three
dimensional subspace which generates a potential field and an isosurface shape.
The surface's genetic definition consists of a single mathematical function. This
function can be represented in the form of a tree (Fig.2), with mathematical

operators as nodes and variables as leaves. Once again, genetic programming techniques can be applied to this tree in order to evolve complex shapes. This has also been tested by Jones [Jon99] or Bedwell and Ebert [BE98]. In these works the subjective judgment of the user was the essential factor of evaluation, and these approaches are very similar to the use of a tree-defined mathematical function on a two-dimensional space to generate art images by Sims [Sim91].

3   Our Interaction Model

Inpired by the previously cited works, we wished to try and develop on this basis a more complete tool of creation. Two axes of development were explored: The development in the Jones-Bedwell-Ebert approach of a broader choice of mathematical operators to move toward a 3-dimensional equivalent of Sims' very complex genetic images [Sim91]. The use of these algebraically defined elements as elementary blocks in a higher level definition of genotypes: CSG compositions of shapes, in the manner of Jacob, Kwong and Wyvill [JKW01], but applied to our complex algebraically defined shapes instead of simple blobs. This combination of algebraic definition of shapes and CSG composition presents an interest that we will expose in the last sections of this paper.

3.1   Algebraic Genotypes and Evolution

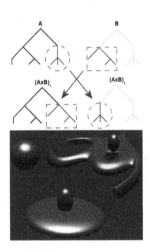

Fig. 3. Crossing operator

In this section we will consider populations of shapes, each of which is defined by a single mathematical function. This function is considered as the shape's genotype. It is defined within a tree structure, as illustrated in Fig 2. The **nodes** of this tree are mathematical operators: **Binary** operators $(+,-,*,/,\%)$, **Unary** operators $(sin(x), cos(x), -x, x^2, x^3, \sqrt{|x|})$, and more complex operators that act as **deformations** of the 3 dimensional space (rotations, translations, twists, warps, tillings...). The **leaves** of the tree are of the form $k * Var$ where k is a mutable constant and Var is either the constant 1 or a variable of the spatial domain in a Cartesian coordinate system (x, y, z) or spherical coordinate system (r, θ, φ). Spherical and Cartesian coordinate systems are used conjointly in the same trees. Several genotypes can be phenotypically equivalent. This is not a particular problem. The purpose of the tool here is to offer the means of creating shapes by iterative experimentation and the underlying mathematics are not relevant to the user. An important aspect however, is to guaranty a certain degree of control and continuity in the creative process. We do want the user to feel that there is a certain logic involved in the creation by genetic manipulations.

The **crossing operator** is applied to two genotypes. It is used to create a set of children shapes whose genotypes are a mix of the genotypes of two parent shapes. This mix is performed by choosing random nodes in the trees defining each parent's genotype and creating new genotypes by swapping the subtrees below these nodes. This operation is illustrated in Fig 3, as well as the result (bottom shape) of a crossing operation performed on a sphere and a more complex shape.

The **mutation operator** is applied to a single genotype. It is used to create a set of children shapes whose genotypes are variations of the genotype of the parent shape. We use different types of mutations: Modifying the **value** of the k parameter associated to a **leaf**, the **type** of a **leaf**, the **type** of a **node** operator while preserving its nature (binary or unary), the **type** and **nature** of a **node**, this last operation implies the creation or destruction of subtree nodes. These mutations are likely to have increasing levels of effect on the generated shape: a mutation creating new nodes or deleting existing ones is likely to generate shapes which look very different from the parent, while simply modifying the type of a leaf will often preserve many characteristics on the shape.

After defining these operators on the genotype space, it is legitimate to question their coherence in the phenotype space: we want genotypes that are similar to generate phenotypes that look alike. Several points can be made on this subject: The phenotype similarities from parent to children is likely to be very weak in the individuals resulting from genetic operations performed on genotype trees of small depth, (therefore we initialize genotypes to trees of a certain depth). To increase the chances of obtaining a coherent result in a crossing or mutation, several of these operations are performed on the chosen parents and the user is presented with a population of different results. Fig 3 and 6 show it is possible to keep a certain level of coherence in the genetic manipulation process.

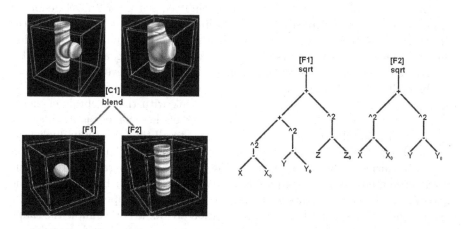

Fig. 4. CSG composition

3.2 CSG Shape Composition and Evolution

The previous paragraphs show briefly how our program manipulates algebraic genotypes to create complex shapes. We are now going to use these shapes in CSG-like compositions (Fig 1). We are therefore using a 2 level genotype representation of our shapes: algebraic definition of elements and CSG composition of these elements. One may choose to now consider the algebraically defined population of shapes as a gene pool from which a different sort of higher-level genotypes and individuals will be defined using CSG operators. In the same way that Bentley [Ben99] defines as genes every elementary block taking part in the definition of his shapes. This combines aspects of the works of Jones[Jon99]-Bedwell-Ebert [BE98] with the work by Jacob, Kwong and Wyvill [JKW01]. The CSG operations are defined in a tree structure once again. The **nodes** of these trees are operators: Union, intersection, blending, translation, symmetries and rotations against the 3 Cartesian axes. **Leaves** of these trees are algebraically defined shapes. The blending operator, which merges smoothly two shapes by simply adding their potential fields, causes some problems in our case. Unlike the common blobby objects, we are dealing with shapes defined by functions that are potentially of very different nature (For example x^{12} and $\sqrt{x}$). A simple addition of potential fields will not blend satisfyingly, as higher power function will dominate lower ones. Potential fields are therefore un-linearly distorted and scaled without affecting the generated shape before being used in the CSG compositions. Mutable parameters are provided to weigh the influence of various shapes in their blending (Fig 5). Crossing and mutation tools on the CSG tree are similar to those described on the algebraic level.

3.3 Implementation Considerations

The previous sections show how we have combined within a 2-level genotype definition of shapes the freedom and tools linked to algebraic implicit surfaces with those linked to CSG and blobby implicit surface manipulation. This section will try to show how this shows on the user-end of the program, and why this is particularly interesting. Our program displays the two levels of populations (algebraically defined shapes and their CSG composition) simultaneously. The CSG individuals keep a dynamically updated link with the algebraic elements from which they are built. As a result when one of these shapes is modified by mutation for example, this mutation propagates to all the CSG individuals that contain this algebraically defined shape in their genotype. This offers new creative possibilities to the editing process. Fig 6 shows the program interface. The user is presented with various populations on which to act: In the center, the algebraically defined elements that compose a library of shapes from which the CSG individuals of the left hand side population are built. For example the shape in the red box of the left hand side CSG population is selected, and the program automatically identifies which individuals from the algebraically defined population it is composed of: here a cylinder and a sphere in the blue boxes of the algebraic element (middle) population. The third population shown here on the

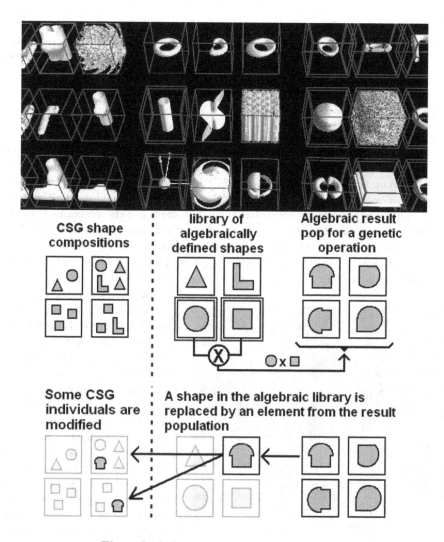

Fig. 5. Links between population components

right hand side is the population used to present results of genetic operations performed on the algebraic shapes. In this particular figure, they present the results of mutations of the torus. Notice how some results from this mutation have little or nothing in common with their parent, as we have mentioned when questioning creation process coherence on the algebraic level. However, since the result from the mutation operation is presented in the form of a sample population, the user is likely to find several shapes resembling the parent, offering some continuity and coherence in the creation process. An individual from this algebraic result population may be selected to take the place of another shape in the algebraic shape library from which CSG shapes are built. If so, all the CSG shapes using the replaced shape will be dynamically updated. The diagrams in Fig 5 illustrate these mechanisms. The 3 populations represented in these diagrams are the populations already described in the previous paragraph.

3.4   Why Two Levels?

There are interests to this two-level editing of shapes. We have mentioned that the level of coherence in the genetic manipulation of shapes can be a little tricky on the algebraic individuals; however, the field of shapes created by genetic manipulations on this level is surprisingly rich. We have not questioned creation process coherence in the case of CSG tree manipulations: the behavior of CSG operators is naturally much more controllable and coherent. For these reasons it seems natural to use a user-based evaluation and constant user control over the algebraic level editing, as done by Bedwell and Ebert [BE98] and Jones [Jon99] and to use the CSG level for the definition of objective characteristics, such as the capacity to be a table, a chair, a pot, as done by Jacob, Kwong and Wyvill [JKW01].

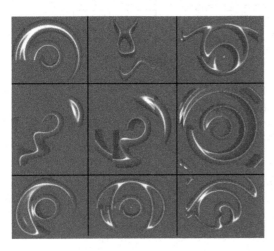

Fig. 6.

Our genotype representation can combine the advantages of both these approaches. Our tool enables a design that partly overlaps the areas that Bentley identified as evolutionary art and creative evolutionary design [Ben99]. A user, by means of subjective selection, genetically edits a set of shapes on the algebraic level of editing, which define *style* and uses genetic operations on the CSG tree population to achieve *purpose*. The user creates a set of shapes on the algebraic level that visually please him regardless of their ability to serve a desired purpose, then searches for a CSG composition of these shapes that serve a purpose. This is demonstrated in the following paragraph.

Fig 6 shows a family of related shapes, generated by mutations on the algebraic level. The algebraic operators we have added to those used in cited articles extend the variety of generated shapes. The creation of these shapes is surprising and interesting, however it is hard to control the process enough to generate objects that serve a defined, objective purpose.

Fig 7 shows a sample of seats generated with our program. They are composed of three algebraic shape elements: two symmetrical side shapes linked with a horizontal shape within a CSG composition. They were generated in the following manner: On the algebraic level, genetic experimentations are performed to obtain a complex and interesting library of shapes, in the same manner that the algebraic shape population in Fig 6 was obtained: iterative crossings, mutations and selections. Simultaneously, the CSG composition individuals are also genetically edited, but less freely than the algebraic shapes: The 3 element structure of the seat object is preserved. Genetic editing on the CSG level is used to generate and test various combinations of algebraic shapes as well as different types of junctions and weights between these elements (blendings with different weights, unions, intersections...).

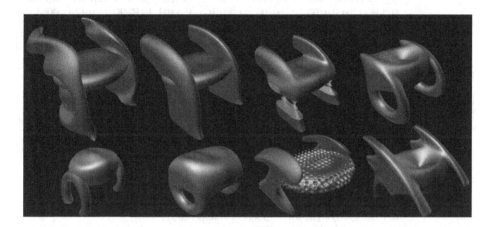

Fig. 7. 2-level genetically evolved shapes: a population of seats

4 Conclusion and Future Work

In this article we have proposed a model which provides expressive ways to explore the vast space of algebraically defined implicit surfaces by genetic programming methods. We have enriched the algebraic genetic definition of surface objects with a CSG level within a single composed genetic structure. The exploitation of this composed genotype enabled us to engender new and interesting editing processes. More particularly, some restrictions on genetic operators performing on the CSG level allowed us to generate functional objects while exploiting the richness and surprising creativity of the algebraic level shapes.

We now work on some extensions of this model to generate constrained shapes responding to a set of constraints. Our aim is not to provide with a completely automatic design process but more to provide a designer with a new interaction model where he can describe both the visual aspect and the technical specifications of a shape. The system will then provide him with a set of solutions than he can rearrange with the operators provided by our model.

5   Related Resources

High resolution images created using our system could be found at
http://www.irit.fr/~herve.luga/

References

[ABGC05]   Alexe, A.-I., Barthe, L., Gaildrat, V., Cani, M.-P.: Shape Modeling
            by Sketching using Convolution Surfaces. In: Pacific Graphics, Macau
            (China) 10/10/05-14/10/05 ACMSIGGRAPH / IEEE (octobre 2005)
[BBB+97]   Bajaj, C., Blinn, J., Bloomenthal, J., Cani.-Gascuel, M.-P., Rockwood,
            A., Wyvill, B., Wyvill, G.: Introduction to Implicit Surfaces. Morgan
            Kaufmann Publishers Inc, San Francisco, CA, USA (1997)
[BE98]   Bedwell, E.J., Ebert, D.S.: Artificial evolution of implicit surfaces, pp.
            261–261 (1998)
[Ben98]   Bentley, P.J.: Aspects of evolutionary design by computers (1998)
[Ben99]   Bentley, J.: Evolutionary Design by Computers. Morgan Kaufmann
            Publishers Inc, San Francisco, CA, USA (1999)
[Bre00]   Bret, M.: Virtual living beings. In: Heudin, J.-C. (ed.) VW 2000. LNCS
            (LNAI), vol. 1834, pp. 119–134. Springer, Heidelberg (2000)
[Dar59]   Darwin, C.: On the origins of species by means of natural selection
            (1859)
[JKW01]   Jacob, C., Kwong, H., Wywill, B.: Toward the creation of an evolution-
            ary design system for implicit surfaces (2001)
[Jon99]   Jones, M.W.: Direct surface rendering of general and genetically bred
            implicit surfaces. In: proc. 17th ann. conf. of eurographics (uk chapter)
            cambridge, pp. 37–46 (1999)
[Kaw05]   Kawaguchi, Y., kawaguchi, Y.: SIGGRAPH '05: ACM SIGGRAPH 2005
            Electronic Art and Animation Catalog, pp. 90–91. ACM Press, New
            York, NY, USA (2005)
[Koz92a]   Koza, J.R.: Genetic programming: on the programming of computers by
            means of natural selection. MIT Press (a Bradford book) Cambridge,
            MA, USA (1992)
[Koz92b]   Koza, J.R.: The genetic programming paradigm: Genetically breeding
            populations of computer programs to solve problems. In: Soucek, B.,
            Group, I.R.I.S. (eds.) Dynamic, Genetic, and Chaotic Programming,
            pp. 203–321. John Wiley, New York (1992)
[Lan89]   Langton, C.G.: Artificial Life: Proceedings of an Interdisciplinary Work-
            shop on the Synthesis and Simulation of Living Systems. Addison-
            Wesley Longman Publishing Co., Inc, Boston, MA, USA (1989)
[LDPB95]   Luga, H., Duthen, Y., Pelle, R., Berro, A.: Extended algebraic surfaces
            generation for volume modelling: an approach through genetic algo-
            rithms. In: Proceedings of Visualisation and Modelling, Leeds, British
            Computer Society (December 1995)
[LG06]   Larive, M., Gaildrat, V.: Wall Grammar for Building Generation. In:
            Spencer, S.N. (ed.) Graphite, 4th International Conference on Com-
            puter Graphics and Interactive Techniques in Australasia and South-
            East Asia, Kuala Lumpur, Malaysia, 29/11/06-02/12/06, ACM Press,
            pp. 429–438 (novembre 2006) http://www.acm.org/

[LLD06]   Lassabe, N., Luga, H., Duthen, Y.: Evolving creatures in virtual ecosystems. In: Pan, Z., Cheok, A.D., Haller, M., Lau, R.W.H., Saito, H., Liang, R. (eds.) ICAT 2006. LNCS, vol. 4282, pp. 11–20. Springer, Heidelberg (2006)

[Sim91]   Sims, K.: Artificial evolution for computer graphics. In: SIGGRAPH '91: Proceedings of the 18th annual conference on Computer graphics and interactive techniques, pp. 319–328. ACM Press, New York, NY, USA (1991)

[Sim94]   Sims, K.: Evolving 3d morphology and behavior by competition. In: Artificial Life IV Proceedings, pp. 28–39. MIT Press, Cambridge, (1994)

[SLD06]   Sanchez, S., Luga, H., Duthen, Y.: Learning classifier systems and behavioural animation of virtual characters. In: Gratch, J., Young, M., Aylett, R., Ballin, D., Olivier, P. (eds.) IVA 2006. LNCS (LNAI), vol. 4133, p. 467. Springer, Heidelberg (2006)

[SLRLG03]   Sanchez, S., Roux, O.L., Luga, H., Gaildrat, V.: Constraint-Based 3D-Object Layout using a Genetic Algorithm. In: 3IA'2003, The Sixth International Conference on Computer Graphics and Artificial Intelligence, Limoges, 14/05/03-15/05/03 (May 2003)

[TL94]   Todd, S., Latham, W.: Evolutionary Art and Computers. Academic Press, Inc, Orlando, FL, USA (1994)

[Whi04]   Whitelaw, M.: Metacreation: Art and Artificial Life. MIT Press, Cambridge, MA, USA (2004)

Data-Embeddable Texture Synthesis

Hirofumi Otori and Shigeru Kuriyama

Toyohashi University of Technology, 1-1 Hibarigaoka, Tenpaku-cho, Toyohashi, Aichi,
441-8580, Japan
{otori,kuriyama}@val.ics.tut.ac.jp

Abstract. Data hiding techniques onto images provide tools for protecting copyright or sending secret messages, and they are currently utilized
as a simple input device of a cell phone by detecting a data embedded in
an image with an equipped digital camera. This paper presents a method
of synthesizing texture images for embedding arbitrary data by utilizing
the smart techniques of generating repetitive texture patterns through
feature learning of a sample image. We extended the techniques so that
a synthesized image can effectively conceal the embedded pattern, and
the pattern can be robustly detected from a photographed image. We
demonstrate the feasibility of our techniques using texture samples including an image scanned from real material.

1 Introduction

The advanced image processing capability of handy cell phones enables a novel
data input tool with images. A QR-code[1] [1] was developed as an efficient and
robust 2D bar code, as shown in Fig. 1(a), and it has become a popular device in Japanese culture for inputting a URL with the photographing capability
equipped on a cell phone. With this device, we can avoid the troublesome operations with the small numerical key-pad of cell phones. However, the meaningless
binary pattern of the QR-code damages the aesthetic quality of the printed images. Some extension methods have been developed to overcome such a defect,
for example, by coloring [2] (Fig. 1(b)) or modifying to small icons (Fig. 1(c));
these methods, however, essentially provide the aesthetic style of a 2D bar
code. Recently, some data-embedding methods onto natural images have been
proposed as a replacement for the QR-code. Some techniques intentionally mod-
ulate the specific color component or frequency channel of the image according
to embedded data. Most methods incorporate either type of numerical techniques developed as watermarking or steganography [3]. The former technique
is utilized for protecting copyright, which requires robustness against intentional
attack through alteration or destruction of images, and the latter is designed to
increase the amount of hidden data (or payload) while sacrificing robustness.

The data-embedding techniques on printed media, like the QR-code, have a
property similar to those of steganography, sacrificing robustness against attacks

---

[1] QR code is a trademark of DENSO WAVE Inc.

A. Butz et al. (Eds.): SG 2007, LNCS 4569, pp. 146–157, 2007.
© Springer-Verlag Berlin Heidelberg 2007

(a) QR code [1]   (b) Color bar code   (c) Design QR [2]

Fig. 1. Examples of two-dimensional bar codes

on copyright, but they require another type of robustness, that is, tolerance for the noise caused by analog transmissions through printing and photographing processes. Such robustness is often obtained by increasing the amount of modulations by sacrificing the quality of original images. Another solution introduces redundancy, for example, the use of the Reed-Solomon code [4], but this strategy is useless when most of the data is undetectable.

The watermarking and steganography mainly treat natural images, and there are few methods developed for artificial images such as cartoons or computer-generated images. For example, data embeddings with run length code [5] or block pattern [6] have been proposed for binary images, but their data detection strategies neglect robustness against noisy data. The steganography on a text document slightly modifies the dots of each letter image [7], but it assumes the high-resolution scanning process of a business copy machine and is hard to extend the capability to arbitrary types of images.

This paper focuses on the texture images for embedding data because texture patterns are widely utilized artificial images. More importantly, texture images can be automatically generated by computing the feature of the iterative patterns of real objects such as woods or cloth, and thus we can embed data by affixing a seal of a synthesized image on a real object in an inconspicuous manner, by which the aesthetic quality of the object's appearance is guaranteed.

Our approach utilizes texture synthesis technique for embedding data so as to be robust against the noise caused by analog transmission. Instead of changing the color component of images, we directly paint the data by converting its numerical value into a dotted colored pattern, and then automatically coat a texture image onto the painted pattern from a sample image (or exemplar) so as to conceal its existence with a natural texture pattern. The recently proposed texture synthesis algorithm [8] and its extensions [9,10] were utilized for synthesizing seamless and continuous images with the constraints of local patterns corresponding to the embedded data.

We first introduce an encoding method with painted patterns in Section 2 as a basic mechanism to embed and detect data. Section 3 explains about smart texture synthesis from an initial painting pattern which is suited to conceal a data-embedded pattern, and we demonstrate the feasibility of our method by showing examples of texture synthesis and data detection by photographing the printed images in Section 4. We finally give conclusions in Section 5.

---

[2] Design QR is a trademark of IT Design Inc. http://d-qr.net/

2   Encoding with Painted Local Binary Pattern

We utilize a feature vector for texture images, called local binary pattern (or LBP) [11]. It was first introduced as a complementary measure for local image contrast, and the definition of pixel neighborhood for computing features is extended to arbitrary circular neighborhoods. The code is computed by comparing the value of a centered pixel against those of neighboring pixels.

We first divide a texture image captured by a digital camera into pre-defined number of square blocks. The LBP is then given for each block by the difference of a pixel value, denoted by $g(\boldsymbol{p})$ at the $\boldsymbol{p}$ coordinates, between a pixel located at the center of the block and the P circular positions at an equal distance (see Fig. 2),

$$LBP_{P.R}(\boldsymbol{p}_c) = \sum_{n=0}^{P-1} s\left(g\left(\boldsymbol{p}_n\right) - g\left(\boldsymbol{p}_c\right)\right) 2^n, s\left(x\right) = \begin{cases} 1 & : x \geq 0 \\ 0 & : x < 0 \end{cases} \quad (1)$$

where $\boldsymbol{p}_c = (x_c, y_c)$ denotes the center position, and the n-th circular position is given by $\boldsymbol{p}_n = \boldsymbol{p}_c + R\left(\cos\left(2\pi n/P\right), -\sin\left(2\pi n/P\right)\right)$ with the distance R from the center. Each $LBP_{P.R}(\boldsymbol{p}_c)$ therefore represents P bits information whose n-th bit has the value of $s(g(\boldsymbol{p}_n) - g(\boldsymbol{p}_c))$. Notice that we simply determine the pixel values by discretizing the coordinate $\boldsymbol{p}_n$ to integers, instead of interpolating the values of neighboring pixels.

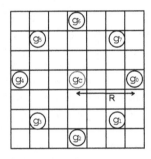

Fig. 2. Pixel sampling positions for computing LBP code (P=8)

The existing technique for analyzing texture images defines the feature by considering rotation invariance pattern and uniformity measure [11]; our method, however, neglects these constraints and allows arbitrary patterns of $LBP_{P,R}(\boldsymbol{p})$. The existing method uses grayscale level or each RGB component as a pixel value, but it can be replaced by an arbitrary color component, if it can be uniquely converted from RGB components. We usually select the component that is insensitive to human vision system; for example, the Cb component on Y-Cb-Cr color space, as the pixel value $g(\boldsymbol{p})$. However, the component must be selected so as to have a high contrast for ensuring the robustness against noisy transmission. The LBP code is then computed by extracting the insensitive component of the color at each pixel and by using equation (1). The extracted LBP codes from all blocks represent all information embedded in the texture image. Therefore, arbitrary data are divided and embedded by painting the pattern of LBP onto each block in their sequence. A texture image is then coated so as to conceal this painted pattern by referencing an exemplar.

3   Texture Synthesis with LBP

3.1   Initial Painting with Embedded Data

The initial paint pattern of a synthesized texture is made from an exemplar. We first extract the insensitive color component as each pixel value $g(\boldsymbol{p})$ and compute the median, denoted by g_m, from all pixels. Every pixel is then divided into two classes: the upper class for $g(\boldsymbol{p}) \geq g_m + T$ and the lower class for $g_m - T \geq g(\boldsymbol{p})$, where the pixel values residing in the middle range; $g_m + T > g(\boldsymbol{p}) > g_m - T$, are neglected in painting LBP. The scalar value T isolates the pixel values in upper and lower classes from the median value g_m, and an increase of T enhances robustness against the noisy variation caused in printing and photographing. However, the larger T narrows down the range of usable colors, and we experimentally found that $T = 30$ ensures good balance for 8-bit pixel values. After categorizing the constituent colors into two classes, the central pixel is always painted by the color whose component is equivalent to the median g_m, and the surrounding pixels are painted by randomly selecting the color whose component belongs to the upper and lower classes for the embedded binary data of 1 and 0, respectively.

Fig. 3(b) represents an example of the initial paint pattern made from the exemplar in Fig. 3(a). We intentionally paint the same value at the nearby pixels of the center and surrounding pixels for increasing robustness against the positional error in sampling. Because each LBP code can represent P bits, embedding data of n bits requires $\lceil n/P \rceil$ image blocks regularly arranged as shown in Fig. 3(b), where $\lceil \; \rceil$ denotes a ceil function.

3.2   Texture Coating with Exemplar

Next, we randomly select the pixel whose value is null and paint it by computing the differences in the insensitive component of the 8 neighboring pixels to the corresponding pixels in the exemplar as,

$$S\left(\boldsymbol{p},\boldsymbol{q}\right) = \sum_{\boldsymbol{r} \in \nu} D\left(\boldsymbol{p},\boldsymbol{q},\boldsymbol{r}\right) \tag{2}$$

$$D\left(\boldsymbol{p},\boldsymbol{q},\boldsymbol{r}\right) = \begin{cases} 0 & \text{if } g\left(\boldsymbol{p}+\boldsymbol{r}\right) \text{ is null} \\ \left(g\left(\boldsymbol{p}+\boldsymbol{r}\right) - \tilde{g}\left(\boldsymbol{q}+\boldsymbol{r}\right)\right)^2 & \text{else} \end{cases}$$

where $\boldsymbol{p}$ denotes the 2D position of the randomly selected pixel, ν is the set of offset vectors for indicating 8 neighbors; $\nu := \{(s,t)|s,t \in (-1,0,1), s \neq t\}$

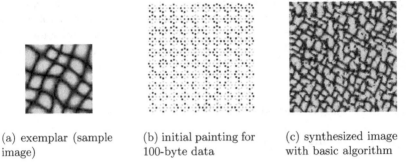

| (a) exemplar (sample image) | (b) initial painting for 100-byte data | (c) synthesized image with basic algorithm |

Fig. 3. Example of texture synthesis

and $\tilde{g}(q+r)$ is the pixel value of the exemplar. Notice that the large $S(p, q)$ corresponds to the dissimilar pattern of neighboring pixels between synthesize texture and exemplar. We then set the pixel value $g(p)$ by those of the most similar pixel of the exemplar that has minimum $S(p, q)$ as

$$\hat{q} = \arg\min_q S(p, q) \ , \ \ g(p) = \tilde{g}(\hat{q}) \tag{3}$$

and the pixel at p is painted by the color whose component corresponds to $g(p)$. The equations (2) and (3) are interpreted as template matching where a 3 by 3 pixels' region at p is regarded as a template and the best matching region is searched within the exemplar. The random selection of p is repeated until all pixels are painted. Fig. 3(c) shows the texture generated by this coating algorithm from the exemplar of Fig. 3(a) and the initial painting of Fig. 3(b).

3.3 Acceleration with Coherence Map

The abovementioned coating algorithm uniquely determines each pixel value by computing the pattern dissimilarity for all pixels in the exemplar; this exhaustive search for minimum $S(p, q)$, however, requires a large amount of computation that proportionally increases for the product of the pixel sizes of the synthesized and exemplar images. We therefore introduce a method [9] that considers the coherency of the exemplar by recording the history of the similarity search onto every pixel.

A coherence map is defined as a set of two-dimensional indices, denoted by $m(p)$, which is assigned to every pixel of a synthesized image for recording the position of the corresponding exemplar's pixel (see Fig. 4(b)). Then the searching space of q in the equation (3) is narrowed down as

$$q \in m(p+r) - r \ \ for \ \ r \in \nu \tag{4}$$

where the index is updated by the position of the most similar pixel as $m(p) = \hat{q}$. The equation (4) is interpreted as the template matching among the exemplar's pixels whose nearby pixel is used for painting the nearby pixel of p in the same adjacency. Notice that we conduct the exhaustive search of q when the index $m(p + r)$ is null. We experimentally confirmed that this coherence-based similarity search can speed up the synthesis by 10 times, compared to the basic coating algorithm.

3.4 Quality Improvement with Similarity Map and Re-coating

The coherence-based similarity search is efficient, but it decreases the quality as a trade-off with drastically narrowing down the searching space of q. We therefore efficiently expand the searching space by considering the similarity inside the exemplar. In particular, we pre-compute the dissimilarity of each square region of N by N pixels inside the exemplar, denoted by $B_N(q, \tilde{q})$, as

$$B_N(q, \tilde{q}) = \sum_{s \in \mu} (\tilde{g}(q + s) - \tilde{g}(\tilde{q} + s))^2 \tag{5}$$

where μ denotes the offset of each pixel in the region from a center position; $\mu := \{(s, t) | s, t \in (-h, .., -1, 0, 1, ..., h)\}$ $h = (N - 1)/2$, and the values of q and $\tilde{q}$ are constrained so that $q + s$ and $\tilde{q} + s$ fall in the pixel range of the exemplar. The size of the square region N for pattern matching is adaptively tuned in a range of 5 to 21 depending on the feature of texture, and we use $N = 15$ as a default.

We next construct a map [10] for indexing a pattern similarity among the pixels in the exemplar by setting the $\tilde{q}$ of the i-th-smallest $B_N(q, \tilde{q})$ to $u_i(q)$, up to the k positions. The most similar pixel in the exemplar is then searched among the positions indexed by the similarity map for the search space given by coherence map in equation (4) as (see Fig. 4(c))

$$q \in u_i (m(p + r) - r) \quad for \ \ r \in \nu \ \ and \ \ i = 0, 1, \ldots, k \tag{6}$$

where $u_0(x)$ represents the identical map; $u_0(x) := x$. With the similarity map, the search space of q is expanded from the similarity record of coherence map to the corresponding k similar pattern in the exemplar. We experimentally confirmed that this expanded search with the similarity map can still speed up the synthesis by 4 times, compared to the basic coating algorithm.

Furthermore, we improve the quality of the synthesized images by repeating the above coating algorithm. After all pixels are painted, we re-coat them all except for the pixels painted for embedding data. The first coating phase determines the most similar pattern only with the painted pixels; in other words, the computation of similarity in equation (2) is inaccurate in the early stage of coating because the effect of many pixels is missed by the rule of $D(p, q, r) = 0$ if $g(p + r)$ is null . In the second coating phase, all pixel values and indices of coherence map $m(p + r)$ have been tentatively determined, and thus the analysis of texture pattern becomes more accurate. We experimentally confirmed that the re-coating in more than the second trial cannot particularly increase the quality of the image, and we therefore execute the re-coating only once.

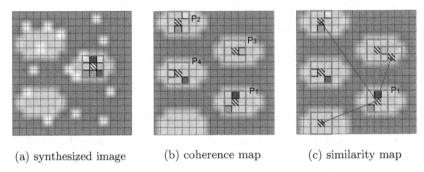

(a) synthesized image   (b) coherence map   (c) similarity map

Fig. 4. Schematic representation of map generations

4   Experimental Results

4.1   Texture Synthesis

The images in Fig. 5 present the synthesized texture from the exemplar and initial painting in Fig. 3 (a) and (b). Figure (a) is synthesized by using the basic algorithm in equation (1) (the same image as in Fig. 3(c)), figure (b) is synthesized with the coherence map, and figure (c) is synthesized by additionally using the similarity map. The texture image in figure (b) shows the increase of conspicuous spots due to the narrow search space with the coherence map, and the image in figure (c) demonstrates the decrease of the spots due to the expanded search space with the similarity map, by which image quality is recovered.

Fig. 6 demonstrates the effectiveness of our random and multiple coating. Figure (a) is synthesized by selecting the unpainted pixels in scan-line order, and figure (b) randomly selects unpainted pixels, which definitely decreases the undesirable spots of LBP. Figure (c) presents the image after re-coating the image of figure (b) in scan-line order at one time, by which tiny noisy spots are removed. These samples are generated using the Cb component of Y-Cb-Cr color space as a pixel value, and the similarity map is constructed with the matching region of $N = 15$ size.

Fig. 7 shows various kinds of texture synthesis, which arranges exemplars (right), textures synthesized through ordinary procedures without embedding data (middle), and data-embedded textures with our method (left). The payload is set to 25 bytes, and the size of the matching region for the similarity map is tuned to $N =$ (a) 7, (b) 15, (c) 11. The color component of (a) Cb, (b) Y, and (c) Cr, is selected as a pixel value, respectively, and the textures without embedding data are synthesized by coating pixels in scan-line order.

Fig. 8 demonstrates the examples synthesized from the exemplar in figure (b) that is generated by scanning the surface of real wooden material in figure (a). Figures (c), (d), and (e) show initial paint patterns for the embedded data of 100, 25, and 16, bytes, respectively, and figures (f), (g), and (h) show the synthesized images using the coherence and similarity maps and re-coating for these paint patterns. These examples clearly show the trade-off between the payload and

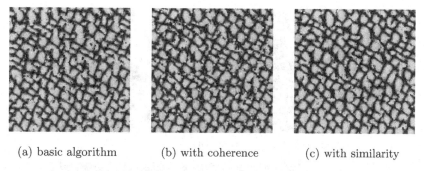

(a) basic algorithm   (b) with coherence   (c) with similarity

Fig. 5. Effect of coherence and similarity maps on synthesized textures

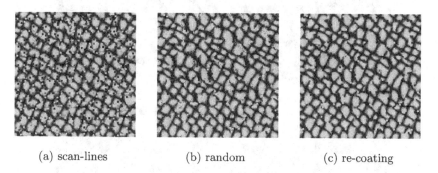

(a) scan-lines   (b) random   (c) re-coating

Fig. 6. Effect of pixel coating strategy

quality. The color space of Y-Cb-Cr of this wooden image has a very low contrast for Cb and Cr components, and we therefore adopted the component Y as a pixel value.

4.2   Accuracy in Data Detection

We have examined the robustness of our data-detecting mechanism. The 100 bytes data-embedded texture images of 200×200 pixels are printed on superfine A4 paper in a 2x2 inch square region with an EPSON PX-G5100 color inkjet printer, and they were photographed with a CANON PowerShotG5 digital camera that is fixed on the tripod in such a way as to be parallel to the paper at a distance of 30 cm, where a fluorescent lamp was used for lighting.

Table 1 shows the result of data detection for the images in Fig. 6(c) and Fig. 8 (f), (g), (h). Error bits were computed by averaging the number of error bits for 10 trials. The embedded data cannot be perfectly detected, but the ratios of error bits are small enough to recover the information with some error correcting techniques such as the Reed-Solomon code.

Next, we have implemented our data-detecting mechanism on a cell phone of FOMA D903i with Doja API, and printed the 25 bytes data-embedded texture image in Fig. 6(c) of 100 by 100 pixels in a 1 by 1 inch square region with the

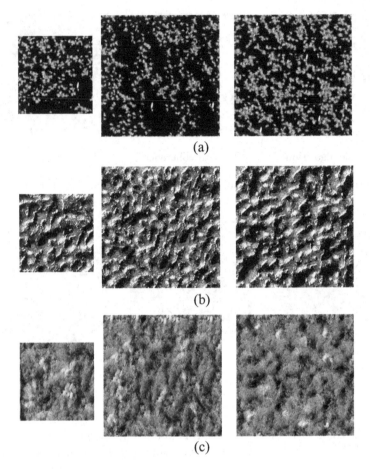

Fig. 7. Examples of exemplar, ordinary synthesis, and data-embedded synthesis

Table 1. Error rate for various size of embedded data

Example	Payload(byte)	Error bits	% of missing data
Fig.6(c)	100	1.2	0.15
Fig.8(f)	100	10.0	1.25
Fig.8(g)	25	0.0	0.00
Fig.8(h)	16	1.0	0.01

same printer. The printed image was captured by the phone's camera with a macro mode of 176 by 144 pixels supported by hand at a distance of 5 to 8 cm. Through 10 trials, we had average error bits of 4.8 where the maximum and minimum of the error bits was 14 and 0, respectively.

Table 2 compares the payload of our method against the existing market products. We can only show a rough comparison due to the lack of detailed

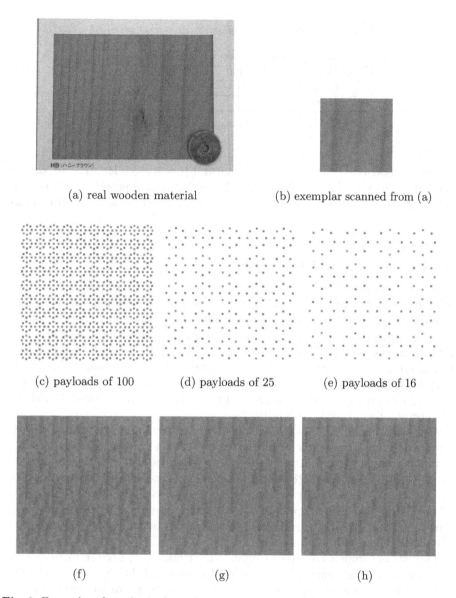

(a) real wooden material   (b) exemplar scanned from (a)

(c) payloads of 100   (d) payloads of 25   (e) payloads of 16

(f)   (g)   (h)

Fig. 8. Examples of synthesized wooden textures. Figure (b) is an image scanned from the material in (a) used as an exemplar. Figures (c), (d), and (e) are initial paintings for given payloads of 100, 25, and 16 bytes, respectively. Textures in figures (f), (g), and (h) are generated from the initial painting in figures (c), (d), and (e), respectively.

specification, and these payloads cannot be fairly estimated because of the difference in measurement conditions in terms of paper-size, resolution of camera, lighting, and so on. The displayed values of payload therefore lack the accuracy in evaluation. However, we can safely conclude that the embeddable data

Table 2. Comparison of payload with market products

Product	Payload(byte)	Methodology
Our method	25 ~ 100	LBP code
QR-Code[1]	3000	2D bar code
Pasha-warp[12]	3	Frequency modulation
FP-code[13]	5	Color modulation

in our method is larger than those in natural image modulations, but smaller than those in the 2D bar code. This shows that our approach based on texture pattern synthesis has the advantage in the payload over natural image modulations.

5   Conclusion and Discussion

We have proposed a novel texture image synthesis for embedding data with little aesthetic defect. Our technical contribution is the introduction of random coating and re-coating to improve the quality of the texture image synthesized from the initial painting of LBP. We have also demonstrated that the efficient computation of pattern similarity using coherence and similarity maps is applicable to our texture synthesis. Our method could be the replacement of QR code in that it can provide visually meaningful images, and also might surpass existing techniques of natural image modulations in payload.

Our algorithm focuses on the textures that are iteratively generated by learning a pattern of an exemplar, and thus is infeasible for a procedurally and randomly generated pattern, for example, those generated using Perlin's noise functions [14]. However, the LBP is still available to extract features of such a class of textures. We successfully embedded the data onto the shape of a histogram of the LBPs that are computed for every pixel inside a divided image block. However, the payload of this method turned out to be far smaller than those of the method proposed in this paper.

Our current implementation requires border lines on a texture image for extracting the square region of a data-embedded area, and this limitation should be removed by developing a technique of automatically determining the square region. The texture pattern is often used as a background, and we should develop a method for coating texture with letter images. The payload of our method should be more accurately estimated in future study.

Acknowledgment

The authors would like to thank the members of Wood One Co., Ltd. for donating the sample of wooden material in Fig. 8(a).

References

1. DENSO Wave. International Standard ISO/IEC18004 (2000)
2. Tack.-don, H., Cheol.-ho, H., Nam.-kyu, L., Eun.-dong, H.: Machine readable code image and method of encoding and decoding the same. United States Patent No. US 7,020,327 B2
3. Provos, N., Honeyman, P.: Hide and Seek: An Introduction to Steganography. IEEE Security & Privacy 1(3), 32–44 (2003)
4. Reed, I.S., Solomon, G.: Polynomial codes over certain finite fields. SIAM J, pp. 300-304 (1960)
5. Hwang, K.-F., Chang, C.-C.: A Run-Length Mechanism for Hiding Data into Binary Images. In: Proceedings of Pacific Rim Workshop on Digital Steganography 2002, pp. 71-74 (2002)
6. Tseng, Y. C., Pan, H. K.: Secure and Invisible Data Hiding in 2-color Images. In: Proceedings of INFOCOM 2001, pp. 887–896 (2001)
7. Fujii, Y., Nakano, K., Echizen, K., Yosiura, Y.: Digital Watermarking Scheme for Binary Image (in Japanese) Japan Patent 2004-289783
8. Wei, L.-Y., Levoy, M.: Fast Texture Synthesis using Tree-structured Vector Quantization. In: Proceedings of SIGGRAPH 2000, pp. 479–488 (2000)
9. Ashikhmin, M.: Synthesizing natural textures. Symposium on Interactive 3D Graphics, pp. 217–226 (2001)
10. Tong, X., Zhang, J., Lui, L., Wang, X., Guo, B., Shum, H.: Synthesis of Bidirectional Texture Functions on Arbitrary Surfaces. In: ACM SIGGRAPH 2002, pp. 665–672 (2002)
11. Mäenpää, T., Pietikäinen, M.: Texture analysis with local binary patterns. Handbook of Pattern Recognition and Computer Vision 3rd ed. World Scientific, pp. 197–216 (2005)
12. Nakamura, T., Ogawa, H., Tomioka, A., Takashima, Y.: Improved Digital Watermark Robustness againt Translation and/or Cropping of an Image Area. IEICE Trans. Fundamentals E83-A(1), 68–76 (2000)
13. Noda, T., Moroo, J., Chiba, H.: Print-type Steganography Technology (in Japanese). Magazine FUJITSU 2006-5 57(3), 320–324 (2006)
14. Perlin, K.: An Image Synthesizer. In: Proceedings of SIGGRAPH '85 85, 287–296 (1985)

Tile-Based Modeling and Rendering

Maki Terai[1], Jun Fujiki[2], Reiji Tsuruno[3], and Kiyoshi Tomimatsu[4]

[1] School of Design, Kyushu University,
[2] Graduate School of Design, Kyushu University,
[3,4] Faculty of Design, Kyushu University,
[1,2,3,4] 4-9-1 Shiobaru, Minami-ku, Fukuoka, 815-8540 Japan
maki@verygood.aid.design.kyushu-u.ac.jp,
fujiki@gsd.design.kyushu-u.ac.jp,
{tsuruno,tomimatu}@design.kyushu-u.ac.jp

Abstract. Generally, 2D computer graphics are suitable for depicting 2D structures. However, computer games generally depict 3D structures using 2D computer graphics. We are interested in such expression. As the overhead view has no 3D geometry data, a mechanism 3D geometry data from the overhead view is proposed. In addition, a tile-based technique for seamless conversion of a two-dimensional graphical expression into a three-dimensional geometric shape is proposed. In the proposed approach, an overhead 2D view defined by tiles on a canvas is converted into groups of 3D forms automatically and distorted according to an arbitrary viewing angle. The derivation and algorithm of the scheme are presented, and example applications are shown.

Keywords: Interaction design, non-photorealistic rendering, computer game, scene description.

1 Introduction

Many computer games are based on "overhead" two-dimensional (2D) computer graphics which are suitable for displaying planar figure(Fig. 1). However, in such graphical engines, three-dimensional (3D) structures are also presented in 2D. In the overhead view, the width of a shape is displayed by a horizontal line, and the height and depth are expressed as a vertical line. Such an expression in not realistic, but is intuitively recognizable, particularly in computer games. In the present study, a technique for converting the overhead view expression into a 3D expression is proposed, and the method is developed so as to allow seamless conversion between the two presentations. A prototype system is demonstrated, and seamless conversion is confirmed. As the overhead view has no 3D geometry data, a mechanism 3D geometry data from the overhead view is proposed. In this system, 3D geometry data recognizable by the user is generated from tiles placed on a canvas. The geometric shape created by the system can be viewed from an arbitrary angle by a gradual warping of the geometry, without the user being aware of the conversion to the 3D expression.

A. Butz et al. (Eds.): SG 2007, LNCS 4569, pp. 158–163, 2007.

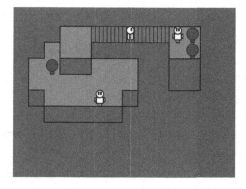

Fig. 1. Overhead view

2 Related Work

A famous modeling method is the sketching interface, which provides an easy way to create a rough model. Zeleznik *et al.* [1] proposed the SKETCH scheme, in which 3D scenes are designed using simple primitives. Igarashi *et al.* [2] proposed the Teddy scheme involving free-form models. Cohen *et al.* [3] proposed the Harold approach, in which a virtual 3D world is generated from 2D input, and Weizhong *et al.* [4] presented a freehand sketch interpreter system for constructing solid 3D models. In addition to these intuitive interface, Fujiki *et al.* [5] propose the Incompatible BLOCK scheme, which is block-based modeling system with intuitive interface but expresses data in a manner impossible in the real world. The modeling system proposed in the present study also employs an expression that is impossible in the real world.

There are many expressions that are not realistic, such as the expression of a shape that is distorted. In computer graphics, many techniques for distorting shape have been represented [6,7,8]. The distortion technique is also employed here, for shapes impossible in the real world.

The present method is similar to that in Ref. [9], where the voxel model representation is used to express the structure of shapes.

3 User Interface

The proposed scheme is a tile-based modeling system. The user designs in overhead view with a view angle to horizon of 45°. The user begins modeling by placing tiles on a canvas in overhead view. The canvas is a uniform square grid, tiles are either green or brown, and the edge pattern has 16 variants (see Fig. 2(a)). Tile color determines depth and height of shapes, and the edge pattern can create closed domains. The basic generation rule for modeling is that the system creates geometric shapes when a group of green tiles are above a group of brown tiles. In each lines, the number of green tiles represents depth, and the number of

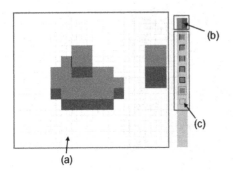 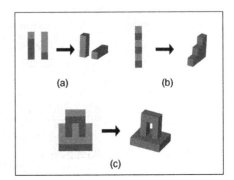

Fig. 2. Left: User interface. (a) Canvas. (b) Panel for changing tile color. (c) Tiles for placement on the canvas. Right: (a) Sample shapes with depth and height. (b) Stair shape. (c) Gate shape.

brown tiles represents height, while the height of the closed domain of green tiles is equal. Therefore, the shape that has not adhered to ground can be created (Fig. 4).

This rule is based on the basic features of the overhead view. Alternating tile arrangements in a row forms a stair (Fig. 2(b)). In addition, the system infers shapes of locations that cannot be observed in overhead view and interpolates shapes.

4 Algorithm

When a user rotates the canvas, the system creates 3D structure data from the arrangement of tiles, seamlessly converting the overhead view into a 3D expression.

4.1 Creating 3D Structures from Overhead View

The system scans all tiles and calculates the closed domain of green tiles. The green tiles in each closed domain are grouped. Each closed domain consists of a number of vertically -arranged tiles, and the system processes the following algorithm for each closed domain. Figure 3 shows such a vertical- arrangement of tiles.

1. The depth of the shape is calculated for each vertically -arranged group of tiles according to the number of continuous green tiles (Fig. 4 (a)).
2. The height of the shape is calculated for each group of vertically -arranged tiles according to the number of continuous brown tiles (Fig. 4 (b)). In each closed domain, the bottom tile of the line with largest height value is the base tile (Fig. 4(c)).

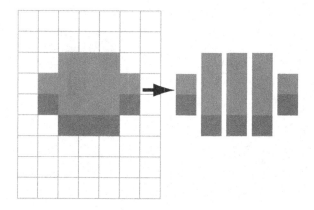

Fig. 3. Vertically-arranged tiles

3. After determining depth and height of all closed domains, the height of the shape is modified. If the base tile is the upper green tile of another closed domain group, the height of the former is added to the height of the latter.
4. The 2D data (2D orthogonal coordinate system) is converted into 3D data. After modifying the height of all shapes, the 3D geometric shape data is calculated using a voxel model in 3D orthogonal coordinate system, the base point in which is calculated from the location of the base tile in the overhead view. Voxel data are determined from the depth and height of the shape data defined.

This procedure converts from overhead view to a 3D view. However, this algorithm does not allow for the definition of locations that cannot be observed in overhead view. Therefore, a complementary algorithm is proposed in which green tiles on both sides of brown tiles of a closed domain group are assigned to that closed domain group (Figs. 4(c,d)). The 3D geometric shape data are thus defined between the green tiles.

4.2   Converting Overhead View into 3D View

In the 3D expression, the shape is distorted depending on the viewpoint, inspired by the View-Dependent Geometry [6] scheme in which the shape is interpolated from multiple views. In overhead view, the sizes of top and front of a cube are equal, corresponding the 3D view at an angle (θ) of 45°. The distortion ratio ($f(\theta)$) is changed according to the viewpoint as follows.

(a)

$$f(\theta) = \frac{(\sqrt{2} - 1)|\theta|}{45} + 1$$

for $0° \leq \theta < 45°, -90° < \theta < -45°$

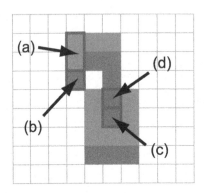 

Fig. 4. Left: (a) Depth (2 in this case). (b) Height (1). (c) Base tile. (c,d) Tile for interpolation. Right: Completed shape.

(b)

$$f(\theta) = \frac{(\sqrt{2}-1)(90-|\theta|)}{45} + 1$$

for $45° \leq \theta < 90°, -45° \leq \theta < 0°$

5 Discussion

In this paper, we have proposed tile-based modeling in overhead view and rendering the created model for viewing at arbitrary angle. We have proposed a rule for generating the shape from overhead view and a technique for seamless conversion from the overhead view to free-angle view. Figure 5 shows some models produced by using our system. It is impossible to convert the arrangement of tiles designed in overhead view into the expected 3D shape precisely. The right figure in Fig. 5 shows that interpolation which cannot be viewed in overhead view. In this figure, (a) is an example shape which seems the expected shape, (b) has a variety of interpolation for 3D.

Our system is associated with the problem of ambiguity. Because overhead view is inherently the ambiguous depiction, it is difficult to infer appropriate shape from the arrangement of tiles in overhead view. In addition, although our system might not be intuitive, the generation rule for modeling is easy and the user who understands the rule can create shape quickly and simply. While some of users had enjoyed to see the unexpected shape, few users were aware of our warping technique for rotating the shape.

In the future, we would like to deal with not only like box shapes but also a variety of shapes. Moreover, we would like to apply the gradual wraping of the geometry scheme to characters and objects put on the shape.

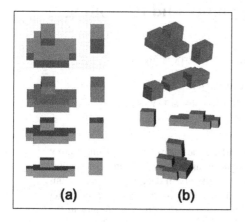 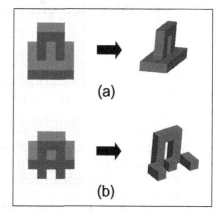

Fig. 5. Left: (a) Vertical rotation. (b) Horizontal rotation. Right: Interpolation of regions not defined in overhead view. (a) Interpolation possible. (b) Interpolation not possible.

References

1. Zeleznik, R.C., Herndon, K.P., Hughes, J.F: SKETCH: an interface for sketching 3D scenes. In: Proceedings of ACM SIGGRAPH96, pp. 163–170. ACM, New York (1996)
2. Igarashi, T., Matsuoka, S., Tanaka, H.: A Sketching Interface for 3D Freeform Design. In: Proceedings of ACM SIGGRAPH99, pp. 409–416. ACM, New York (1999)
3. Cohen, J.M., Hughes, J.F., Zeleznik, R.C., Harold.: A world made of drawings. In NPAR 2000: First International Symposium on Non-Photorealistic Animation and Rendering. In: Fekete, J.-D., Salesin, D.H. (eds.) ACM SIGGRAPH, pp. 83–90. ACM Press, New York (2000)
4. Liu,W., Kondo,K., Mitani,J.: A Freehand Sketch Interpreter System for Constructing 3D Solid Models, IPSJ Symposium Series, vol. 2005(4), pp. 159–160
5. Fujiki, J., Ushiama, T., Tomimatsu, K., gIncompatible BLOCK: Wonders Accompanied Interfaceh, ACM SIGCHI2006 (April 2006)
6. Rademacher,P.: View-Dependent Geometry. In: Proceedings of SIGGRAPH 99, pp. 439–446 (1999)
7. Zorin, D., Barr, A.H.: Correction of geometric perceptualdistortion in pictures. In: SIGGRAPH95 Conference Proceeding, Annual Conference Series, pp. 257–264. ACMSIGGRAPH, AddisonWesley (August 1995)
8. Wood, D., Finkelstein, A., Hughes, J., Thayer, C., Salesin, D.: Multiperspective Panoramas for CelAnimation. In: Proceedings of SIGGRAPH 97, pp. 243–250. ACM, New York (July 1997)
9. Mitani, J., Suzuki, H., Uno, H.: Computer aided design for Origamic Architecture models with voxel data structure. IPSJ Magazine 44, 1372–1379 (2003)

Visualization of Uncertainty and Reasoning

Torre Zuk and Sheelagh Carpendale

University of Calgary
{zuk,sheelagh}@cpsc.ucalgary.ca

Abstract. This article gathers and consolidates the issues involved in uncertainty relating to reasoning and analyzes how uncertainty visualizations can support cognitive and meta-cognitive processes. Uncertainty in data is paralleled by uncertainty in reasoning processes, and while uncertainty in data is starting to get some of the visualization research attention it deserves, the uncertainty in the reasoning process is thus far often overlooked. While concurring with the importance of incorporating data uncertainty visualizations, we suggest also developing closely integrated visualizations that provide support for uncertainty in reasoning.

1 Introduction

Uncertainty and its complement certainty are fundamental parts of any analytic or reasoning process and relate to important cognitive constraints in using any visualization. To inform the design process we review and coalesce many important aspects of reasoning under uncertainty and discuss these with regard to implications for visualization. For each of these aspects we consider reasoning and representational requirements and assess the potential for exploiting visual support. Based on our analysis of the impact of uncertainty in the reasoning processes, we propose that these receive increased consideration in the design of visualization systems. For instance, when appropriate this could include an additional visual component focusing on reasoning uncertainty and support for introspection. For this reasoning support we contribute design considerations and describe an example system for medical diagnosis.

In the analytic reasoning process, often choosing the visual representation drives the exploration for an iteration of searching, comprehension building, or hypothesis testing. The inability to transform or change this representation is the representational primacy that Amar and Stasko consider a limitation of many current visualizations [1]. In addition to options for alternate representations, it is important to augment a representation with uncertainty in order to allow potential interpretations of the data to be considered. Hepting has described an analogous process for visual interfaces as "begin with an incomplete articulation of a context and allow the user to interactively develop and refine it" [16]. Leaving uncertainty out of a data visualization promotes assumptions that lead to more uncertainty in the reasoning process and the viewer may not be aware of this uncertainty. With insight problems (e.g. the 9-dot problem [30]) searching representation space may be key and Gestalt may even hinder the process [30]. Thus providing cues about uncertainty in representation may promote consideration of other representations and help further the exploration. Based on and extending the impact of data uncertainty visualization, we suggest that representing the reasoning process may aid

A. Butz et al. (Eds.): SG 2007, LNCS 4569, pp. 164–177, 2007.
© Springer-Verlag Berlin Heidelberg 2007

in determining both the next reasoning step, and the assessment of the solution. Further this visual representation specifically designed to support the reasoning process should also incorporate uncertainty to provide transparency of confidence.

Given that both knowledge and representation are coupled to uncertainty, we will present arguments to illustrate that uncertainty of reasoning as well as uncertainty in data should be visualized and if possible integrated in a manner that supports the reasoning process. Even well-defined problems such as proving a premise using predicate logic usually requires an external aid (visualization, such as hand drawn sketches) due to the limits of working memory. When adding the complexity of uncertain data or actions, one would expect Bayesian reasoning or some form of satisficing [37] would also benefit from visualization support.

2 Cognition, Uncertainty, and Visualization

In this section we have gathered together the central components of several discussions of reasoning and cognition and discuss them in light of uncertainty visualization. For our discussion we define reasoning very loosely and consider how *knowledge constructs, heuristics and biases*, and *temporal constraints* impact reasoning and discuss the potential for uncertainty visualization. We close this section by delineating types of reasoning uncertainty.

2.1 Knowledge Constructs

Thomas and Cook describe three higher order knowledge constructs: *arguments, causality*, and *models of estimation* [38]. Arguments are "logical inferences linking evidence and other reasoning artifacts into defensible judgments of greater knowledge value" [38]. Causality is an understanding of the action-reaction relationship. Models of estimation provide for the use of powerful abstractions in interpreting the data and providing estimates of solutions. We will discuss these three constructs in terms of their relationship to visualization.

Arguments and Visualization: Visualizing an argument formalizes it for introspection and collaboration. *Arguments* are one of the reasoning steps of problem solving, and the presence of uncertainty is what creates an ill-structured problem. Paraphrasing van Bruggen [44], an ill-structured problem has: an ambiguous and incomplete problem specification, a lack of clear stopping criteria, multiple information sets and representations with no clear indication of relevance, and incomplete knowledge of operations or solution path. Solving ill-structured problems often requires non-linear progression, partial solutions, and representational refinement [44], for which extra cognitive support will be beneficial.

Complex problems and arguments are also more likely to require external assessment or benefit from collaborative refinement. Without a representation of the current uncertainty in different analytic strategies resource management is difficult. By visualizing which areas have uncertainty and are making the problem ill-structured, users may more easily monitor progress and decide to divert resources to reduce the most significant uncertainty.

Causality and Visualization: More causality may be perceived than your visualization intends. *Causality* is often perceptually linked to temporality. Michotte [27] found that with the movement of patches of light, the relative timing of motion could create the strong perception of causal relationships. Likewise with less abstract occurrences people will often assume causality based on temporal relationships. Due to this perception, animation may enhance the communication of causality and should be used carefully if causality is not to be inferred.

Reasoning about causality under uncertainty may also utilize heuristics that are prone to error and bias. Tversky and Kahneman found that if one event (C) was naturally viewed as a cause of another (E), then even if they had equal probabilities their participants would be biased in favor of causal inferences over diagnostic inferences (i.e. believe $P(E|C) > P(C|E)$ even though $P(C) = P(E) \Rightarrow P(E|C) = P(C|E)$) [43]. Furthermore they found that people were biased toward weighing evidence for causal impact in the future versus diagnostic reasoning about the past. Kahneman and Miller hypothesize that alternatives to the effect are more available to the mind than alternatives to the cause [20], and so leading the user to consider more causes could reduce this bias. When there is an effect with an uncertain cause this might be visually induced by showing additional dangling links back from the effect.

Models of Estimation and Visualization: A visualization is a model which adds its own uncertainty. Applying any *models of estimation* requires a jump from the concrete to the abstract. This may likely increase uncertainty by requiring assumptions, introducing translation errors, or adding in the stochastic variability of a model. Any uncertainty this abstraction process introduces should be visualized to keep under consideration when interpreting the model results. The propagation of errors is also important to consider when using models as the input uncertainty will often be increased, potentially by something as simple as the addition of variables.

2.2 Reasoning Heuristics and Biases

An exemplar of reasoning heuristics and biases may be found from user prediction calibration. Griffin and Tversky [14] state in the assessment of evidence that overconfidence often resulted when the evidence strength (extremeness) was high and weight (predictive validity) low. For example, there may be a bias toward rejecting the null hypothesis when the means are very different even when there are large standard deviations. Under-confidence often resulted when the strength of evidence was low but the weight high (i.e. a moderate impression based on extensive data) [14]. An example may be the failure to confidently communicate the need to address climate change. One might help address these biases by showing the merged strength-weight visually.

For information systems Turpin and Plooy [42] review the decision-making heuristics and biases: *representativeness*, *availability*, *adjustment and anchoring*, *problem or decision framing*, and *automation*. Their literature review found real world examples providing some evidence for each of these types. They touch on the role of how information systems may elicit biases as well as aid in debiasing, and also suggest innovative representations and decision process support may reduce bias. They conclude by calling for more field research to better quantify the effects of these biases in relation to other problems such as data quality. The debate continues as to how frequently these heuristics and biases occur outside the laboratory [14], but they are certainly relevant to design when considering user constraints.

We provide a subset of these heuristics and biases, most from the foundational collections on the subject [14, 19], and others as cited. We have organized these into three categories based on visualization strategies that may potentially mitigate them. The categories are: *associations*, *ignorance of rules*, and *application of rules*. Mental associations have a conscious and subconscious influence on reasoning. Rules encompass the simple cognitive constructs for inferring information (e.g. a theorem) all the way up to methods for forming arguments. We will describe each in turn along with visualization strategies that may be beneficial.

Associations and Visualization: A visualization is impacted both positively and negatively by associations it triggers. *Associations* may bias the reasoning process in various ways. One major type is the *affect* or reliance on the associated "good" or "bad" response to a stimulus [36], which Norman has recently discussed in relation to its impact on design [29]. *Availability* of instances in the mind for estimating probability form another type: retrievability of instances is important when the size of a set is estimated by availability of instances [19]; if instances are not available, the ease of imagining them will act as availability [19]; *illusory correlation* when the frequency of co-occurrence may be estimated based on strength of association [19], and a *recency bias* results in the overweighting of recent events [41].

Visualizations can provide access to huge amounts of data and thereby reduce the biases of one's own limited associations. By providing high density visual queries that can be quickly modified one may be influenced less by expectations and let the data provide its own associations. Using a computer to analyze the data and make a visualization based on a fixed set of rules inherently reduces these types of biases.

Ignorance of Rules and Visualization: If a visualization does not convey to the viewer the meanings of its representation(s) the user may fail to form the correct interpretations and arguments. *Ignorance of rules* (often statistical) can also lead to poor reasoning and the *representativeness* heuristics [19]. These include: insensitivity to prior probabilities (e.g. Bayes' rule not applied); small sample expected to be as representative of population as a larger sample; failure to consider regression to the mean; misconceptions of chance (e.g. representativeness of a random process as a whole expected in short sequences); irrelevant data may be used as a predictor; and the *illusion of validity* where redundancy in inputs reduces accuracy but increases confidence.

While visual representations themselves may not promote statistical ignorance, they rarely go the one step further to aid statistical interpretation. Even the basic box and whisker plots tailored for hypothesis testing are in rare use. Visualizations have the potential to alleviate these issues by integrating realizations of other potential outcomes and integrating statistical information with drill downs.

Application of Rules and Visualization: Direct visual support for reasoning may assist with the application of rules. Any given strategy or *application of rules* may provide an inferior result, as is possible with the *adjustment and anchoring* set of heuristics. A selection of these are: insufficient adjustment when an initial estimate is weighted too strongly during subsequent revisions (and may be based on irrelevant data) [6, 19]; adjustment from single event probability produces overestimate of conjunctions and underestimate of disjunctions [19]; a tendency to be overconfident in decisions or estimates [8, 17]; *automation* or technology dependency leading to errors of omission and commission [4, 33, 42]; and overestimated confidence in the ability of a priori predicting past events (i.e. hindsight is 20:20) [8]. Similar to the application of rules category, the use of heuristics in software programs dealing with complex problems is also common-place and they need to be understood by the user to avoid introducing interpretation errors.

Many visualizations do not include visual explanations of the mapping of data, algorithms and uncertainty, but this is crucial for avoiding these types of biases. This class of reasoning shortfalls will be greatly aided by a visualization of the reasoning process itself. Any reasoning visualization may provide grounds for review, analysis, and collaboration; thereby opening up what might be a hidden and flawed decision process. Just as MacEachren noted for visualization errors [23], we can group reasoning errors into Type I, reaching conclusions that are not supported, and Type II, failure to reach conclusions that are supported.

When these biases or heuristics are likely to manifest in a user's reasoning, we can make attempts to debias or provide alternative heuristics (or algorithms). Fischhoff reviewed some of these attempts for *overconfidence* and *hindsight* bias, and found only partial success [8]. The review was organized around three categories: faulty tasks (attempts such as raise stakes, clarify instructions, ...), faulty judges (warn of problem, train extensively, ...), and mismatch between judge and task (make knowledge explicit, search for discrepant information, ...). There is greater potential for cognitive support with visualization systems as the offloaded tasks may use algorithms that do not suffer from these issues, and may dynamically attempt debiasing, but the danger of the *automation* heuristic also needs to be considered.

For many problems, heuristics can provide fast and accurate enough approximations for the task at hand. Gigerenzer et al. compared some satisficing methods (fast and frugal heuristics) against some "optimal" algorithms (e.g. Bayesian networks) representing unbounded rationality [13]. With complete knowledge and across 20 real-world scenarios some simple heuristic strategies (*minimalist* and *take the best*) were found to perform comparably to the algorithms [13]. If specific heuristics are accepted for use as standard operating procedures we may look at providing visualization support to enhance them further or to reveal when they can not be trusted.

Arnott [2] has provided a taxonomy of biases and proposed a general decision support design methodology utilizing these theories. Watkins [45] also reviewed many cognitive heuristics and biases and believed that they are worth considering for uncertainty visualization. While we agree that they are an important design consideration, especially when providing a decision support tool, we should be wary of their potential impact on the analysis and discovery process, and so should perform research on their role in visualization in general.

If we assume two cognitive models of reasoning: associative and rule-based [34], then some issues may be more related to one system. The associative system may be directly affected by Gestalt and a visualizations' ability to convey the required uncertainty for immediate processing and consideration. There may be the flexibility in rule-based reasoning to use methods that avoid the drawbacks of potential heuristics and biases.

With the more general rule-based reasoning we have the potential to learn and utilize problem solving "programs" that have been validated to some extent, but perhaps at the cost of sacrificing creativity and imagination (associative). A graphical or visualization system should try to provide assistance to both systems but avoid leading users to the *automation* heuristic.

2.3   Uncertainty and Reasoning Time-Frames

One fundamental constraint on the reasoning process is time. Time stress and other situational attributes can distort our perception leading directly to biases [25]. This distortion adds uncertainty, confounding the uncertainty that may have led to the time stress. Strategies will vary based on the amount of time resources available. At a high level it may be similar to game strategies in which search space (e.g. minimax tree) is pruned based on the time allowed. Cognitive models such as Cohen et al.'s Metarecognition [3] have been proposed for time limited decision-making. In these cognitive models visualizations may illustrate uncertainty of the data, but visual support of meta-reasoning may be the area where they can contribute the most.

Watkins created and analyzed an uncertainty glyph to depict three types of uncertainty and their sum in a decision support system [45]. One interesting finding was that all analyst participants agreed somewhat or stronger that in general "uncertainty visualization would degrade the ability of most analysts and decision-makers to respond to or 'interpret a scenario' in a timely manner". The majority thought, however, it would not overload decision-makers in less time-constrained situations, and were not comfortable adding data with associated uncertainty to a knowledge base without an uncertainty visualization.

Delay is also Lipshitz and Strauss' first conceptual proposition: uncertainty in the context of action is a sense of doubt that blocks or delays action [22]. They cite Dewey's statement that problem solving is triggered by a sense of doubt that stops routine action [5], but dropped the important aspect that uncertainty triggers problem solving that necessitates neither blocking or much delay. One should note that changes in uncertainty may trigger action, and that delay can be the optimal "action". An example of this may be the space shuttle Challenger disaster, for which the criticality of data quality has been discussed by Fisher and Kingma [9]. Tufte has also analyzed the space shuttle Challenger and Columbia disasters from a visualization point of view [40, 41], and one may argue the most significant uncertainty was not in the data but in the reasoning.

2.4   Types of Reasoning Uncertainty

There are many taxonomies of uncertainty to be found in different domains. Lipshitz and Strauss found in a study of military decision makers that they distinguished between *inadequate understanding*, *incomplete information*, and *undifferentiated alternatives* [22]. Different strategies were employed based on these types of uncertainty. Thus task considerations may dictate the types of uncertainty that are significant. Hence we would suggest a user and task centered approach be taken with uncertainty issues.

Thomson et al. have constructed a typology for visualizing uncertainty in geospatially referenced data [39]. They considered Pang et al.'s low-level classification [31]

Table 1. Extending Thomson et al.'s typology of uncertainty [39] to reasoning

Uncertainty Category	Reasoning Definition
Currency/Timing	temporal gaps between assumptions and reasoning steps
Credibility	heuristic accuracy & bias of analyst
Lineage	conduit of assumptions, reasoning, revision, and presentation
Subjectivity	amount of private knowledge or heuristics utilized
Accuracy/Error	difference between heuristic & algorithm (e.g. Bayesian)
Precision	variability of heuristics and strategies
Consistency	extent to which heuristic assessments agree
Interrelatedness	heuristic & analyst independence
Completeness	extent to which knowledge is complete

and Gershon's high-level taxonomy [10] and provide a typology to be instantiated based on task, giving examples from intelligence analysis. They advise a hierarchical approach for instantiating this typology across multiple domains or tasks. We extend the definitions of their typology to the reasoning process in Table 1, demonstrating how their typology is useful at the level of reasoning as well. Considering how this typology applies to reasoning can extend its intended purpose of guiding the development of visual representations for uncertainties.

Dynamic data is the main reason why *currency / timing* is tied to uncertainty. Thereby the error between prior observations and the current state generally increases over time. In some cases the duration of observation allows for a trade-off between uncertainties in attributes (e.g. Heisenberg's Uncertainty Principle). Temporal constraints are a major reason why completeness of knowledge can not be fully attained. Past decisions, assumptions, and arguments often form the a priori knowledge base. Visualizing the impact time constraints had on this prior information can greatly influence its usage. Opacity is often used for temporal encoding where data fades out over time as it becomes dated.

For *credibility*, *lineage*, and *subjectivity*, all levels from data gatherers to decision-makers should be considered in the reasoning instantiation of the framework. When the decision processes span multiple levels of management or government these aspects are especially important to consider. One example was when the director of the NASA Goddard Institute for Space Science (a climatologist) had the qualitative certainty and causality in his report on climate change strongly diluted by the U.S. White House Council on Environmental Quality [18] (See Figure 1). In this case the reader would

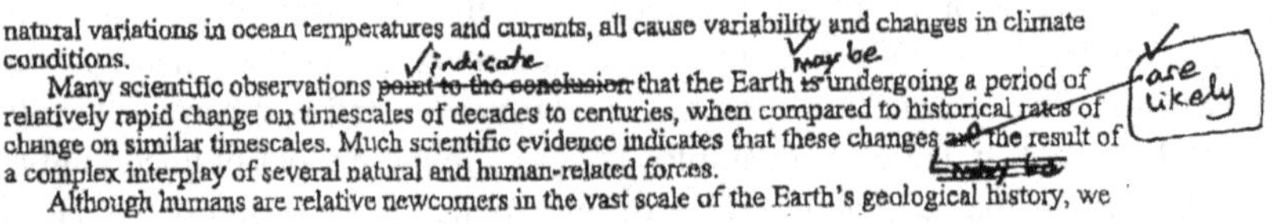

natural variations in ocean temperatures and currents, all cause variability and changes in climate conditions. ~~indicate~~ *indicate*   ~~may be~~ *may be*
Many scientific observations ~~point to the conclusion~~ that the Earth ~~is~~ undergoing a period of ~~are~~ *are likely*
relatively rapid change on timescales of decades to centuries, when compared to historical rates of
change on similar timescales. Much scientific evidence indicates that these changes ~~are~~ the result of ~~likely to~~
a complex interplay of several natural and human-related forces.
Although humans are relative newcomers in the vast scale of the Earth's geological history, we

Fig. 1. Draft copy showing hand editing of scientific confidence. Changing of definite wording "is" to speculative "may be" among the 3 revisions in the paragraph shown.

assume the credibility and subjectivity of the scientist authors, with no way of knowing that a non-scientist had revised the scientific judgment. The final decision makers (U.S. Congress) would benefit from visualizing the uncertainty in credibility, lineage, and subjectivity of reasoning. Ignorance of any of these types of uncertainties may directly impact the ability of decision-makers to make good decisions, and therefore guidelines mandating the visualization of such uncertainty should be considered.

To visualize *accuracy / error* one must consider the effects of potential heuristics and biases, as discussed in Section 2.2. The visualization of reasoning accuracy will likely not be possible unless tools are used for the reasoning in which heuristics and strategies are made explicit. Error itself is not usually known a priori and so would be visualized as a post mortem task. Visualizing *consistency* and *precision* in heuristics or strategies is important for decision confidence. Precision of a single heuristic may be difficult to assess as cognitive strategies themselves may not be precisely defined. The same visualization of reasoning heuristics that provides an estimate of precision, could likely reveal inter-heuristic consistency.

Visualizing *interrelatedness* may allow results from analysts working in teams to be collectively considered. It may be useful for the interrelatedness of many data points to be visualized using preattentively processed visual cues. For example, connectedness (from Gestalt theory) may allow one to consider linked reasoning artifacts holistically, potentially reducing the risk of over weighting redundant findings. As *completeness* includes comprehension (ignorance) some aspects are dependent on all the other types of uncertainty being visualized. Similar to error, in advance it will usually only be estimated. A good example of the cost of unvisualized uncertainty is the wasted resources in duplicated research caused by the lack of publishing on scientific failures.

3   Visual Support for Uncertainty in Reasoning

Numerous methods have been proposed integrating uncertainty into data for visualization [31], and some have been evaluated for specific tasks [15, 26]. However there has been less research into how well these provide decision support. How best to provide reasoning and meta-reasoning support that incorporates uncertainty is an open question.

3.1   Problem Solving

Newell and Simon [28] provided a high level organization of a problem solver for a generic information processing system. We have used this organization to highlight aspects of uncertainty in the process of reasoning in general as shown in Figure 2. While uncertainty likely exists in some form in all aspects of the organization, the method selection process is important (shown in bold red in the figure) in that it is affected by both data and problem representational uncertainties as well as potential ambiguity in the relationship of methods to goals. Our looser interpretation of their general problem solver allows the method selection to require problem solving (a recursive invocation) and methods would include all heuristics and strategies (top-down, bottom-up, etc.). Visual aids for the method selection process would likely be beneficial as this complex

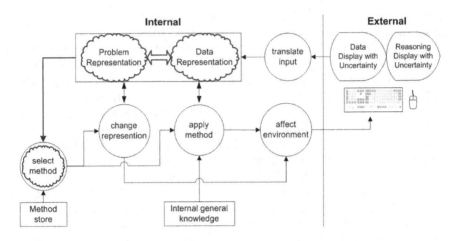

Fig. 2. Organization of problem solving with uncertainty. Revision of Newell and Simon's general organization of a problem solver [28] highlighting where uncertainties likely exist.

"phase" requires the consideration of sub-goals and the actions related to them, while still considering their context in the overall problem. There is the potential for change in both internal and external representations of the problem and of the data [32].

While traditional graphics and HCI research has focused on the external part, more considerations need to be made for the internal part. The visualization system should also produce the artifacts that may assist introspection on the cognitive process. As these processes are tightly coupled, the ability to monitor and aid the reasoning process will add additional requirements to the visualization. Visualizations may need to be modified in order to allow parallel support both data and reasoning process visualization, which might be useful to think of as a larger task context. This support could tie both direct visual artifacts in with meta-data artifacts recording a history of exploration and the discovery processes that were used.

3.2 Analytic Processes

Amar and Stasko's [1] precepts for design and evaluation of information visualizations provide a set of principles on how visualizations can better support the analytic process. The three main weaknesses of current systems were stated as: limited affordances, predetermined representations, and the decline of determinism in decision-making. These weaknesses or gaps in the analytic process were to be addressed by the Rationale Precepts: expose uncertainty, concretize relationships, and expose cause and effect; as well as the Worldview Precepts.

All the above precepts deal with complex issues and appear to pertain to reasoning as a whole, thus providing guidelines for reasoning visualizations and support as well as information visualizations. Bridging the analytic gaps and extending ideas in current information visualization systems to reasoning visualizations will likely require the linking of these types of tools, or developing additional integrated cognitive

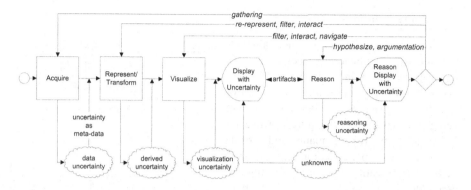

Fig. 3. Reasoning extensions to Pang et al.'s data visualization pipeline with uncertainty [31]

support, while ensuring consistent cognitive styles to avoid a huge context switch. We propose for complex problem solving that reasoning support with uncertainty should be built into the visualization pipeline. This integration could be as light-weight as virtual sticky notes for one's ideas that are colour coded based on certainty. Figure 3 shows our extension to Pang et al.'s visualization pipeline [31] to include reasoning support with uncertainty. This integration provides benefits by simplifying the backtracking (revaluation and searching) phases of the sense-making loop. Thus uncertainty in one case or hypothesis would be easily reviewable by another user. Visualizations for uncertainty in both the data and reasoning pipelines could use consistent representations and/or metaphors for the same types of uncertainty to reduce cognitive load. The complexity and constant evolution of visualization tools promotes specialized systems to handle specific sub-tasks. Therefore this pipeline may cross multiple visualization systems and so providing visual consistency will add design constraints. Independent applications will require support for restoration of data, operations, and viewing parameters.

The link between visualization and reasoning pipelines should be bidirectional to allow for feedback from the reasoning process for potential integration into the visualization tools. This could be as simple as the goal or larger context in the reasoning process that may be provided with text or graphically. It could also communicate a strategy of exploration which the data visualization tool could then dynamically facilitate. In a collaborative setting this might be valuable to provide awareness of strategy changes when one is focused on a small scale task. While this concept has been implemented to a limited extent (e.g. BAE Systems' POLESTAR), most visualizations provide little or no direct reasoning support or are not linked to one that does.

Using a participatory design approach we have developed a prototype system for evidence-based medicine diagnostic support that provides this parallel (reasoning/data) visualization approach. The parallel visualizations are in the form of multiple views, two of which are shown in Figure 4. It utilizes a decision tree as a GUI with integrated reasoning and data uncertainty. The reasoning visualization can be viewed along with other data and its uncertainty in multiple other views. This design provides transparency of the uncertainty in the Bayesian reasoning that may assist in this difficult task.

3.3 Representations

Visual representations of data uncertainty allow for the amplification of cognition (e.g. parallel processing, increased working memory), and when time frames allow introspection, we suggest similar benefits will acrue from visual representations of reasoning uncertainty. Kirschenbaum and Arruda [21] found an ellipse was more accurate than verbal quantification in communicating uncertainties in a spatial problem. With non-spatial uncertainty, Watkins [45] found his glyph (which distinguished: unreliability, ignorance, and analytical input) was rated well by analysts but with some qualifications. Finger and Bisantz [7] compared degraded icons (levels of blur) against the degraded icons with text probability, and full detail icons with text probability, for the task of hostile/friendly target classification with evolving target probabilities. They found for their task that the addition of text did not provide a statistical advantage, and the degraded icons without text were in general better. As the number of uncertainty levels that need to be read are task specific, this should drive the representational requirements [46].

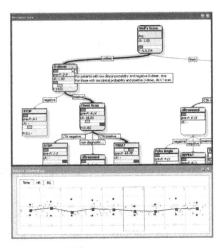

Fig. 4. Integrated data and reasoning visualizations for evidence-based medicine. Reasoning view (upper) and test data view (lower).

In the field of Geographic Information Systems (GIS), which has been at the forefront of uncertainty visualization, frameworks have been put forth that recommend visual representations of the uncertainty based on the data and uncertainty types [24]. Even though their spatial considerations and constraints limit the general problem, there are still no accepted standards. For general visualization including reasoning, user and task considerations will drive the best way to create uncertainty visualizations. Some representations may be more natural for expressing uncertainty as meta-data such as opacity, fuzziness, and colour saturation [23, 24], but when distinguishing different types of uncertainty, or for integration with multivariate data, these options may not be optimal.

Representations will afford a set of methods and actions that allow one to proceed to a solution. Gigerenzer suggested that natural frequency representations may have inherent cognitive support in the brain as posing conditional probability questions in the form of natural frequencies helped more people solve the problems [11]. More recent arguments and research have indicated that it is more likely that the computational complexity, due to the transparency of the information structures, that is key to a person's ability to find the correct Bayesian solution [35]. This does not contradict the finding that natural frequencies may be a more efficient representation for promoting Bayesian reasoning [12].

Cognitive support may be given by providing uncertainty or ambiguity in representations to provide clues to potential representational transformations or new representations. User interactivity in selecting the representation, while often difficult to provide in a visualization, implicitly communicates to the viewer that there is uncertainty in the optimal representation(s). At a meta level, visualizing your own reasoning process can also reveal a bias or suggest a new strategy. Representations of the reasoning process which illustrate uncertainty will help one perform this introspection.

4   Conclusion

We have described how the cognitive issues of reasoning under uncertainty relate to various aspects of visualization and provided some guidance as to how one may address these issues. As a result of the complexity and uncertainty in the reasoning process we see potential in the integration of data and reasoning visualizations. This integration of the discovery process and sense-making loops, would provide a direct visualization of the entire analytic process, and might facilitate the exposure of analytic gaps. Without this type of cognitive support monitoring the effect of uncertainty in the data and the analytic process will be extremely difficult.

When we create new support there is a potential hazard if the external visualization does not diminish cognitive load, it may in fact raise it, thereby preventing the formation of schemata [44]. Therefore when the performance of sub-tasks require complete attention this level of integration may be more useful as an analytic context or an audit trail. Multiple views or the easy movement of reasoning artifacts between the two visualization systems could maintain this context without adding cognitive load. The visualization we briefly introduced (medical diagnostic support) illustrated that for some problem areas a reasoning component can exist as a natural and central component of the interface. As uncertainty abounds in the reasoning process we expect that visualization of the uncertainty will enhance problem-solving and decision-making.

Acknowledgements

We gratefully thank NSERC for funding this research and the Government Accountability Project for providing source material.

References

[1] Amar, R., Stasko, J.: Knowledge precepts for design and evaluation of information visualizations. Visualization and Computer Graphics, IEEE Trans. on 11(4), 432–442 (2005)

[2] Arnott, D.: Cognitive biases and decision support systems development: a design science approach. Information Systems Journal 16, 55–78 (2006)

[3] Cohen, M.S., Freeman, J.T., Wolf, S.: Metarecognition in time-stressed decision making: Recognizing, critiquing, and correcting. Human Factors 38(2), 206–219 (1996)

[4] Cohen, M.S., Parasuraman, R., Freeman, J.T.: Trust in decision aids: A model and its training implications. In: Proceedings 1998 Command and Control Research and Technology Symposium (1998)

[5] Dewey, J.: How We Think. Dover Publications (1997)

[6] Edwards, W.: Conservatism in human information processing. In: Kahneman, D., Slovic, P., Tversky, A. (eds.) Judgment under Uncertainty: Heuristics and biases, pp. 359–369. Cambridge University Press, Cambridge (1982)

[7] Finger, R., Bisantz, A.M.: Utilizing graphical formats to convey uncertainty in a decision making task. Theoretical Issues in Ergonomics Science 3(1), 1–25 (2002)

[8] Debiasing, B.F.: In: D. Kahneman et al editor, Judgment under Uncertainty: Heuristics and biases, pp. 422–444. Cambridge University Press, Cambridge (1982)

[9] Fisher, C.W., Kingma, B.R.: Criticality of data quality as exemplified in two disasters. Information and Management 39, 109–116 (2001)

[10] Gershon, N.: Short note: Visualization of an imperfect world. IEEE Computer Graphics and Applications 18(4), 43–45 (1998)

[11] Gigerenzer, G., Hoffrage, U.: How to improve bayesian reasoning without instruction: Frequency formats. Psychological Review 102(4), 648–704 (1995)

[12] Gigerenzer, G., Hoffrage, U.: Overcoming difficulties in bayesian reasoning: A reply to Lewis and Keren (1999) and Mellers and McGraw (1999). Psychological Review 106(2), 425–430 (1999)

[13] Gigerenzer, G., Czerlinski, J., Marignon, L.: How good are fast and frugal heuristics. In: Gilovich, T., et al.(ed.) Heuristics and Biases: The Psychology of Intuitive Judgment, pp. 559–581. Cambridge University Press, Cambridge (2003)

[14] Griffin, D., Tversky, A.: The weighing of evidence and the determinants of confidence. In: Gilovich, T., et al. (ed.) Heuristics and Biases: The Psychology of Intuitive Judgment, pp. 230–249. Cambridge University Press, Cambridge (2003)

[15] Grigoryan, G., Rheingans, P.: Point-based probabilistic surfaces to show surface uncertainty. IEEE Transactions on Visualization and Computer Graphics 10(5), 564–573 (2004)

[16] Hepting, D.H.: Towards a visual interface for information visualization. In: Information Visualisation, 2002. Proc. Sixth International Conference on, pp. 295–302. IEEE Computer Society Press, Los Alamitos (2002)

[17] Howell, W.C., Burnett, S.A.: Uncertainty measurement. Organizational Behaviour and Human Performance 22, 45–68 (1978)

[18] C.B.S. Broadcasting Inc.: Rewriting the science. 2006. (visited April 2007) http://www.cbsnews.com/stories/2006/03/17/60minutes/main1415985.shtml

[19] Kahneman, D., Slovic, P., Tversky, A. (eds.): Judgment under Uncertainty: Heuristics and biases. Cambridge University Press, Cambridge (1982)

[20] Kahneman, D., Miller, D.T.: Norm theory: Comparing reality to its alternatives. In: Gilovich, T., Griffin, D., Kahneman, D. (eds.) Heuristics and Biases: The Psychology of Intuitive Judgment, pp. 348–366. Cambridge University Press, Cambridge (2003)

[21] Kirschenbaum, S.S., Arruda, J.E.: Effects of graphic and verbal probability information on command decision making. Human Factors 36(3), 406–418 (1994)

[22] Lipshitz, R., Strauss, O.: Coping with uncertainty: A naturalistic decision-making analysis. Organizational Behaviour and Human Decision Processes 69, 149–163 (1997)

[23] MacEachren, A.M.: Visualizing uncertain information. Cartographic Perspective 13, 10–19 (1992)

[24] MacEachren, A.M., Robinson, A., Hopper, S., Gardner, S., Murray, R.: Visualizing geospatial information uncertainty: What we know and what we need to know. Cartography and Geographic Information Science 32(3), 139–160 (2005)

[25] Mandel, R.: Perception, Decision Making and Conflict. University Press of America, Washington, D.C. (1979)

[26] Masalonis, A., Mulgund, S., Song, L., Wanke, C., Zobell, S.: Using probabilistic demand prediction for traffic flow management decision support. In: Proceedings of the 2004 AIAA Guidance, Navigation, and Control Conference. American Institute of Aeronautics and Astronautics (2004)

[27] Michotte, A.: The Perception of Causality. Methuen, London, Translated by T. Miles and E. Miles (1963)

[28] Newell, A., Simon, H.A.: Human Problem Solving. Prentice-Hall Inc, New Jersey (1972)

[29] Norman, D.A.: Emotional Design: Why We Love (Or Hate) Everyday Things. Basic Books (2003)

[30] Novick, L.R., Bassok, M.: Problem solving. In: Holyoak, K.J., Morrison, R.G. (eds.) The Cambridge Handbook of Thinking and Reasoning, pp. 321–349. Cambridge University Press, Cambridge (2005)

[31] Pang, A.T., Wittenbrink, C.M., Lodha, S.K.: Approaches to uncertainty visualization. The. Visual Computer 13(8), 370–390 (1997)

[32] Scaife, M., Rogers, Y.: External cognition: how do graphical representations work? Int. J. Human Computer Studies 45, 185–213 (1996)

[33] Skitka, L.J., Mosier, K.L., Burdick, M.: Does automation bias decision-making? Int. J. Human-Computer Studies 51, 991–1006 (1999)

[34] Sloman, S.A.: Two systems of reasoning. In: Gilovich, T., Griffin, D., Kahneman, D. (eds.) Heuristics and Biases: The Psychology of Intuitive Judgment, pp. 379–396. Cambridge University Press, Cambridge (2003)

[35] Sloman, S.A., Over, D., Slovak, L., Stibel, J.M.: Frequency illusions and other fallacies. Organizational Behaviour and Human Decision Processes 91, 296–309 (2003)

[36] Slovic, P., Finucane, M., Peters, E., MacGregor, D.G.: The affect heuristic. In: Gilovich, T., Griffin, D., Kahneman, D. (eds.) Heuristics and Biases: The Psychology of Intuitive Judgment, pp. 397–420. Cambridge University Press, Cambridge (2003)

[37] Stirling, W.C.: Satisficing Games and Decision Making. Cambridge University Press, Cambridge, UK (2003)

[38] Thomas, J.J., Cook, K.A. (eds.): Illuminating the Path: The Research and Development Agenda for Visual Analytics. IEEE Computer Society (2005)

[39] Thomson, J., Hetzler, E., MacEachren, A., Gahegan, M., Pavel, M.: A typology for visualizing uncertainty. In: Proc. SPIE & IS&T Conf. Electronic Imaging. Visualization and Data Analysis 2005, vol. 5669, pp. 146–157 (2005)

[40] Tufte, E.R.: Visual Explanations. Graphics Press, Cheshire, CT (1997)

[41] Tufte, E.R.: Beautiful Evidence. Graphics Press, Cheshire, CT (2006)

[42] Turpin, M., du Plooy, N.: Decision-making biases and information systems. In: Decision Support in an Uncertain and Complex World: The IFIP TC8/WG8.3 International Conference 2004, pp. 782–792 (2004)

[43] Tversky, A., Kahneman, D.: Causal schemas in judgements of uncertainty. In: Gilovich, T., Griffin, D., Kahneman, D. (eds.) Heuristics and Biases: The Psychology of Intuitive Judgment, Cambridge University Press, Cambridge (2003)

[44] van Bruggen, J.M., Boshuizen, H.P.A., Kirshner, P.A.: A cognitive framework for cooperative problem solving with argument visualization. In: Kirshner, P.A. (ed.) Visualizating Argumentation: Software Tools for Collaboration and Educational Sense-Making, pp. 25–47. Springer, Heidelberg (2003)

[45] Watkins, E.T.: Improving the analyst and decision-maker's perspective through uncertainty visualization. In: Master's thesis, Air Force Institute of Technology, Wright-Patterson Air Force Base, Ohio (2000)

[46] Zuk, T., Carpendale, M.S.T., Glanzman, W.D.: Visualizing temporal uncertainty in 3D virtual reconstructions. In: Proc. of the 6th International Symposium on Virtual Reality, Archaeology and Cultural Heritage (VAST 2005), pp. 99–106 (2005)

DIVA: An Automatic Music Arrangement Technique Based on Impression of Images

Kisa Ohyama and Takayuki Itoh

Ochanomizu University
2-1-1 Otsuka, Bunkyo-ku, Tokyo 112-8610 Japan
{kisa,itot}@itolab.is.ocha.ac.jp

Abstract. This poster reports our first approach for automatic music arrangement based on the impression of input images. Given a digital image and keywords of objects shot in the image, the technique selects a rhythm pattern associated from the keywords and color distribution of the image. As a preprocessing, the technique first provides sample colors, images, and keywords to users, and then collects the feedback of selection of rhythm patterns associated from them. The technique then leads equations to calculate the association of rhythm pattern from arbitrary input images. Finally, the technique automatically calculates the association scores of all prepared rhythm patterns from the images, and provides music arranged applying the associated rhythm pattern.

Keywords: Automatic music arrangement, Digital image, Standard MIDI File(SMF), Color contradistinction.

1 Introduction

Impression-based matching of music and image is a potential research topic. For example, several multimedia player software show arbitrary movies while playing the music, but users often complain the combination of music and movies. We think good matching of music and image will make multimedia software more fun. Recently many studies in this research area have been presented, such as music search engine based on impression of scenes, correlation of music and images via impression-related words, icon selection based on properties of music, and some sonification works; however, we think there are several more applications to be discussed.

This poster presents DIVA (Digital Image Varies Arrangement), a technique for automatic music arrangement based on impression of images. Input and output of DIVA are defined as follows:

Input: A standard MIDI File(SMF) consists of four parts, including melody, harmony, bass, and percussions. A raster image with some keywords of objects shot in the image.

Output: An arranged SMF whose melody and harmony are same as the input SMF, but bass and percussions are arranged based on the impression of the input image.

A. Butz et al. (Eds.): SG 2007, LNCS 4569, pp. 178–181, 2007.

DIVA consists of preparation and actual stages. Preparation stage provides sample colors, images, keywords, and music arranged applying the prepared rhythm patterns, to users. It collects the selection of rhythm patterns from the users, as their feedback. It then leads equations to calculate association of music arrangement, from colors and keywords of arbitrary input images. Actual stage calculates associations of rhythm patterns from a given input image, and finally arranges the input music applying the most associated rhythm pattern.

2   Implementation

DIVA posterizes images into predefined 66 colors, and then leads equations to calculate association of rhythm patterns from colors. Our implementation defines the 66 colors as follows. It divides HSB color space into 63 subspaces, by dividing Hue into 7, Saturation into 3, and Brightness into 3, and then selects one color in the each subspace. Moreover, our definition includes 3 monochrome colors (white, gray, and black). Experimentally we found that the definition was good, since more colors did not bring more satisfaction of users, but fewer colors might decrease their satisfaction.

DIVA then calculates importance of i-th color C_i in an image, for each of 66 colors. Current implementation considers of color contradistinction to calculate C_i, by applying the following idea to consider of them:

Contradistinction of brightness. Often we feel a color brighter if it is surrounded by dark colors. To apply this mechanism, our implementation introduces the variable b for bright colors. If the bright color occupies small parts of an image, and it is surrounded by larger parts of dark colors, our implementation applies the value $b > 1$ to the pixels of the bright colors. Otherwise, it applies the value $b = 1$ for each pixel.

Forward and backward movement. Often we feel forward movement for warm colors, and backward movement for cool colors. To apply this mechanism, our implementation introduces the variable p for each of 66 colors, which applies the value $p > 1$ for warm colors, and $p = 1$ for cool colors.

Applying the above two variables, our implementation calculates C_i using the following equation:

$$C_i = \sum_{j=1}^{N} b_j p_j f_j \tag{1}$$

Here, N is the total number of pixels in the image, b_i and p_i are the values of b and p at the j-th pixel, and f_j is a binary value, where $f_j = 1$ if j-th pixel is i-th color, otherwise $f_j = 0$.

After calculating C_i, our implementation leads the following equations to calculate association of rhythm patterns from an input image:

$$P_j = a \sum_{i=1}^{66} C_i R_{ij} + b \sum_{k=1}^{M} Q_{kj} \tag{2}$$

Here, P_j denotes the association of j-th rhythm pattern, a and b are constant positive values, R_{ij} is the association of i-th color to the j-th rhythm pattern, M is the number of keywords, and Q_{kj} is the association of k-th keyword to the j-th rhythm pattern.

The preparation stage obtains the values of R_{ij} and Q_{kj} by the combination of the following procedures.

Procedure 1. DIVA shows a list of keywords to users, and collects the feedback of values of Q_{kj} for each combination of keyword and rhythm pattern.

Procedure 2. DIVA shows the 66 colors to users, and collect the feedback of values of R_{ij} for each combination of color and rhythm pattern.

Procedure 3. DIVA shows many sample images (25 images in our experiments) to users, and collect the feedback of values of P_{jl}, the association between j-th rhythm pattern and l-th sample image. Then it obtains optimal R_{ij} values, by applying an optimization scheme to the following equation:

$$P_{jl} = \sum_{i=1}^{66} C_{il} R_{ij} \qquad (3)$$

Here, C_{il} is the importance of i-th color in the l-th sample image.

The actual stage calculates P_j values of the all rhythm patterns for an input image, using equation 2 with the values of R_{ij} and Q_{kj} obtained by the preparation stage. It then selects the rhythm pattern that obtained the highest P_j value.

Finally, DIVA arranges the input music applying the selected rhythm pattern. We assume that input SMF consists of four parts, melody, harmony, bass, and percussions. Our current implementation simply replaces bass and percussions parts by the selected rhythm pattern, without applying any modifications for melody and harmony parts.

3   Experiments

This section shows our experiments with DIVA, preparing 7 rhythm patterns, 10 keywords, and 25 sample images. The keywords include the names of objects shot in the images, such as sunset, flower, and snow. We prepared four types of preparation stages as follows.

Preparation 1. We applied procedure 1 to obtain Q_{kj}, and let $R_{ij} = 0$.

Preparation 2. We applied procedure 2 to obtain R_{ij}, and let $Q_{kj} = 0$.

Preparation 3. We applied procedure 3 to obtain R_{ij}, and let $Q_{kj} = 0$.

Preparation 4. We applied procedure 3 to obtain R_{ij}, and procedure 1 to obtain Q_{kj}.

For the evaluation of automatic arrangement results, we provided all 7 arrangements to users, and collected the selection of arrangement associated from the input images. After that, we applied DIVA to the input images, and calculated the ratio of concordance between users' and DIVA's choices of rhythm patterns.

We asked the above procedures to 8 experimental users, including 3 male and 5 female, 3 workers and 5 students, 5 experts and 3 non-experts in music. Ages of all experimental users were 20's.

Table 1. Ratio of concordance between users' and DIVA's choices

Preparation 1	Preparation 2	Preparation 3	Preparation 4
0.11	0.28	0.44	0.71

The result shows that DIVA provided good results, since random selection will bring 0.14 of ratio of concordance in average, and the above results were much better than the random selection.

This result also gives some suggestions: The ratio of concordance is better when we apply both color distribution and keywords for the calculation of association of rhythm patterns. Also, it is better to provide sample images rather than predefined colors to users.

We observed that experimental users can be divided into the following two patterns:

- Some users present higher association between colors and rhythm patterns.
- Others present higher association between keywords and rhythm patterns.

We modified the constant values as $a > b$ in equation (2) for former users, and $a < b$ for latter users, and observed that the ratio of concordance got higher.

4   Conclusion

This poster presented a technique for automatic music arrangement, which selects the rhythm pattern most associated from color distribution and keywords of input images. A part of our experimental results are shown at http://itolab.is.ocha.ac.jp/ kisa/diva1/index_e.html.

Our future works include: larger experimental tests with more sample images and more rhythm patterns, more detailed analysis of feedback of experimental users, more sophisticated implementation of color contradistinction, and more sophisticated calculation of R_{ij} values in procedure 3.

Multi-modal Interface for Fluid Dynamics Simulations Using 3–D Localized Sound

Robyn Taylor[1], Maryia Kazakevich[1], Pierre Boulanger[1], Manuel Garcia[2], and Walter F. Bischof[1]

[1] Advanced Man-Machine Interface Laboratory,
Department of Computing Science, University of Alberta
T6G 2E8 Edmonton, Alberta. Canada
{robyn,maryia,pierreb,wfb}@cs.ualberta.ca
[2] Department of Mechanical Engineering, EAFIT University
Medellin, Colombia
mgarcia@eafit.edu.co

Abstract. Multi-modal capabilities can be added to a simulation system in order to enhance data comprehension. We describe a system for adding sonification capabilities to a real-time computational fluid dynamics (CFD) simulator. Our system uses Max/MSP modules to add sonic properties to CFD solutions. The enhancements described in this paper allow users to locate sound sources in a 3–D environment using stereo auditory cues to identify data features.

1 Introduction

High-performance computing allows us to generate complex simulations in real time, producing large, detailed and dense data sets that are rich with information. Although visualization is often an expressive and effective tool for illustrating data sets or for communicating computational results, it can be difficult to communicate multi-dimensional data using visualization alone. When data sets become highly multi-dimensional, the number of visual features required to illustrate data properties can become confusing or unintelligible to the user. This issue is commonly known as the "curse of dimensionality."

We have created a distributed simulation system that is designed to facilitate multi-modal data communication. The system allows large-scale simulations to be rendered in real-time on a high-performance computational platform, then communicated to the user via a multi-modal workstation. The current system uses visualization and sonification to communicate data to the user, and is also equipped with a haptic interface which will be integrated at a later stage. This paper discusses our sonification strategies for enhancing the presentation of dense multi-dimensional computational fluid dynamics (CFD) data.

There are a number of projects involving the sonification of scientific data sets that are similar to our own approach. The research of Klein and Staadt [6] is particularly relevant as they are also concerned with the sonification of vector fields. They examine how best to sonify local areas of interest as the user

A. Butz et al. (Eds.): SG 2007, LNCS 4569, pp. 182–187, 2007.
© Springer-Verlag Berlin Heidelberg 2007

navigates through large data sets, using parameters of frequency and amplitude to manipulate generated white noise.

Obrenovic *et al.* [7] address sound spatialization in their research, undertaking a user study in order to assess whether sonified data (spatialized sound and amplitude modified by position) helps users to locate a specific target in a data set. Their findings indicate that the use of spatialized and positional sound sources help users find targets more quickly and accurately.

Hunt *et al.* [3] [4] offer an alternative method for data sonification. They introduce the concept of a Model-based Sonification system, whereby the sonification properties are generated directly from the acoustical properties of the simulation. We theorize that an acoustically based approach could produce interesting sonification mappings in a CFD scenario and plan to investigate this strategy at a later date.

As described by Kazakevich *et al.* [5], we have previously experimented with sonification in our CFD system, providing users with auditory feedback when searching for the center of a vortex in a visualized CFD dataset. Our strategies are currently being evaluated in a formal user study to determine their effectiveness. The results indicate that there is an increase in the efficiency of locating the center of a vortex using sound and visualization. Visualization allows users to rapidly locate the rough vortex location, while sonification helps the users refine their identification of the vortex center. This paper presents our continuation of this previous work, introducing new sonifications to the simulation.

2   Structure of the Simulation System

The sonification interface developed for this project serves as a front-end to a large-scale, collaborative computational steering system [1]. This system allows users to access supercomputer systems in order to perform complex CFD simulations in real-time and then using a specialized solution server, transmit the results of their computations to remote users via a high-bandwidth connection. The application we are developing is a simulated "Virtual Wind Tunnel" that allows users to visualize the behaviour of a fluid (air, water, etc.) and to observe how it interacts with virtual objects or terrains.

Visualization and Interactivity. The visualization component of our multi-modal interface is a simple 3D rendering created using OpenGL Performer. Wind velocity and direction are represented by mapping the velocity vectors to arrow glyphs which are colored according to each vector's magnitude.

The user can interact with the visualization using two input devices. A mouse is used for navigation, and a haptic tracker is used to interact with the sonification mechanism. The tracker controls the on-screen pointer that represents the user's virtual position in the simulation. The sonification system considers the user's virtual position when computing the auditory feedback that is provided in order to illustrate properties in the dataset. Currently no haptic force-feedback is provided (this functionality will be implemented at a later date.)

Sonification Interface. The sonification component of the system was developed using Max/MSP [2]. Max/MSP is a music and sound analysis and generation development environment with a visually programmed interface that makes it suitable for rapid prototyping and evaluation. Max/MSP applications are developed by drawing lines to connect modules (known as 'objects') to describe the way audio data flows between object components. Max/MSP contains a number of sound synthesis objects which one can use inside a sonification system. The sonified data is transmitted to the user via a stereo headset, allowing sound to be spatialized in two dimensions.

3   Sonification Strategies

The client module that is used to communicate data from the solution server and the position of the haptic device to the sonification module contains the following outputs:

1. Up to 20 data points can be simultaneously sonified. For each point, several pieces of information are available for sonic rendering:
   - the magnitude of the velocity vector;
   - the horizontal distance between the data point and the user's pointer in screen space;
   - the distance (in XYZ coordinate space) between the data point and the user's pointer.
2. The dot product produced by determining the difference between the velocity vector representing the user's pointer's movement in space and the velocity vector closest to the pointer

Using these parameters, we have defined several strategies to associate data exploration with auditory feedback.

3.1   Spatialized Rendering of Sound Sources

We used sound spatialization in the auditory interface in order to provide users wearing stereo headphones with additional cues regarding data location. The Max/MSP toolkit provides capabilities for panning amongst multiple speakers, so we were able to easily integrate stereo sound into the rendering environment.

Targeting Regions of Interest. We devised a sonification strategy to allow users to target the spatial location of regions of interest in a simulation. For the purposes of investigation, we determined regions of interest to be regions of high vorticity. We chose to sonify the 20 points of highest vorticity in a simulation and created a sonification scheme that allowed the user to 'hear' the data points from any position inside the simulation. Distance to/from the regions of interest is communicated to the user in several ways:

- The closer to a point the user's pointer is, the louder that point sounds
- The user's pointer position relative to the each sonified point determines how the sound is balanced between the stereo headphones
- The intensity of the sonified point is relayed to the user via frequency modulation of the sound

Each sonified point is associated with a "pink noise" sound, generated using the MSP `pink~` object [2].

Distance Sonified Through Amplitude. The amplitude of the signal associated with each point is manipulated based on its distance from the user's pointer. To do this, the sonification module is supplied with an input which describes the distance between the user's pointer and the point being sonified. The cube root of this distance is determined, so that amplitude increases non-linearly as the user approaches the data point. This increases the user's ability to perceive the increase in amplitude and is based on psycho-physical considerations, as is discussed by Kazakevich *et al* [5].

Velocity Sonified Through Frequency. To manipulate the frequency component of the sounds associated with each data point, we adjust a `lowres~` low-pass filter which affects the presence of high frequency components on the audio stream and manipulates the perceived "pitch" of the sound. In this way, one can map point velocity to the maximum frequency found in the auditory output stream, causing the points with the highest velocities to be sonified by the highest pitched pink noise stream.

Stereo Sonification. The sonification module is given a parameter reflecting the left-right position of the data point relative to the user's pointer in screen-space. This parameter is then mapped to the input of the Max/MSP `pan~` object, so that Max/MSP outputs the sound through the stereo headphones proportionally to the distance the data point appears to the left or right of the user's pointer. Data points that are far to the left are sonified primarily through the leftmost headphone speaker, but as the user changes position, the left-right balance becomes more equal, or shifts to the rightmost speaker if the user's pointer crosses to the opposite side of the data point.

Stereo sonification gives the user an additional cue as to whether or not he or she is moving closer or farther to the sound source, and in which direction he or she should move the pointer in order to reduce the distance to the region of interest.

The spatialization provided interesting auditory feedback regarding the position of the data points in space, despite the fact that it was rudimentary (a surround-sound 3-dimensional system would be more effective.) The drawback to this sonification scheme is that the global maximum is not clearly evident, since the sonified data points are all associated with similar sounds, making it difficult to distinguish fine features in the data. For this reason, we experimented with an alternative sound generation strategy in the next sonification.

3.2   Frequency Targeting for Sound Sources

This scheme was proposed as a way to rapidly identify the global maximum in a data set by using frequency modulation and stereo spatialization to guide the user towards the data element with the highest velocity value.

To create this sonification, only one data point (the maximum) was sonified, and the user's distance to the target point affected the frequency output by Max/MSP. Stereo sound was also used to guide the user in the direction of the target point.

In order to generate the sound mapping between distance and frequency, sine waves were generated using the Max/MSP `cycle~` object. The sine waves were generated at several frequencies to provide the user with a complex tone rather than a single pure sine wave. As the user's pointer approached the target data element, the frequency of the sine waves increased causing the user to perceive an increase in pitch. Conversely, if the user moved the pointer further away from the target, the pitch of the sound decreased.

This sonification scheme appeared to assist a user in locating the target point in the data set. The stereo spatialization helped identify the point's location at large distances, and changes in the sonified frequency helped the user to fine-tune their search.

3.3   Consonance and Dissonance When Traversing Flow

This sonification scheme was devised as a way to indicate to the user whether he or she was moving with or against the airflow in the simulation as described by the direction of the velocity vectors in the fluid field.

To determine this, the user's movement vector was determined by monitoring the distance between his or her current position and his or her position in the previous timestep. This movement vector could then be compared to the nearest velocity vector in the simulation. The dot product between the two vectors indicates the difference between them, and it can be used to determine whether the user is moving with or against the velocity vectors in the simulation. When the dot product between the two vectors is negative, the user is moving against the airflow; when it is positive, he or she is moving with the airflow.

To sonify this information, a series of sine tones were created. The tones were separated by a consonant interval when the dot product is positive and the user is moving with the airflow, and a dissonant interval when the dot product is negative and the user is moving against the airflow.

This is done by layering several sine waves created using the Max/MSP `cycle~` object. The sine waves corresponding to the consonant and dissonant components of the sonification are triggered on and off based on the value of the dot product, causing the user to perceive a consonant sound when travelling with the direction of flow, and a dissonant sound when travelling against the direction of flow.

After some exploration of this sonification strategy, our team theorized that the use of consonance and dissonance in relation to flow direction could aid in the comprehension of a simulation which used streamlines to describe continuous airflow. We plan to explore this use of sonification in future project development.

4   Future Work

While the sonification strategies presented in this paper appear to be useful, user studies are required to validate their effectiveness in improving users' comprehension and exploration of multi-dimensional data sets.

Currently, a user study is underway evaluating our previously developed sonification strategies described by Kazakevich *et al.*[5]. Extending the user study to evaluate our new sonification methods is required in order to assess their merit and refine their parameters to achieve the optimal configuration for each strategy.

In the future, we would like to expand our multi-modal platform to include not only sonification strategies, but also haptic strategies that would allow the user to obtain force-feedback information about their interactions with the data set, and provide them with a more concrete spatial understanding of the rendered solution. It is our hope that incorporating multi-modal interaction will allow us to give users a better understanding of the complex simulation data that our solution server is capable of computing and distributing to collaborative research groups.

References

1. Boulanger, P., Garcia, M., Badke, C., Ryan, J.: An advanced collaborative infrastructure for the real-time computational steering of large CFD simulations. In: European Conference on Computational Fluid Dynamics ECCOMAS CFD, Egmond aan Zee, The Netherlands (2006)
2. Cycling '74. Max/MSP.http://www.cycling74.com/
3. Hunt, A., Hermann, T.: The importance of interaction in sonification. In: Proceedings of ICAD 04 – Tenth Meeting of the International Conference on Auditory Display, Sydney, Australia (2004)
4. Hunt, A., Hermann, T., Pauletto, S.: Interacting with sonification systems: Closing the loop. In: Proceedings of the Eighth International Conference on Information Visualization, pp. 879–884. London, UK (2004)
5. Kazakevich, M., Boulanger, P., Bischof, W., Garcia, M.: Multi-modal interface for a real-time CFD solver. In: HAVE 2006 – IEEE International Workshop on Haptic Audio Visual Environments and their Applications, pp. 15–20. Ottawa, Canada (2006)
6. Klein, E., Staadt, O.: Sonification of three-dimensional vector fields. In: Proceedings of the SCS High Performance Computing Symposium, pp. 8–15. Arlington, USA (2004)
7. Obrenovic, Z., Starcevic, D., Jovanov, E.: Experimental evaluation of multimodal human computer interface for tactical audio applications. In: Proceedings of the IEEE International Conference Multimedia and Expo, pp. 29–32. Lusanne, Switzerland (2002)

Focus+Context Resolution Adaption
for Autostereoscopic Displays

Timo Ropinski, Frank Steinicke, Gerd Bruder, and Klaus Hinrichs

Visualization and Computer Graphics Working Group (VisCG),
Department of Computer Science, University of Münster
Einsteinstr. 62, 48149 Münster, Germany
{ropinski,fsteini,g_brud01,khh}@math.uni-muenster.de

Abstract. In this paper we introduce concepts in order to enhance the resolution of autostereoscopic displays for performing routine tasks. Our *Sim2D3D* technique presented earlier allows users to work with any 2D or 3D application in an autostereoscopic desktop environment. We have conducted a user study to investigate the impact of this technique on routine tasks performed using autostereoscopic displays. The problems identified in this user study led us to further improve the design of autostereoscopic user interfaces by increasing the effective resolution for context areas.

Keywords: autostereoscopic displays, user interfaces, multi-resolution.

1 Introduction

Nowadays ASDs are mainly used in research institutions working on stereoscopic visualization or in isolated fields like oil and gas exploration, photogrammetry and medical visualization ([3]). This indicates that the potential of these displays has not yet been unleashed for routine work, e.g. with text processing and spread sheet applications, but also internet browsing, gaming, etc. There are mainly three reasons which have prevented the breakthrough of ASD technologies so far. First of all, ASDs cannot be used to display plain 2D content. Since the lenticular sheet or the parallax barrier usually attached in front of the display makes both eyes see different regions of the screen, plain images are perceived distorted. Therefore applications have to be adapted to be used with ASDs. There are two groups of such adapted applications. Applications of the first group separate 2D and 3D content and require beside the ASD used to visualize the 3D content an additional regular display for the 2D content. These applications have the advantage that the user can control the application by using the well known GUI elements provided by the OS. However, problems arise when decoupling the visualization and user interface elements to different displays: the user has to change focus when performing an interaction task addressing both 2D and 3D content. This focus change takes time, since every change towards the ASD requires the user to find the *sweet spot*, which is the region in front of the display in which a correct stereoscopic image can be perceived. Furthermore,

A. Butz et al. (Eds.): SG 2007, LNCS 4569, pp. 188–193, 2007.

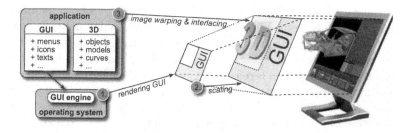

Fig. 1. Illustration of the autostereoscopic user interface framework showing 2D and 3D content simultaneously. The GUI is rendered by the OS using half the native ASD resolution (1), and scaled to the native resolution (2). Image warping is used to generate a stereo pair (3).

using context menus on top of the 3D canvas is not possible, since these menus would be displayed distorted. The other group of applications addressing ASDs provides custom user interface elements which are rendered stereoscopically. Although these widgets have been developed according to the underlying OSs, in most cases they cannot match the look and feel and therefore require the user to deal with slightly different interface concepts. Because of the required extra implementation effort only very few applications have been adapted to be used with ASDs. The second drawback of ASDs is their reduced resolution which is inherent to stereoscopic visualization. Since on the same amount of screen space images for the left and the right eye - and eventually for multiple viewers - have to be displayed, it is obvious that the resolution is reduced by the factor $2 \cdot v$, where v is the number of simultaneous viewers supported. Finally the user has to be in the sweet spot in order to perceive correct stereo images and to minimize the interference patterns otherwise occurring at the border of the display. Although this drawback can be resolved by exploiting head tracking, appropriate head tracking technologies require a continuous adaptation of the lenticular sheet or parallax barrier, and hence they emit noise which may be distracting to the user.

2 Related Work

The concepts introduced in this paper are based on the *Sim2D3D* stereoscopic user interface framework [4]. As mentioned above currently ASDs have been used mainly to present 3D content which has been specially adapted to meet the requirements of the used display technology. To allow simultaneous viewing we need to modify the monoscopic content in order to make it perceivable on ASDs and generate a stereo pair out of the 3D content. Since these are diverse image processing operations first we have to separate the 2D from the 3D content. To achieve this separation, our technique acts as an integrated layer between the rendering application and the OS. By using this layer we ensure that the OS takes care of rendering the 2D GUI elements in a native way and preserves the look and feel. To achieve a correct display of 2D content on ASDs it has to be processed with respect to the corresponding structure, e.g., a lenticular sheet, attached to the panel. We have to generate two half images so that the user perceives the same information with both eyes, resulting in a flat 2D image embedded in the image plane which sometimes is referred to as the focal plane. The overall process for preparing 2D content for vertically interlaced ASDs can be summarized as depicted in step 1 and step 2 shown in Figure 1. To allow proper viewing of 2D content on the ASD, we render these elements into a virtual desktop having a quarter of the resolution of the ASD (step 1). Later on the generated image is scaled uniformly by a factor of 2 before it is written to the main desktop (step 2). Since only a few 3D applications natively support stereoscopic viewing on ASDs, in most cases we have to adapt also the 3D content. We use image warping to generate the stereoscopic half images (see Figure 1 (step 3)). This technique performs a reprojection of the monoscopic image depending on the values stored in the depth buffer.

3   Comparing ASD Resolutions

To make ASDs usable for performing routine tasks it is necessary to allow simultaneous viewing of 2D and 3D content in such a way that a 3D application containing 2D GUI elements can be viewed without any distortion (see Section 2). Under these prerequisites it can be evaluated how users work with ASDs in their usual working environment. Performing routine tasks with standard software applications on single user vertical interlaced ASDs results in a resolution decrease by a factor of 2. The goal of our study is to find out if and how far the clean separation of the two half images can be neglected by introducing an overlap and thus saving display space. Assuming that the user exploits knowledge in the perception process ([2]) a certain amount of overlap may be possible by still allowing a good comprehension with a reasonable cognitive effort.

The most obvious approach for generating content for ASDs is to provide non overlapping half images, one for each eye. In a single user vertical interlaced ASD setup this is equivalent to rendering images with half the resolution in width and height into a virtual desktop, and scaling them uniformly by a factor of 2 when writing to the main desktop. In our study we used a *SeeReal Technologies Cn 20"* display having a native resolution of 1600×1200, and a virtual desktop having a resolution of 800×600. To increase the effective resolution, the resolution of the virtual desktop into which the GUI elements are rendered can be changed, and a different scaling factor can be used when writing these elements onto the main desktop. To obtain a uniform scaling and thus avoid deformation we have ensured that these resolutions have the native aspect ratio of the ASD, which in our case is $4 : 3$. Finding the best suitable resolution for the virtual desktop is a tradeoff between the usage of screen space and the time a user can work with the system without suffering eye-strain. A resolution of half the native ASD resolution would minimize eye-strain, since two completely distinct half images are displayed, while a higher resolution would provide more screen space.

Table 1. Averaged results of the questionnaires measured on a five point Likert scale, where 5 means that the user agreed with the statement in the left column and 1 means that the user disagreed

Statement	800 × 600	1024 × 768	1280 × 960	1600 × 1200
text is well perceivable	4.50	$4.00^1/3.80^2$	$1.83^1/2.33^2$	1.00
little to no eye-strain occurring	4.50	$3.16^1/3.00^2$	$1.66^1/1.66^2$	1.00
2D tasks can be fulfilled	3.50	$2.66^1/2.80^2$	$1.16^1/1.66^2$	1.00
combined 2D/3D tasks can be fulfilled	3.75	$3.33^1/3.80^2$	$2.00^1/2.00^2$	1.00
could use more than one hour	4.25	$3.00^1/3.20^2$	$1.50^1/1.66^2$	1.00
static head position not restrictive	4.00	$3.50^1/3.20^2$	$3.16^1/1.33^2$	$-^3$
interference pattern did not disturb	3.50	$3.00^1/3.00^2$	$2.16^1/1.33^2$	$-^3$

[1]: bilinear interpolation, [2]: bicubic interpolation, [3]: no meaningful values given

To make the tradeoff we have conducted a user study in which 7 users had to perform a text reading task on the ASD. All users were male, 5 of them were wearing glasses or contact lenses. Their experience with stereoscopy and ASDs ranges from novices having no experience up to experts with high knowledge in this domain. Accomplishing the task, the users had to read texts with a varying length from 398 to 410 words on different ASD setups, i.e., having different resolutions of the virtual desktop. The word count of the used texts ensured that no scrolling was necessary to navigate and the user could concentrate on the reading task itself, while at the same time the entire display width was filled with text requiring the user to look at different regions on the screen. In addition to the resolution of the virtual desktop we also altered the interpolation method applied when scaling its content to fit the main screen having the native resolution of 1600×1200. We tested resolutions of 800×600, 1024×768, 1280×960 and 1600×1200 pixels, and we used bilinear as well as bicubic interpolation for the 1024×768 and the 1280×960 resolutions. Each subject had to read one out of six different texts with different screen resolutions and (if applicable) bilinear or bicubic interpolation. Furthermore all texts were extracted from the same news source in order to make their comprehension requiring about the same effort. During the tests the users had to sit in front of the ASD, reading the text aloud, and we recorded the reading process in order to measure the required time and to identify subjective comments and mistakes. We used different permutations of the text extracts and display resolutions in order to exclude a possible coherence. After the texts have been read, we have conducted a survey with each user. Among others the survey targeted the degree of eye-strain and in how far the users could imagine to work with this setup. Therefore we have confronted the users with statements and they had to express their agreement on a five point Likert scale, were 1 means that they not agree at all while 5 means agreement (see Table 1).

The results clearly show that the users prefer the 800×600 resolution to all other setups. The users could read the text best at this resolution and eye-strain was minimal. The users have stated that 2D as well as 3D tasks can be accomplished comfortably using this setup and assumed to be able to work with the 800 × 600 resolution for at least one hour. The restriction of the head position as well as the perceived interferences have been revealed as not very disturbing. Only when using the 1600 × 1200 resolution, these drawbacks where less disturbing. However, this is due to the fact that the users canceled the test early since almost nothing could be read. Although the results of the 1024 × 768 resolution were not as good as for the 800 × 600 resolution, the difference is not that significant. For example, users could imagine to perform work that involves 2D as well as 3D tasks at the 1024 × 768 resolution with bicubic interpolation as well as with the 800 × 600 resolution. In general, the alternative between a bilinear or a bicubic interpolation has not shown a significant impact on the perception of 2D content. Therefore, the results indicate that bilinear interpolation is sufficient in most cases, in particular when considering the higher computational complexity when using bicubic interpolation. Due to the low number of participants we have omitted a complete statistical evaluation. However, the results give good cues about the benefits and drawbacks of the different setups and match with the experience with users working almost daily with these displays, as reported informally.

4   Focus+Context Resolution Adaption

The results of the user study indicate that text can be read best at half the resolution of the native ASD display which ensures that both eyes perceive exactly the same image. However, the results likewise indicate that a resolution of 1024 × 768 with a scaling factor of 1.56 also leads to good readability and an acceptable amount of eye-strain. Hence we decided to integrate a multi-resolution based focus+context mechanism into our autostereoscopic user interface framework ([1]). The goal is to provide the user with the best perceivable resolution in the focus area of the screen, by still giving a good contextual overview of the rest of the desktop. We have chosen to use 1024 × 768 as the resolution for the virtual desktop. In addition we apply different scaling factors to the visible windows. While we will use a scaling factor of 2 for the window being in focus and a scaling factor of 1.56 for the background, we linearly interpolate the scaling factors for all other windows in the order they do overlap. Hence we have to identify a front-to-back order of all windows starting with the one being in focus. After the scaling factors have been determined we traverse all windows currently visible, copy the appropriate image data from the virtual desktop, apply the determined scaling factor and write the transformed image data to the main desktop. Figure 2 shows two examples of the same desktop setup, once without and once with the window scaling approach being applied. Although the improved readability can only be perceived when using an ASD the different window sizes can be seen clearly.

(a)   (b)

Fig. 2. The desktop shown (a) without and (b) with front-to-back order window scaling

5   Conclusions and Future Work

In this paper we have presented concepts developed with the goal to make ASD technologies more suitable to perform routine tasks. Based on our proposed autostereoscopic user interface framework *Sim2D3D* we were able to conduct 2D text reading experiments in order to discover the influence of the resolution adaptation of ASDs to text perception. We could show that, although displaying two identical images for both eyes led to the best perception of 2D content, using a higher resolution leading to an overlap of the two half images still allows to perceive the text very well. Based on these findings we have developed a multi-resolution focus+context display model for ASDs, where the focus window is displayed with two completely separated half images, while the context information is displayed using different degrees of overlap. Thus we were able to increase the effective resolution of these displays, by still allowing good perception.

References

1. Baudisch, P., Good, N., Stewart, P.: Focus plus context screens: combining display technology with visualization techniques. In: UIST '01: Proceedings of the 14th annual ACM symposium on User interface software and technology, pp. 31–40. ACM Press, New York (2001)
2. Gregory, R.L.: Knowledge in Perception and Illusion. Phil. Trans. R. Soc. Lond. 352, 1121–1128 (1997)
3. Halle, M.: Autostereoscopic Displays and Computer Graphics. ACM SIGGRAPH Computer Graphics 31(2), 58–62 (1997)
4. Ropinski, T., Steinicke, F., Bruder, G., Hinrichs, K.H.: Simultaneously viewing monoscopic and stereoscopic content on vertical-interlaced autostereoscopic displays. In: Poster-Proceedings of the 33rd International Conference on Computer Graphics and Interactive Techniques (SIGGRAPH06), ACM Press, Boston (2006)

Feature Extraction from the Mesh Model with Some Noise

Zhong Li[1], Lizhuang Ma[2], Zuoyong Zheng[2], and Wuzheng Tan[2]

[1] Department of Mathematics and Science, Zhejiang Sci-Tech University,
Hangzhou, China, 310018
lizhongzju@hotmail.com
[2] Department of Computer Science and Engineering, Shanghai Jiao Tong University, Shanghai,
China, 200030
ma-lz@cs.sjtu.edu.cn, {Oliver.zheng,Tanwuzheng}@sjtu.edu.cn

Abstract. This paper presents a new feature extraction method on the mesh model with some noise. Firstly, we compute Mesh saliency value of every vertex on the mesh model. Then we set it as the weighted factor and employ the weighted bi-quadratic Bézier surface to fit the vertex and its neighborhood by the least square method. So we obtain the smoothed principal curvature and principal direction of every vertex, which can be used for detecting and extracting the feature point. The advantage of our method is that we can achieve the better feature extraction result from the mesh model with some noise.

1 Introduction

On a smooth surface, we can define the ridges as the locus of points where the maximal principal curvature takes a positive maximum along its curvature line and the valleys as the locus of points where the minimal principal curvature attains a negative minimum along its curvature line. We uniformly call them crest lines [1]. Undoubtedly, triangular mesh model has been the popular representation form in Computer Graphics and Computer Aide Design, and the feature extraction from the mesh model has many applications in medical image, object recognition, shape analysis, mesh segmentation, etc [2].

Recently, the feature extraction from the mesh model has gotten the broad attention and research. The popular methods are based on the point extraction. These methods firstly search points with the large curvature change as the feature points, then connect them to form the feature line. Or they calculate the principle curvature of each vertex by building the local coordinate system or the local fitting surface, then detect the feature point according to the principle curvature derivatives [3,4]. In these methods, the precise principal curvature computation is the key operation for the feature point detection. And these methods only rely on the local neighborhood information, which don't consider other globe information. Other popular methods are based on the surface extraction [5,6]. These methods firstly look for some feature seeds, then create the surface with similar geometric character such as the normal vector or curvature by the region growing method. At last, the feature line is gotten by

A. Butz et al. (Eds.): SG 2007, LNCS 4569, pp. 194–199, 2007.
© Springer-Verlag Berlin Heidelberg 2007

the surface intersection method. In these methods, the surface intersection is the key operation during the whole feature extraction process. For all above methods, the feature extraction results are not desirable when the mesh model has some noise because the noise and the feature point are treated simultaneously. Current methods normally do the feature extraction operation after the mesh model is denoised and smoothed. But the smooth process probably causes the distortion of the mesh model and brings the error accumulation for the feature extraction [7]. So how to directly extract the feature lines from the mesh model with some noise is still a big challenging for researchers.

With the further research and development for 3D mesh models, some novel ideas can be applied for the mesh feature extraction. In 2005, Lee et al [8] proposed a Mesh saliency method, which merges the perceptual criteria by the low-level human visual system curs with geometric properties based on discrete differential geometry for 3D mesh, it can successfully capture salient regions in meshes.

In this paper, we set Mesh saliency of each vertex as the weighted factor, which can describe the salient character of mesh vertex, and use the weighted bi-quadratic Bézier surface to fit each vertex and its neighborhood. The new smoothed principal curvatures and principal directions are used for the detection of feature point. Compared to other feature extraction methods, our method can obtain the better feature extraction results for the mesh model with some noise.

2   The Feature Extraction Based on Mesh Saliency

The main idea of our feature extraction method is that we firstly calculate Mesh saliency value of each vertex, then set it as the weighted factor and use the weighted bi-quadratic Bézier surface to fit each vertex and its neighborhood. The smoothed principal curvature and principal direction are used for the detection of feature point by modified Stylianou's method. Firstly, we can use Lee's method to obtain the Mesh saliency of each vertex on the mesh model [8].

2.1   The Local Fit by the Weighted Bi-quadratic Bézier Surface

After getting the Mesh saliency of each vertex, we should fit each vertex and its neighborhood on the triangular mesh with some noise, the popular methods use the quadratic or cubic algebraic surface [4,6] through the least squares method. Here we use the bi-quadratic Bézier surface to fit the vertex and its neighborhood. The advantages of parametric surface fitting are that it can be designed easily and conveniently, and for the mesh surface with some noise, we can add the adjusting matrix and factor to fit the local area, which can obtain the more accurate fitting surface [9].

When using the bi-quadratic Bézier surface to fit the vertex and its neighborhood, we set all vertexes in the 2-ring neighborhood of vertex p_i as the fitted points. To fit these vertex p_i and other vertexes in the 2-ring neighborhood, we should compute the control point b_{ij} positions of the bi-quadratic Bézier surface according to these given vertexes. Supposing the parameter of the given vertex in the fitted surface is (u_i, v_i), first of all, we require to know all parameters of these given vertexes, these parameters can be gotten by projecting vertexes onto a tangent plane and scaling them to the [0,1] range.

Supposing there are n vertexes in the 2-ring neighborhood of vertex p_i, firstly, we compute the approximate normal vector N on p_i by the arithmetic average of all normal vectors on given vertexes. Then, we construct a tangent plane which is vertical to N and set p_i as the origin of coordinate. If some projected points of n vertexes in the tangent plane are on the same position, we change the origin of coordinate to get the new tangent plane until all projected points are not on the same position. Then we build up the local Cartesian coordinates in this plane so that the coordinates of all projected points are enclosed by a min-max box, which can be scaled to the [0,1] range. The coordinates of projected points in this range are regarded as corresponding parameters of given vertexes.

For vertex p_i and other vertexes in its 2-ring neighborhood, after obtaining corresponding parameter (u_i, v_i) of these vertexes, we can construct a linear equation system $Ax=B$, where

$$A = \begin{bmatrix} B_0^2(u_0)B_0^2(v_0) & B_0^2(u_0)B_1^2(v_0) & \cdots & B_2^2(u_0)B_2^2(v_0) \\ B_0^2(u_1)B_0^2(v_1) & B_0^2(u_1)B_1^2(v_1) & \cdots & B_2^2(u_1)B_2^2(v_1) \\ & & \vdots & \\ B_0^2(u_n)B_0^2(v_n) & B_0^2(u_n)B_1^2(v_n) & \cdots & B_2^2(u_n)B_2^2(v_n) \end{bmatrix},$$

$$x = [b_{0,0} \quad b_{0,1} \quad \cdots \quad b_{2,2}]^T, \ B = [p_0 \quad p_1 \quad \cdots \quad p_n]^T.$$

From this equation system, we compute x to get the control points b_{ij}, which can construct the bi-quadratic Bézier surface.

Because there exist some noise in the original mesh model, the fitting surface by above method may be not precise. We can add the adjusting matrix and the adjusting factor to modify the fitted surface by the least square method. The modified equation system is as follows

$$\begin{bmatrix} \alpha A \\ (1-\alpha)S \end{bmatrix} [x] = \begin{bmatrix} \alpha B \\ 0 \end{bmatrix}$$

where A, x, B are the above definitions, the matrix S is added to make each of the four quadrilaterals formed by the $b_{i,j}$ as close to a parallelogram as possible, which can be set as

$$S = \begin{bmatrix} 1 & -1 & 0 & -1 & 1 & 0 & 0 & 0 & 0 \\ 0 & 1 & -1 & 0 & -1 & 1 & 0 & 0 & 0 \\ 0 & 0 & 0 & 1 & -1 & 0 & -1 & 1 & 0 \\ 0 & 0 & 0 & 0 & 1 & -1 & 0 & -1 & 1 \end{bmatrix}$$

The factor α is added to adjust in [0,1] depending on the intensity of noise in the mesh model. When noise is dense, α is set lower. Whereas, α is set higher. Here, α can be chosen according to the Mesh saliency value in its neighborhood. When the Mesh saliency values vary obviously, there may be much noise in this neighborhood, so we set the lower α value. When the Mesh saliency values vary unconspicuously, we set the higher α value. Supposing the maximum and minimum of Mesh saliency in the neighborhood are $Saliency_{max}$, $Saliency_{min}$, here α is chosen as $Saliency_{min}$ / $Saliency_{max}$.

For the above equation system, we can use the least square method to get the control points so that we obtain the fitting surface $B(u, v)$. At this time, vertex p_i is namely the corresponding point $B(u_i, v_i)$.

2.2 The Feature Point Detection from the Smoothed Mesh Model

For the mesh model with some noise, when we use the weighted bi-quadratic Bézier surface to fit each vertex and its neighborhood, it can be called as the denoising and smoothing process of each vertex. According to the differential geometry formula, we can compute the Gaussian curvature and mean curvature of the point $B(u_i, v_i)$ on the fitted bi-quadratic Bézier surface. Then we can get two smoothed principal curvatures and corresponding principal directions from Gaussian curvature and mean curvature.

Now, we detect the feature point by the new principal curvature of each vertex after being denoised and smoothed. Normally, the feature point judgement is related to the calculation of curvature values and their derivatives. Suppose e_{max} and e_{min} are the derivatives of the principal curvature k_{max} and k_{min} along their corresponding curvatures directions t_{max} and t_{min}, namely

$$e_{max} = \partial k_{max} / \partial t_{max} \, , \, e_{min} = \partial k_{min} / \partial t_{min} \, .$$

The ridge point is given by

$$e_{max} = 0, \, \partial e_{max} / \partial t_{max} < 0, \, k_{max} > | k_{min} |$$

and the valley point is gotten by

$$e_{min} = 0, \, \partial e_{min} / \partial t_{min} > 0, \, k_{min} < - | k_{max} | .$$

Above two formulations state that a point is the feature point if its largest curvature (absolute value) is locally maximal in its corresponding direction. But for the triangular mesh model, we can not explicitly calculate curvature derivatives on each vertex. Here, we modify Stylianou's method [10] to detect the feature point by following steps.

Step 1. Compute the intersection points between the normal plane generated by t_{max}, n and the 1-ring neighborhood of p. Supposing the intersection points are a and b, we denote corresponding two mesh vertexes, for example, vertexes p_i , p_{i+1} for point a.

Step 2. Calculate the maximal principle curvature at a and b by the interpolation method. Supposing the maximal principle curvatures are kp_i and kp_{i+1} at vertexes p_i, p_{i+1}, the maximal principle curvature k^a_{max} at a can be gotten by linear interpolation of kp_i and kp_{i+1}.

Step 3. If $(k^p_{max})^2 - (k^a_{max})^2 > e$, $(k^p_{max})^2 - (k^b_{max})^2 > e$, then vertex p is a ridge point, where $e > 0$ is a threshold. Different from Stylianou's method which sets the constant value $e = 0.01$, here, e is chosen as $Saliency_{min}$ / $Saliency_{max}$, where $Saliency_{max}$,

Saliency$_{min}$ are the maximum and minimum of Mesh saliency in vertex's 1-ring neighborhood. Because the mesh saliency describes the salient character of local area, it can be used for the threshold value of the feature point. When vertex p is the boundary point, there may be only one intersection point between the normal plane and its 1-ring neighborhood. In this case, we only judge one condition for the ridge point detection.

Step 4. We can use similar method for the detection of the valley point. The difference is that we set t_{min} as minimal principle curvature.

3 Experiment Results

We use VC6.0 language and OpenGL Graphic tools to implement our algorithm for the feature extraction from the triangular mesh model. Here, the main computer configuration is with CPU P4/1.8 G and EMS memory 512 MB. We use some different mesh models to test and explore the efficiency and robustness in the proposed algorithm. In Fig. 1(a), there is the feature extraction result by Stylianou's method for smooth Fandisk model. Fig. 1(b) is the feature extraction result by our method for the same mesh model. We find some feature lines in our result are longer than those in Stylianou's method. Fig. 1(c) and Fig. 1(d) are the feature extraction results between Stylianou's method and our method for Fandisk model when adding some noise. We find some short pseudo feature lines in our result are fewer than those in Stylianou's method. Compared to direct feature extraction method, our method is more effective for the smooth mesh model and the mesh model with some noise.

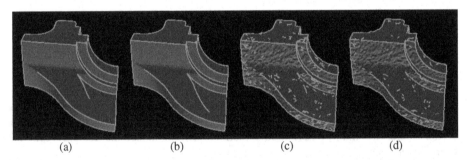

| (a) | (b) | (c) | (d) |

Fig. 1. Fandisk mesh model

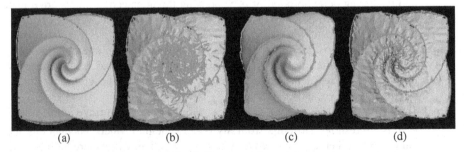

| (a) | (b) | (c) | (d) |

Fig. 2. Flower mesh model

In Fig. 2(a), there is the feature extraction result by our method for the smooth flower mesh model. Fig. 2(b) is the result by direct feature extraction for the flower model with some noise. We notice that there are some blur feature lines in the center part of flower model. In Fig. 2(c), there is the result by firstly smoothing the mesh model, then extracting the crest line by Stylianou's method. We find the feature lines appear some distortions caused by the smoothing process. Fig. 2(d) is the result by our method for the flower mesh model with some noise. Comparatively, our feature extraction method is better than other methods for the mesh model with some noise.

4 Conclusion and Future Work

We present a novel feature extraction method for the mesh model with some noise. By setting Mesh saliency as the weighted factor, we construct the weighted bi-quadratic Bézier surface to fit each vertex and its neighborhood. The smoothed curvature is used for the detection of feature extraction.

Because we add the computation of Mesh saliency of each vertex and the local fitting by the bi-quadratic Bézier surface, the whole algorithm is slower than direct feature extraction method. How to improve our algorithm's time complexity is the future work of our researches.

Acknowledgements

This research was supported by National Natural Science Foundation of China (No. 60573147) and Natural Science Foundation of Zhejiang, China (Y106207).

References

1. Ohtake, Y., Belyaev, A., Seidel, H.: Ridge-valley lines on meshes via implicit surface fitting. ACM Trans Graphics 23(3), 609–612 (2004)
2. Mao, Z.: Research on several algorithms of digital geometry processing [D]. Shanghai Jiao Tong University (2006) (in Chinese)
3. Milroy, M., Bradley, C., Vickers, G.: Segmentation of a wrap-around model using an active contour. Computer-Aided Design 29(4), 299–320 (1997)
4. Goldfeather, J., Interrante, V.: A novel cubic-order algorithm for approximating principal direction vectors. ACM Trans Graphics 23(1), 45–63 (2004)
5. Sapidis, N., Besl, P.: Direct construction of polynomial surfaces from dense range images through region growing. ACM Trans. On Graphics 14(2), 171–200 (1995)
6. Chen, Y., Liu, C.: Quadric surface extraction using genetic algorithms. Computer-Aided Design 31(2), 101–110 (1999)
7. Belyaev, A., Anoshkina, E.: Detection of surface creases in range data. Eleventh IMA Conference on The Mathematics of Surface (2005)
8. Lee, C., Varshney, A., Jacobs, D.: Mesh saliency. In: Proceedings of SIGGRAPH (2005)
9. Razdan, A., Bae, M.: Curvature estimation scheme for triangle meshes using biquadratic Bézier patches. Computer-Aided Design 37(14), 1481–1489 (2005)
10. Stylianou, G., Falin, G.: Crest lines for surface segmentation and flattening. IEEE Trans Vis. Comput Graphics 10(5), 536–544 (2004)

Effects of Space Design Visualization on Users' Subjective States

Shigeyoshi Iizuka and Yusuke Goto

NTT Cyber Solutions Laboratories, NTT Corporation
1-1 Hikarinooka Yokosuka-Shi Kanagawa Japan
s.iizuka@lab.ntt.co.jp, goto@y510.net

Abstract. We developed a system that visualizes how design of interior space affects user's subjective states when they are communicating personal information on a computer. After measuring the subjective reassurance of users while they were communicating information, we used the results to plot and create personal information spaces. Then the subjective aspects of workspace design were visualized based on these personal information spaces. Designers can intuitively understand the subjective aspects of space design visualized based on a user's subjective states using our system.

Keywords: Space Design, Visualization, Subjective States.

1   Introduction

Technologies are being developed to ensure secure online transfer of information, but risks remain when people enter highly confidential information such as personal data into systems in public areas. Complete security means both communication and physical security. We are conducting a study of secure space design technology in response to the need for physical spaces where people can use these services securely (Iizuka, 2004). Generally, the success or failure of a design depends on whether the completed item performs the function for which it was conceived during the planning stage. However, because a computer user's subjective states cannot be seen, it is hard to determine how well a space design supports users' subjective needs. We developed a system that visualizes the subjective characteristics of space design based on users' subjective states while they are communicating information. First, to obtain the basic data, we measured the subjective reassurance of the user when he was communicating information. That is, visual representations of personal information space were created based on experimental results. Then, the subjective effects of space design were visualized based on those personal information spaces. Below, we describe how we identified a user's subjective data and propose a system that enables designers to easily visualize users' subjective reactions to a designed space.

A. Butz et al. (Eds.): SG 2007, LNCS 4569, pp. 200–203, 2007.

2 Measurement of a User's Subjective States

We hypothesized that the position of a stranger in relation to a user affects the user's feelings of reassurance about public work environments and that these feelings affect "personal space" (Sommer, 1959; Shibuya, 1985). We set up a user's hypothesized personal space perimeter, positioned a stranger at different points on and inside it, and measured the user's feelings of reassurance with the stranger at each position. We used direction and distance as the parameters for the stranger's position.

2.1 Measurement

The ten points at which the stranger was positioned during the trials (five direction times two distance points) are shown in Figure 1.

We measured feelings of reassureance for four kinds of information a user might communicate. These four information classifications are based on four criteria that affect a user's feelings of reassurance when communicating information in a public space and were obtained by our previous research (Iizuka, 2005).

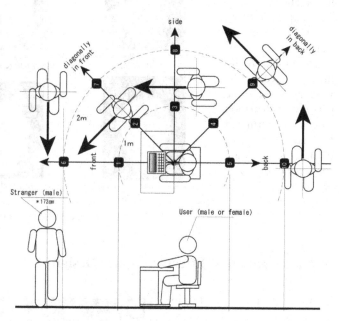

Fig. 1. Experimental set-up

- Person-specific and money-related information
  - Name, address, credit card number
- Present circumstances and history-related information
  - Occupation, birthplace, education
- Preferences and behavior-related information
  - Hobbies, current destination, favorite stores
- Work-related information
  - Employer name (office), address, phone number, and mailing address

In this experiment, the user was alone, and there was always one other person (the stranger) around. The four sorts of information mentioned above were presented to the user by displaying them on a PC screen. The participants were 10 males and 10 females in their 20's, 30's, 40's and 50's. Each participant rated their feelings of reassurance for all types of information with the stranger at all evaluation points.

2.2 Personal Space Creation

We tried to determine a personal information space by the expression of which degrees (levels) of reassurance felt by the user can be visualized. The personal information spaces determined for each type of information are shown in Figure 2.

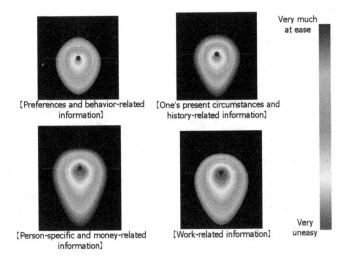

[Preferences and behavior-related information]   [One's present circumstances and history-related information]

[Person-specific and money-related information]   [Work-related information]

Very much at ease

Very uneasy

Fig. 2. Personal Spaces for Communicating Information

3 Visualization of Effects of Space Design

Figure 3 illustrates our results for personal information space. We tried to visualize how reassured users would feel using computers in a space designed in a particular way.

First, we looked at a floor plan for a public space with seats for computer terminals. Then, we mapped previously

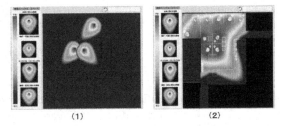

(1)   (2)

Fig. 3. Personal Information Space Mapping

generated personal information spaces onto the floor plan. Personal information space is mapped onto all seats shown on the floor plan (Figure. 3(1)), and the mapped personal information spaces are overlapped (Figure. 3(2)).

4 Effect of Seat Rearrangement on Users' Subjective States

The following example illustrates how visualization eases design of workspace that takes account of a user's subjective states. The effect (increased feelings of reassurance) of a different arrangement of seats can be visualized by applying personal information spaces to floor plans before and after seats are rearranged. Using such visualization enables designers to intuitively understand the effects of rearrangement.

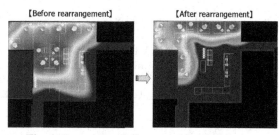

Fig. 4. Comparison Before and After Renovation

5 Conclusion

We developed a system that visualizes the effects of space design on users' subjective states while they are communicating information. First, to obtain the basic data, we measured users' feelings of reassurance with a stranger standing in different positions and at different distances, which are considered to greatly affect a user's feelings of reassurance. Using the results, we expressed a user's degree of reassurance as a personal information space. Then, we visualized the effects of space design on personal information spaces. Using our system, designers can intuitively understand the effects of space design on users' states.

We think this visualization system can be used to redesign actual work environments. We also think that we can improve the credibility of the visualization by further testing of personal information spaces. Therefore, we plan to increase the size of our sample and conduct an experiment in a real-world environment. We also want to develop a structure that automatically creates personal information spaces and visualizes space design effects.

References

Iizuka, S., Nakajima, S., Ogawa, K., Goto, Y., Watanabe, A.: Reassurance When Using Public Terminals in Public Spaces. In: Proceedings of the 66th National Convention of Information Processing Society of Japan (IPSJ) 4-451-4-452 (2004)

Iizuka, S., Ogawa, K., Nakajima, S.: A study to develop public work environment design guidelines for handling personal information. In: Proceedings of HCI International 2005, incl. in CD-ROM (2005)

Shibuya, S.: A Study of the Shape of Personal Space. Bulletin of Yamanashi Medical University 2, 41–49 (1985)

Sommer, R.: Studies in Personal Space. Sociometry 22, 247–260 (1959)

Multi-view Sketch-Based FreeForm Modeling

Florian Levet, Xavier Granier, and Christophe Schlick

IPARLA project (INRIA futurs - LaBRI),
UMR 5800, Université Bordeaux 1; 351, cours de la Libération
33405 Talence, France
{levet,granier,schlick}@labri.fr

Abstract. For the generation of freeform 3D models, one of the most intuitive solution is to use sketch-based modeling environments. Unfortunately, since the user interface relies upon the analyse of sketches in order to determine which action is requested by the user, the possible amount of different operations can be limited. In this paper, we present a 3D sketching system based on multiple views. Each view is specialized on a component of the modeling process (like the skeleton, the profile, etc.), and is based on specific sketching interactions. With this approach, an user could improve its understanding of the modeling process and perform a larger range of modeling operations.

Keywords: Sketch-based 3D Modeling.

1 Introduction

In order to create simpler interfaces, new approaches for 3D modeling have been developed, based on the human ability to quickly draw a global overview of an object. These approaches are commonly referred as *3D Sketching*. Their principle is to infer the shape of a 3D model and add details thanks to different editing operations (e.g., cutting, extrusion), all based on sketched 2D curves.

One of the limitations of these systems is due to their exclusive use of sketches. Since they are only strokes drawn by the user, their shape and the operations that they perform are obviously limited. While classic 3D modelers have dozens of possible operations made available by cascading menus and buttons, each 3D sketching system can only perform few operations based on its analysis of the strokes.

In this paper, we present a new 3D sketching interface based on multiple views for the creation 3D freeform models. Each view provides is a specialized into a component of the complete modeling process. Since each view has its dedicated sketching interactions, our system allows a larger variety of sketch-based modeling tools compared to existing systems. Our system is based on the following goals: (1) he has to preserve and further develop the sketching interaction of the editing operations for each view, (2) he has to present all the characteristics of the models thanks to the distinct views and, finally, (3) he has to provide an easy switch between the different views.

A. Butz et al. (Eds.): SG 2007, LNCS 4569, pp. 204–209, 2007.
© Springer-Verlag Berlin Heidelberg 2007

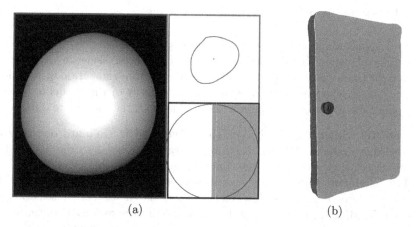

Fig. 1. (a) Three different views are used in our system: the 3D view (left frame) that shows the 3D object under construction, the skeleton view (upper-right frame) which shows the outline of the object and its skeleton and, the profile view (bottom-right frame) that shows the profile currently used to create the object. (b) A door created with two objects. Their positionning was done in the 3D view.

2   Previous Work

Teddy [3] is the precursor of 3D freeform modeling tools based on gestures and curves. From a sketched 2D silhouette, the system extracts a skeleton and infers the 3D mesh of the object based on a circular profile. Moreover, a gesture grammar converts drawn curves into corresponding modeling operations: extrusion, deformation, cutting, etc. Since the system is totally based on sketches, it is easy to create interesting objects even for non-expert users of 3D modeling softwares. But, since some editing operations are difficult on meshes, many following works are based on alternative geometric representations of their objects. For instance, Owada et. [7] used voxels in order to create internal structures. Many approaches (e.g., [4,9,8]) use implicit surfaces because of their nice mathematical properties: these systems define the 3D object as a set of implicit primitives stored in a tree structure and with an easy fusion between different primitives.

More recently, some systems [9,2,6] have introduced profile editing for sketch-based modeling. Their goal is to remove the usual blobby aspect of 3D models created with sketch-based modeling tools. Nevertheless, one main limitation of all these systems is that they only present one single view (or a pop-up window which is closed after the editing operation [6]) during the modeling task. Thus, only a part of the object information is displayed at a given time.

In traditional 3D modeling systems (e.g., 3DS Max, Blender), possible geometry misunderstandings can be solved by using multiple 2D views of the same scene. Moreover, some editing tasks can be performed more efficiently and accurately on 2D views. In this paper, we propose to extend this idea to sketching systems.

3 3D Sketching with Multiple Views

Figure 1 shows a snapshot of our prototype system. Currently, it is based on three different views: the 3D view (see the left frame), the skeleton view (see the upper-right frame) and the profile view (see the bottom-right frame). As said in Section 1, each views is specialized into a component of the modeling process and defines its own sketching interactions. Moreover, their aims are different:

- **The 3D view:** This is the common view used in standard one-view 3D sketching systems. All the sketching operations related to the 3D mesh of the object (cut, extrusion, etc...) are implemented in this views.
- **The skeleton view:** This view is related to the skeleton of the object. In this view, users can either select an area on the object by selecting the corresponding region on the skeleton, or modify the extracted skeleton.
- **The profile view:** In this view, users can change the profile of either the complete object or the currently selected region.

3.1 The 3D View

The 3D view is very similar to the standard one-view of other 3D sketching systems and, is mainly used to perform three tasks: (i) the visualization of the 3D objects, (ii) the positionning of these 3D objects (either by moving them - see Figure 1(b) - or by defining a new 2D plane for the silhouette curve) and, (iii) 3D editing of the objects with all the Teddy-like operations such as cutting, extrusion or fusion.

3.2 The Skeleton View

When the user has finished to sketch the 2D silhouette of an object, this curve is first sampled and, then, the silhouette points are transferred to the skeleton view. Starting from them, a two-step process is used to compute the skeleton. First, the pointset is approximated with a 2D variational implicit surface [10]. The gradient of this implicit surface is then used to determine the vanishing points (points where the gradient drops to zero) that are the skeleton seeds. Since we know the neighboring relations between them, we can easily construct axial edges between neighboring seeds as well as radial edges that link the axial edges to the silhouette curve (see [5] for more details about this technique).

Although this process can be totally automatic, we prefer to let the user influence the creation of the resulting skeleton. Therefore, users are allowed to either move, discard or create skeleton points.

3.3 The Profile View

All the operations related to the profile curve are defined on the profile view which is the last view provided by our system. More precisely, users have just to draw a 2D sketch to define a new profile. In our current implementation, only half

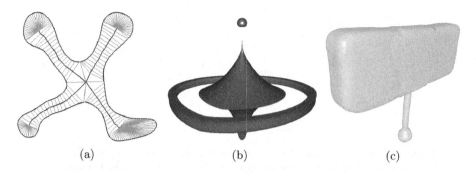

Fig. 2. (a) Final skeleton with axial edges (in black) and radial edges (in grey). (b) A genus 2 object obtained with only one silhouette and one profile curve. (c) A hammer created with our system.

of the curve has to be drawn and the other half is reconstructed by symmetry [6]. Besides, since users may want to create a 3D blobby object by only sketching a silhouette curve, we have designed a default circular profile curve which is loaded at the beginning of our system session. Once the profile curve has been generated, it is then sampled and the sample points are transferred to the 3D view to be applied on the current selected area. If no local area of the object has been selected (see Section 4), the new profile curve is applied on the whole object. Note that our system allows the definition of disconnected components for the profile curve in order to get objects which genus is more than 0 (see Figure 2(b)).

4   Interactive Session

The use of three different views, each one with a specific sketching interaction, leads to a better understanding of the characteristics of the 3D model under construction. Indeed, having all these informations (silhouette curve, profile curve, axial and radial edges) displayed at the same time in the same view would be disturbing for the user. Moreover, some occlusions can occur between these different elements. By having three views, we separate the information and we can display all the elements at the same time.

Note that it is possible to change the position of the three views, as the 3D view is not necessary the more important view for a specific operation. In some case, the user may want to have the skeleton or the profile view as the principal view. So, we offer a straightforward sketch-based interface to swap the position of two different views: this is done by starting a stroke in one view, and finishing it in the other one (see Figure 3).

A usual session of our system starts with the interactive sketching of the silhouette curve. Then, the system determines the seed points of the skeleton, as well as their initial relationship. The user may want to influence the creation of this skeleton, as explained above, or just let the system perform it automatically.

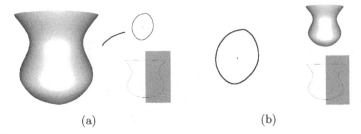

(a)   (b)

Fig. 3. (a) The default setting of the system with the 3D view as the principal view. (b) The user has swapped the skeleton view and the 3D view by sketching a stroke.

Afterwards, the axial edges and the radial ones are computed from the skeleton and, finally, the system infers the volume of the object by using the profile curve designed in the profile view.

After having defined a first version of the 3D object, the user can still modify its global shape by editing either the silhouette curve, the seed points or the profile curve. This basically redefines the mesh of the 3D object from scratch. For more local editing, we offer another possibility that works by selecting a subset of radial edges and applying a new profile curve on them, which only involves displacement of mesh vertices.

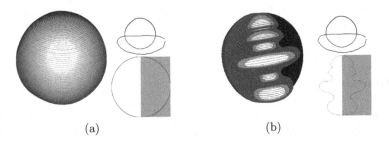

(a)   (b)

Fig. 4. (a) A radial edge selection has been done on the skeleton view (the bounding stroke). (b) Selected points have been moved to match the new sketched profile curve.

Figure 4 presents an example of such local editing. The selection of a subset of radial edges has been easily performed in the skeleton view since it's a 2D view (see Figure 4(a)). This task would have been painful to realize in the 3D view. Then, a new profile curve is sketched in the profile view, leading to the modification of the corresponding selected points of the mesh (see Figure 4(b)). Since, the three views are displayed, the user can easily understand the effects of this editing operation.

Finally, users can obtain models which have a genus greater than 0 (see Figure 2(b)) by drawing a profile curve with disconnected components. More complex models are easily obtained by combining different primitives as can be seen with the door of Figure 1(b) and the hammer of Figure 2(c).

5   Conclusion and Future Work

In this paper, we have presented a new 3D sketching system that uses multiple views, where each one provides some kind of specialization of the complete modeling process. Displaying all the degrees of freedom of a 3D model in a single view can be disturbing and hardly understandable. This is the reason for which we split the display and only present relevant information to each component. However, because all the views are displayed at the same time, our system provides efficient visual clues to the user to understand how the creation of the 3D model is performed. Moreover, each view defines a specific sketching interaction, enabling a much larger variety of editing operations.

Two directions of research are focusing our attention right now. First, we plan to further develop the sketching interface of the already defined views. For instance, we want to offer more interaction in the skeleton view to give a better control over the skeleton computation. Finally, we think that we can use even more views with our system. For instance, we plan to design a specialized view which define a suggestive interface [1]. The aim of this view would be to suggest different results (related to the possible operations) when a user draw a stroke.

References

1. De Araujo,B.,Jorge, J.: Blobmaker: Free-form modelling with variational implicit surfaces. In: Proc. of Encontro Português de Computação Grafica" (EPCG) pp. 17–26 (October 2003)
2. Cherlin,J.J., Samavati,F., Sousa,M.C., Jorge, J.A.: Sketch-based modeling with few strokes.In: SCCG '05: Proc of the 21st spring conference on Computer graphics pp. 137–145 (2005)
3. Igarashi, T., Matsuoka, S., Tanaka, H.: Teddy: a sketching interface for 3d freeform design. In: Proc. of ACM SIGGRAPH '99, pp. 409–416. ACM Press, New York (1999)
4. Karpenko, O., Hughes, J., Raskar, R.: Free-form Sketching with Variational Implicit Surfaces. Computer Graphics Forum (Proc. of Annual Eurographics Conference 2002) 21(3), 585–594 (2002)
5. Levet,F., Granier,X.: Improved skeleton extraction and surface generation for sketch-based modeling. In: GI (Graphics Interface) (2007)
6. Levet, F., Granier, X., Schlick, C.: 3d sketching with profile curves. In: Butz, A., Fisher, B., Krüger, A., Olivier, P. (eds.) SG 2006. LNCS, vol. 4073, pp. 114–125. Springer, Heidelberg (2006)
7. Owada, S., Nielsen, F., Nakazawa, K., Igarashi, T.: A Sketching Interface for Modeling the Internal Structures of 3D Shape. In: Butz, A., krüger, A., Olivier, P. (eds.) SG 2003. LNCS, vol. 2733, pp. 49–57. Springer, Heidelberg (2003)
8. Schmidt,R.,Wyvill, B., Sousa,M.C., Jorge, J.A.: ShapeShop: Sketch-Based Solid Modeling with BlobTrees. In: Eurographics Workshop on Sketch-Based Interfaces and Modeling, pp. 53–62 (2005)
9. Tai, C.-L., Zhang, H., Fong, C.-K.: Prototype Modeling from Sketched Silhouettes based on Convolution Surfaces. Computer Graphics Forum 23(1), 71–83 (2004)
10. Turk,G., O'Brien,J.: Variational implicit surfaces. Technical Report GIT-GVU-99-15, Georgia Institute of Technology (1998)

Jigsaw Texture Synthesis

Minh Tran and Amitava Datta

School of Computer Science & Software Engineering
The University of Western Australia
35 Stirling Highway Crawley, W.A. 6009, Australia
{minh,datta}@csse.uwa.edu.au

Abstract. Texture synthesis aims to seamlessly extend a sample texture. This can be achieved by reproducing the texture's recognisable patterns along with minimising the occurrences of undesirable image characteristics such as disjoint image features. Presently, patch-based methods have consistently produced the most impressive results. These methods involve aligning and stitching texture patches together. However, image inconsistencies exist when image features are misaligned; they are either fused together or abruptly cut off. Our method minimises the occurrences of these anomalies by using image edges to align patches and redefine their boundaries to preserve texture features. This implementation requires little to no user-defined variables or iterations and can be practically scalable given some pre-computation.

1 Introduction and Previous Work

Texture is an image characterised by a distinguishing pattern; we use these image characteristics to compare and differentiate between two textures. Since the placement, orientation, scale and colour of these features are so important, they are the parts of the image which texture synthesis aims to replicate effectively. However, there is a certain balance that is involved. If a texture's pattern is reproduced too infrequently, the output deviates from its source as the result may contain more unfamiliar pixels than familiar pixels. If the features are reproduced too frequently, there is a risk that the synthesised image will be dominated by repeated features. This may be useful if repetition is a characteristic of the texture itself, like a brick wall for example, but for more naturally occurring textures like flowers and tree bark, this repetition can be perceived as unnatural and uncharacteristic. Therefore the aim of texture synthesis is to imitate the recognisable visual features of a texture such that the output and the sample look as though they've been extracted from the same source.

A successful texture synthesis method can generate textures to an arbitrary size. These in turn, can be used in image processing, image compression and the visual aesthetic enhancement and rendering acceleration of various computer graphics and visualisation applications. However, depending on its intended use, a texture synthesis runs into the familiar problem of quality vs. efficiency. Typically, fast methods generate approximate results [8, 10, 3] while a more accurate

A. Butz et al. (Eds.): SG 2007, LNCS 4569, pp. 210–215, 2007.

synthesis requires a number of user-specified variables and interaction. For example, some methods require many iterations of the output in order to obtain a satisfactory result [5, 11]. Also, due to the immense variation in textures available, current approaches suit certain types of texture and therefore, perform unfavourably for other classes of textures [1,7,8]. Our method is simple the only required user-defined variable is the output size. However, our jigsaw method runs into similar difficulties in regards to replicating a wide range of textures.

Our method aims to generate large textures fairly quickly for applications for large data sets such as immersive environments. This paper discusses our work in developing a patch-based method that uses feature edges to minimise image discontinuity between neighbouring patches. A number of methods [9,11,4,6] use image features in their synthesis method and our results, where it works well, are comparable to current published results.

2   Our Approach

Our texture synthesise implementation employs a patch-based approach. This method applies the idea that once a pixel has been generated, the next or neighbouring pixels have already been predetermined since each pixel is characterised by its neighbours. Our approach uses the entire image as the patch. This can potentially produce repetitive results so we place rotated versions of the same texture together with the intention of creating an intermediary patch, called the middle patch, to ease the transition between the two images. This approach creates two areas of intersection per patch pair, instead of one where the two patches meet. The advantage this has is that the corresponding middle patches of all the possible combinations of unique patch pairings can be determined beforehand. The output can then be generated to a larger size relatively quickly by placing random combinations of the input using the corresponding pre-computed middle patches to link these patches together. This pre-computation pays off when the size of the output is more than four times larger than the input size.

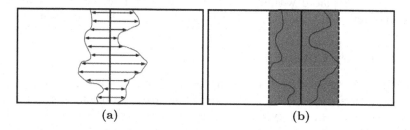

(a)   (b)

Fig. 1. A diagram of how the size of the middle patch is determined. In Image (a), the features cut off at the intersection or the join of these two patches is found by extending perpendicular lines from each pixel along the join to the nearest texture edge. Image (b) shows the bounding box (in grey) encapsulating the identified edges.

2.1 Edge Detection

The preservation of texture pattern from sample to output is vital in obtaining a favourable comparison between the two images. Therefore we are interested in using texture features in our matching criteria for aligning the middle patch with its neighbouring patches. These features can be identified by the rapid colour change in the image which signifies its presence. Instead of matching these features by colour, we outline their location, shape and structure by finding these areas of high intensity gradients. Detecting edges is another area of research and there are myriad approaches. We have chosen to use the well established Canny edge detector [2] to identify edges within the image.

2.2 Patch Matching

To maintain image continuity, instead of removing or morphing the edges [9, 4], we redefine a new boundary using the retrieved edges. By restricting the boundary path to areas of high intensity gradients, we maximise the chances of preserving entire texture elements and minimise the occurrences of texture fusions, cut-off texture elements.

Fused or truncated texture features typically occur at the boundaries of misaligned patches. By finding the features located between two patches, we can identify the region that is disrupting the image fidelity. Replacing this area with a corresponding matching patch resolves the discontinuity and links the two patches together. The cut off features are found by tracing the edges that extend from the image extremities. This process is illustrated in Figure 1 where the features cut off at join are found by drawing a vector perpendicular to the join line and finding the nearest edge that intersects it. The resulting path encapsulates the incomplete features and identifies the area requiring replacement.

The middle patch is searched for within the two images or patches, both horizontally and vertically. The match returned is the patch with the most coincident edges within the bounding box identified in Figure 1b. Once this is found, the middle patch is placed within the bounding box forming two joins within the image pair and additional steps must be taken to ensure image fidelity.

2.3 Boundary Cutting

To minimise image feature discontinuity, a new boundary is defined that follows the path of the enclosed edges situated close to the two joins formed by the middle patch. The boundary cut is determined in the same manner as identifying the features cut off at the image join described in the section 3.2. The resulting path may itself be rather disjoint because neighbouring intersected edges may not form a closed path. Therefore the area enclosed by these lines and nearby edges form a more continuous pathway. The same can be done for the other side of the join.

The directions in which the new boundary cut can form is restricted to two directions: either the patch seeps into the middle patch or the middle patch seeps outward into the original neighbouring patches. To minimise the amount of spatial intrusion, the boundary cut with the least amount of overlap area is chosen. As a result, the inward boundary is favoured over the outward boundary since the outward moving boundary has potentially more room to invade. There can be a situation where the resultant inward boundary cut extends towards and includes the original patch join. Since this reveals the area of discontinuity we are trying to replace, the method chooses the outward boundary cut instead.

2.4   Jigsaw Texture Synthesis

Joining two patches or images together can be extended to a random array of patches with each join of neighbouring patches connected in this jigsaw style. Starting from the top left patch, the middle patch of the horizontal join is determined first, then the vertical join corrected next. Images can either be rotated or, for rotationally invariant textures, sub-images can be used to form the image array. The final step in the synthesis process is smoothing the patch boundaries with a median filter.

3   Results and Discussion

The results discussed in this section were generated using Matlab on an Intel Pentium D 3GHz 1GB RAM machine.

Figure 2 displays synthesis results for textures which do not perform well. A disadvantage to this method is that since patches are paired randomly, maintaining the structure of the features can be difficult; hence this method is more suited to textures with clustered texture elements. If the paired patches are misaligned by default, a meticulously cut boundary may not be able to hide the overall structural incongruity, see Figure 2a) and b). Also, sample images with lateral or disconnected texture elements makes boundary cutting difficult and the cut meanderings are uncharacteristic and therefore are discernible, see Figure 2c) and d).

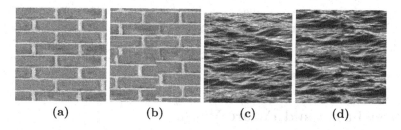

(a)   (b)   (c)   (d)

Fig. 2. This figure shows examples of the types of textures which are not suited to the jigsaw synthesis method

Results of this method using rotated versions of the texture as input can be viewed in Figure 3. Feature inconsistencies at these borders still exist although, for some of these textures, they are difficult to identify given the scattered structure of the texture features. There is still room for improvement. In particular, the effectiveness of the boundary cutting needs to be more prudent than the current implementation.

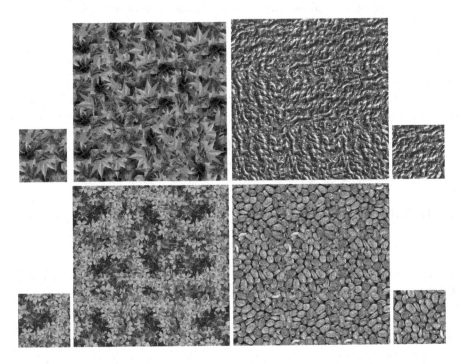

Fig. 3. Synthesis results where the output is 3 times the original texture size

In relation to the rotated versions of the texture as input, the patch size is automatically determined. Textures with dense features and therefore dense edges could potentially produce smaller bounding boxes and reduce pre-computation times. Pre-processing times for input textures (64×64–256×256) ranged from $O(nlog(n))$ to $O(n)$. Synthesis times were linear relative to the size of the output with eight different 128×128 input images producing outputs of 768×768 in an average time of 1.04sec.

4   Conclusion and Future Work

The jigsaw patch-based method is a work in progress. Since patch boundaries are defined along edges where sharp colour changes are expected, the visibility of the re-cut boundary is masked. This minimises the occurrences of texture feature fusing and cut-offs which is a recurring anomaly in patch-based methods. Large textures can be generated in little time if the patch connectors are determined beforehand. Results have produced pre-processing times ranging from $O(nlog(n))$ to $O(n)$ at best, with very quick synthesis times. Although this method does not suit all types of textures, it performs well for textures with clustered texture elements. Presently, the results of this method are comparable to recent patch-based methods, with the advantage of it being a simple implementation. The output size is the only user-defined variable. Not all results are favourable, however, so more work is still needed to refine the method to suit a wider range of textures.

Acknowledgements

This research is being supported by a WA CSIRO Postgraduate Scholarship.

References

1. Ashikhmin,M.: Synthesizing natural textures. In: Symposium on Interactive 3D Graphics, pp. 217–226 (2001)
2. Canny, J.F.: Finding edges and lines in images. Master's thesis, MIT AI Labs (1983)
3. Cohen, M.F., Shade, J., Hiller, S., Deussen, O.: Wang tiles for image and texture generation. ACM Trans. Graph. 22(3), 287–294 (2003)
4. Fang,H., Hart,J.C.: Textureshop: texture synthesis as a photograph editing tool. In: SIGGRAPH '04: ACM SIGGRAPH 2004 Papers, pp. 354–359 (2004)
5. Kwatra,V., Schodl,A., Essa,I., Turk,G., Bobick,A.: Graphcut textures: Image and video synthesis using graph cuts. In: Proceedings of SIGGRAPH 2003 (2003)
6. Lefebvre,S., Hoppe,H.: Appearance-space texture synthesis. In: SIGGRAPH '06: ACM SIGGRAPH 2006 Papers, pp. 541–548 (2006)
7. Liu,Y., Tsin,Y.: The promise and perils of near-regular texture. In: 2nd International Workshop on Texture Analysis and Synthesis, associated with the European Conference on Computer Vision (2002)
8. Wei,Li.-Yi., Levoy, M.: Fast texture synthesis using tree-structured vector quantization. In: Akeley,K.(ed.) Siggraph 2000, Computer Graphics Proceedings, ACM Press / Addison Wesley Longman, pp. 479–488 (2000)
9. Wu,Q., Yu,Y.: Feature matching and deformation for texture synthesis. In: Proc. of SIGGRAPH 2004 (2004)
10. Zelinka, S., Garland, M.: Jump map-based interactive texture synthesis. ACM Trans. Graph. 23(4), 930–962 (2004)
11. Zhang, J., Zhou, K., Velho, L., Guo, B., Shum, H.-Y.: Synthesis of progressively-variant textures on arbitrary surfaces. ACM Trans. Graph. 22, 295–302 (2003)

Synthesis of Dancing Character Motion from Beatboxing Sounds

Kyung-Kyu Kang and Dongho Kim

Department of Media, Soongsil University
511 Sangdo-dong, Dongjak-gu, Seoul, Korea
{rcrookie,dkim}@ssu.ac.kr

Abstract. This paper describes a real-time system to synthesize a dancing character that is matched with beatboxing sounds. It is easier for humans to make a rhythmical sound with their mouth and vocal like a beatboxing than playing musical instruments. The system extracts rhythm features from dancing motion clips contained in a motion clip database at a preprocessing step. While performing beatboxing in real time, the system extracts rhythm features from those sounds and then finds appropriate a clip in the database whose rhythm features are matched to the sounds.

Keywords: character animation, sound analysis, motion synthesis.

1 Introduction

Recently many researchers have focused on the methods to synthesize new dancing characters based on the background music [1], [2]. Results of those researches need a lot of processing time to make dance motions, and besides, use a background music that is made by a professional musician. This paper proposes a new approach for synthesizing dancing characters matched with an ad-lib musical performance such like *beatboxing* in real-time.

We extract rhythmic features from dancing motion clips and beatboxing sounds. The voice percussion is used to express rhythmic phrase of the performer only using their mouth and voice without any musical instruments and knowledge about composing. Beatboxing sounds are simple to analyze rhythmic features because they have a few components of voice drum like a real drum set. The rhythmic features of dancing motion clips are extracted from Hands gestures. The gestures are important as a way of emotional expressions. It is an interesting and novel work to make dancing characters matching with beatboxing sounds for everyone.

2 System

Our system consists of off-line and on-line parts. The system analyzes every dancing motion clip in a motion database for extracting rhythm features in off-line part. While

A. Butz et al. (Eds.): SG 2007, LNCS 4569, pp. 216–219, 2007.

a user is performing beatboxing, the system tracks a beat structure of the audio signal, and then finds a motion clip whose rhythm features are matched to the structure of the sound in on-line (Fig. 1.).

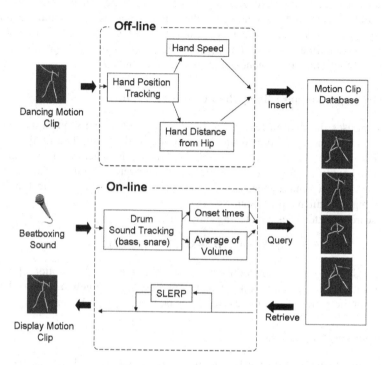

Fig. 1. System overview. After extracting rhythm features of dancing motion clips, the data are inserted into the database (off-line part). The system queries the database with features of beatboxing sounds to retrieve a dancing clip matched with it (on-line part).

2.1 Motion Analysis

We extract rhythm features from the hand positions vector of a dancing character (Fig. 1 off-line part). Hand positions are the most important elements of expressing the rhythmical emotion of human beings. When a person is performing a beatboxing, we can see a rhythmical hand action. Additionally, the hand position vector has only 6 elements- left-hand's position(x, y, z) and right-hand's position(x, y, z) -, which make easy to compute. We extract two rhythmic features from the hands vector of a motion, M. One is the number of big movements per second, M_M and the other is the speed of hand's movements, M_S. The movement means distances between hands and the hip as a root segment of a character structure. It can be computed by calculating the length of the hand position vector.

2.2 Beatboxing Analysis

Beatboxing sounds normally can be separated into three components, i) bass drum, ii) snare drum, and iii) high hat, which are similar to a real drum set. We consider bass and snare drum sounds as the key of rhythm features of beatboxing sounds. These elements are extracted from the frequency spectrum calculated with Fast Fourier Transform (FFT). We read onset times of bass and snare drum's frequency ranges. The onset times can be detected by a process of the frequency analysis [3], [4], [5].

The On-line part of Fig. 1 analyzes the onset times as the rhythm features of beatboxing sounds. We also extract two features from the sound signal, B. One is the number of onset times per second, B_O and the other is the average power of the frequency of the drum component sounds in a few seconds, B_P.

2.3 Searching a Motion Clip by the Beatboxing Features

The system uses the rhythm features of beatboxing sounds and sends a query to find an appropriate dancing motion from the motion clip database. The rhythm features extracted from the analysis of beatboxing sounds are matched with the features of motion clips extracted from the onset times and the average volume. The goal of the searching step is to find a speedy motion clip if the beating speed is fast and find a clip with big movements if the sound is loud.

This searching step uses a matching function S:

$$S(B,M) = (B_O - kM_S) + (B_P - hM_M),$$

where k and h are proportional constants. The system tests every motion clips in the database and find a new motion that has the smallest S. If the new motion is the same motion with the current motion, this step finds new one except this one.

2.4 Displaying Motion Clips

If the rhythm features from the beatboxing sound have a big change or the current motion clip ends in one second, searching a next motion clip while the system executes the present motion clip determined by the current sound features. Then current and next motion clips are blended within about one second overlapped, using spherical linear interpolation (SLERP) for every joint's rotation.

3 Conclusion

We introduced a real-time technique to synthesize a dancing character that is matched with beatboxing sounds. We need to enhance the technique of analyzing beatboxing sounds so that it can support complex sounds such as disk jockey's scratching sounds. The most important part of our system is the matching part, so we need to improve algorithms for matching information of music sounds with motions. We also plan to research a technique how to synthesize dancing characters reacting to the background music in real-time as well as beatboxing.

Acknowledgements. This work was supported by grant No. R01-2006-000-11214-0 from the Basic Research Program of the Korea Science & Engineering Foundation.

References

1. Kim, T.H., Park, S.I., Shin, S.Y.: Rhythmic motion synthesis based on motion beat analysis. ACM Transactions on Graphics 22(3), 392–401 (2003)
2. Shiratori, T., Nakazawa, A., Ikeuchi, K.: Dancing - to - Music Character Animation. In: EUROGRAPHICS 2006, Computer Graphics Forum 25(3), 449–458 (2006)
3. Goto, M.: An Audio-based Real-time Beat Tracking System for Music With or Without Drum-sounds. In Journal of New Music Research 30(2), 159–171 (2001)
4. Kapur, A., Benning, M., Tzanetakis, G.: Query-by-beat-boxing: Music retrieval for the DJ. In: The International Conference on Music Information Retrieval, pp. 170–177(2004)
5. Sinyor, E., McKay, C., Fiebrink, R., McEnnis, D., Fujinaga, I.: Beatbox Classification using ACE. In: The International Conference on Music Information Retrieval, pp. 672–675 (2005)

Sketch-Based Virtual Human Modelling and Animation

Chen Mao, Sheng Feng Qin, and David Wright

School of Engineering and Design, Brunel University, Uxbridge, UB8 3PH, UK
{Chen.Mao, Sheng.Feng.Qin, David.Wright}@brunel.ac.uk

Abstract. Animated virtual humans created by skilled artists play a remarkable role in today's public entertainment. However, ordinary users are still treated as audiences due to the lack of appropriate expertise, equipment, and computer skills. We developed a new method and a novel sketching interface, which enable anyone who can draw to "sketch-out" 3D virtual humans and animation. We devised a "Stick Figure→Fleshing-out→Skin Mapping" graphical pipeline, which decomposes the complexity of figure drawing and considerably boosts the modelling and animation efficiency. We developed a gesture-based method for 3D pose reconstruction from 2D stick figure drawings. We investigated a "Creative Model-based Method", which performs a human perception process to transfer users' 2D freehand sketches into 3D human bodies of various body sizes, shapes and fat distributions. Our current system supports character animation in various forms including articulated figure animation, 3D mesh model animation, and 2D contour/NPR animation with personalised drawing styles. Moreover, this interface also supports sketch-based crowd animation and 2D storyboarding of 3D multiple character interactions. A preliminary user study was conducted to support the overall system design. Our system has been formally tested by various users on Tablet PC. After minimal training, even a beginner can create vivid virtual humans and animate them within minutes.

Keywords: Sketching interface, Virtual human modelling and animation, Storyboarding, User study.

1 Sketch-Based Human Modelling and Animation Pipeline

1.1 Intuitive Graphics Pipeline

Natural figure sketches are featured by foreshortening, contour over-tracing, body part overlapping, shading and shadow, etc. To decompose the complexity of direct 3D modelling and animation from fully rendered sketches, we designed a "Stick Figure [1]→Fleshing-out→Skin Mapping" pipeline (see Fig. 1). This is inspired by the drawing sequence recommended by many sketch books and tutorials. Meanwhile, in principle, it echoes the modelling and animation pipeline in commercial packages (i.e. Maya, 3D Studio Max). Regarding our current design, functionalities at different levels were gained for different users. Thus they can choose to make simple stick figures, create delicate 3D surface models, or explore further to animate these sketch-generated creatures. Moreover, models can be exported to commercial packages at any level, to be refined by their powerful function kits.

A. Butz et al. (Eds.): SG 2007, LNCS 4569, pp. 220–223, 2007.

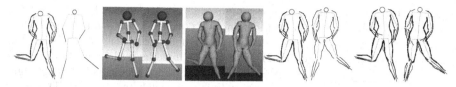

Fig. 1. Users first draw stick figure key frames to define a specific motion. Then, they can "flesh-out" any existing stick figure with body profiles to portray an imaginative character. The system can automatically "perceive" the body size (skeleton proportion) and shape (body profile and fat distribution) from the sketched figure, and transfer it into a 3D virtual character. The resulting 3D skin surface can be mapped onto each of the posed stick figure key frames, which can be further interpolated as the final 2D and 3D character animation.

1.2 Preliminary User Study

A preliminary user study (including *Questionnaire* and *Sketching Observation*) was conducted to explore design questions, identify users' needs, and obtain a "true story" of figure sketching. 60 questionnaires were collected and processed; and 14 sketching observations were conducted with 14 users (including artists, designers, animators, graduate students, and researchers) in the pre-defined drawing scenarios. The study outcomes were adopted to develop a natural and supportive sketching interface.

1.3 Sketch-Based 3D Stick Figure Modelling and Animation

Maintaining the correct proportion and foreshortening is a common challenge in figure sketching for not only novice but also skilled artists. To help overcome this difficulty, we provide an on-line drawing assistance, which is based on the utilisation of template skeleton and the real-time body part recognition and length control. We developed a "Multi-layered Back-front Ambiguity Clarifier", which utilises figure perspective rendering gestures, human joint ROM (Range of Motion), and key frame coherence to identify user intended 3D poses from 2D stick figure drawings. Since a quick and imprecise sketching may accidentally generate physically impossible poses, we offer a "Figure Pose Checking and Auto-correction" routine to detect ill-posed body parts, highlight them, and give proper corrections based on human body joint ROM and balance. Once obtaining a series of 3D stick figure poses, user can interactively sketch-out motion paths and timing, and add their favoured sound/background to enhance the 3D virtual world. The resulting 3D animation can be automatically synthesised in VRML after a single user click.

2 Fleshing-Out to Create Various Human Body Models

2.1 From 2D Raw Sketches to 3D Human Body Models

Users can depict the visual appearance of a virtual character through "fleshing-out" a single stick figure with body profiles. Improved on [2], which enables sketch-based spherical object modelling, we investigated a "Creative Model-based Method", which performs a human perception process to model irregular/complicated human skin surfaces. Through this method, the system can perceive the body size (skeleton proportion) and shape (body fat distribution) of a sketched figure and transfer it into a plausible 3D counterpart model through continuous graphical comparisons and generic model morphing (see Fig. 2). We created a three-layered (skeleton-fat tissue-skin) anatomical generic model, which can be transformed sequentially through rigid morphing, fatness morphing, and surface fitting to match the original 2D sketch. Moreover, we offer an auto-beautification function to regularise 3D asymmetrical bodies made by users' drawing imperfections. Users can interactively refine their 3D models by over-sketching 2D figure profiles. Modifications can be made at any time and on any key frame sketch to achieve the updated 3D model.

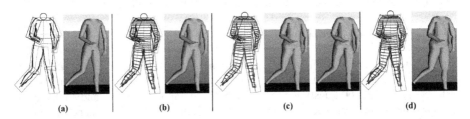

(a)   (b)   (c)   (d)

Fig. 2. (a) The input 2D freehand sketch and the 3D model after rigid morphing. **(b)** Graphical comparison to get the fat distribution measurements and the fatness morphed model **(c)** Graphical comparison to get the surface fitting measurements; the model with and without system auto-beautification **(d)** Overtracing body contour (right lower torso, left lower leg, and right leg) to modify an existing 3D surface model.

2.2   Generic Model Acquisition and Specification

Our generic model is reconstructed from cadaveric cross-section images from the Visible Human Project® of the National Library of Medicine. The preparation of this multi-layered anatomical model includes: *Virtual Skeleton Registration, Skin Mesh Recovery, Template Fat Distribution Digitisation.*

3   Sketch-Based Multi-level Character Animation

Our system supports character animation in multiple levels, including articulated figure animation, 3D mesh model animation, and 2D contour animation, and 2D personalized NPR animation (see Fig. 1). Following the "Stick Figure→Fleshing-out→Skin Mapping" pipeline, a 3D virtual human animation is accomplished by wrapping the sketch-generated skin surface onto a series of posed stick figures, which can be further interpolated via VRML with the associated graphical motion definition. 2D NPR animation is generated by successively interpolating the extracted key figure contours (with the mapped fleshing-out contours) and playing their in-betweens on sketching interface. This approach is different from the traditional cel animation, and users do not need to render each key frame once a single key figure is fleshed-out.

4 Sketching-Out Crowd Animation and Character Interactions

In our system, users can build their own 3D character and motion library, and animate a population of virtual humans through motion retargeting and a sketch-based actor allocation in 3D space [3]. Moreover, users are able to sketch-out character interactions in each story scene (by either stick or full figure drawing). The system can deliver an immediate 3D scenario, in which virtual actors are acting and interacting with each other.

5 User Experiences

This system has been tested by 10 different users (including artists, an animator, undergraduates and postgraduates, and a 12-year-old boy) through *performance tests*, *sketching observation*, and *user interviews*. After a short tutorial, users rapidly learned the modelling process and began to sketch-out their own virtual human animation on Tablet PC within minutes. Only *6.27* and *6.75* minutes were taken on average to create a *3-frame stick* and *full figure animation* respectively. Through sketching observation and user interviews, our sketching interface is proved by users to be easy to learn and use, and enjoyable for fast 3D virtual human modelling and animation.

6 Conclusion

Human modelling and animation is a recognised challenge and labour-intensive task, which has been, until now, confined to the domain of professionals. This research draws on existing drawing skills of ordinary users to create and animate their own characters through 2D freehand sketching. Preliminary user study and formal user tests were conducted to ensure the usability and functionalities of this sketch-based modelling and animation interface.

References

1. Mao, C., Qin, S.F., Wright, D.K.: A Sketch-based Gesture Interface for Rough 3D Stick Figure Animation. In: Proc. of Eurographics Workshop on Sketch Based Interfaces and Modeling, pp. 175–183 (2005)
2. Igarashi, T., Matsuoka, S., Tanaka, H.: Teddy: A Sketching Interface for 3D Freeform Design. In: Proc. SIGGRAPH '99, pp. 409–416 (1999)
3. Mao, C., Qin, S.F., Wright, D.K.: Sketching-out Virtual Humans: from 2D Storyboarding to Immediate 3D Character Animation. In: Proc.of ACM SIGCHI International Conference on Advances in Computer Entertainment Technology, Hollywood, Los Angeles (2006)

Perceptually Adaptive Rendering of Immersive Virtual Environments

Kimberly Weaver and Derrick Parkhurst

Iowa State University
1620 Howe Hall
Ames, IA 50011
{weaverk,derrick}@iastate.edu

Abstract. When rendering immersive virtual environments, it is necessary to limit the geometric complexity of the scene in order to retain interactive frame rates. Both reduced frame rendering rates and reduced geometric complexity have been shown to have a negative impact on task performance. We present a perceptually adaptive rendering system which optimizes rendering performance in immersive virtual environments. Our system currently uses three discrete levels of detail for each model, which are created prior to run time. We use head position and orientation in the 3D environment to determine the appropriate geometric level of detail (LOD) of the objects in the scene. Based upon the thresholds used to trigger a change between two LODs, interactivity can be significantly improved without overtly distracting the user.

Keywords: perceptually adaptive rendering, level of detail, virtual reality.

1 Introduction

Virtual environments which are geometrically complex tend to exhibit more visual realism than lower complexity renderings. The time required to render any scene is proportional to that scene's geometric complexity.When creating virtual environments, it is often necessary to limit the geometric complexity of the scene in order to maintain frame rates which support natural interactivity. Psychophysical studies have demonstrated that both reduced rendering rates and reduced geometric complexity have the ability to impede task performance [1]. With immersive virtual environments, the importance of balancing the tradeoff between interactivity and displaying a sufficiently complex scene is amplified because it is necessary to render multiple display surfaces simultaneously.

Our approach employs gaze-contingent perceptually adaptive rendering. The LOD for the objects in the current frame are determined by the direction of the gaze at that point in time. Another type of perceptually adaptive rendering involves saliency (what objects in the scene are most likely to be the focus of attention) and renders objects with the most saliency with more detail that objects with low saliency. The saliency approach is more task-dependent; therefore the gaze-contingent approach is more desirable in an environment whose main purpose is general exploration.

A. Butz et al. (Eds.): SG 2007, LNCS 4569, pp. 224–229, 2007.

Using perceptually adaptive rendering techniques can increase frame rendering rates and thus interactivity without reducing the perceived quality of the display. Such techniques exploit the limitations of human visual perception to mask any changes in complexity that may be made [2]. Not all of the visual input received by the human visual system is processed. Additionally, very little of the visual field is processed in high detail because of the physiological organization of the visual system from the retina to the cortex. As the eccentricity from the point of gaze increases, the resolution of the information received as well as the extent to which that information is processed decreases. Information at the point of gaze is processed most fully and is represented at the highest resolution. Visual information from the periphery is processed the least and is represented at the lowest resolution.

Our perceptually adaptive rendering system uses this information to optimize rendering performance in immersive virtual environments. This system is designed to work primarily in the C4 and C6, Iowa State University's (ISU) four-sided and six-sided CAVEs, which are housed at the Virtual Reality Application Center (VRAC). Currently, the system increases overall frame rendering rates by reducing the geometric level of detail (GLOD) of objects situated in the user's visual periphery. Previous research using a desktop virtual reality display has shown that reducing GLOD of an object in proportion to the distance from the point of gaze (established using an eye tracking system) enhances interactivity while maintaining perceptual quality [3]. Given the vastly larger display size of CAVEs, which spans the user's entire field of view, the benefits of using perceptually adaptive rendering are much greater than using the same techniques on desktop displays.

Fig. 1. The virtual environment displayed in a four-sided CAVE

2 Implementation

The rendering software is built using VR Juggler (http://www.vrjuggler.org), which handles the coordination and configuration of input and output devices. OpenSG (http://www.opensg.org) is used to maintain the scene graph and control the switching between different LODs. Physical simulation of objects in the environment is implemented using the Open Physics Abstraction Layer (http://opal.sourceforge.net)

and the Open Dynamics Engine (http://www.ODE.org) libraries. This allows for easier rearrangement of objects in the environment as well as creation of multiple unique arrangements of objects.

The geometry of the objects at each LOD is computed prior to runtime using QSlim (http://graphics.cs.uiuc.edu/~garland/software/qslim.html). The attribute deviation metric provided by the MeshDev package (http://meshdev.sourceforge.net) is used to ensure that the mean error across all models is consistent for any given level of detail. Fig. 2 shows five of the models currently being used and their three levels of detail. Smooth meshes with a high vertex count can be reduced drastically. Objects with fewer vertices, cannot be reduced as drastically, but they also carry a lower computational burden to start with. This method does not work as well with objects possessing extreme surface variation such as the brain gear in Fig. 2.

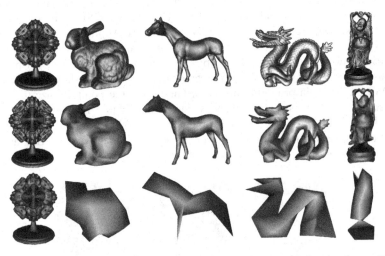

Fig. 2. The 5 models (*from left to right: brain gear, bunny, horse, dragon, happy Buddha*) rendered at their three levels of detail high (*top*), medium (*center*), low (*bottom*)

The current system uses head position and orientation within the 3D environment as a proxy for gaze direction. Both head position and orientation are commonly tracked in CAVEs because they are used in the calculations for rendering the scene properly based on the user's viewpoint. The appropriate GLOD of the objects in the environment is chosen based on the angular distance (θ) between the vector defined by the user's current head position and direction, and the vector from the current head position to the geometric center of the relevant object. Three discrete levels of detail (LOD_{high}, LOD_{medium} or LOD_{low}) are currently used in our implementation. Depending on the angular thresholds chosen to trigger a reduction in GLOD (t_l and t_u), interactivity is significantly improved without causing a distraction to the user. The highest LOD, LOD_{high} is chosen to be rendered if the angular distance, θ, is less than or equal to the lower threshold, t_l. If θ is greater than t_l and less than or equal to the upper threshold t_u, then LOD_{medium}, the middle GLOD is chosen to be rendered. Finally, if θ is greater than t_u, then the lowest GLOD, LOD_{low} is selected.

In the current implementation, t_l is equal to 1 radian (approximately 57 degrees) and t_u equals 2 radians (approximately 115 degrees). The change to LOD_{low} occurs outside of the user's field of view. We feel that LOD_{low} should still be rendered. Otherwise, the light emitted by the virtual environment might distract the user from the area of the scene he or she is currently inspecting. Also the cost of rendering such a low-polygon-count model is negligible.

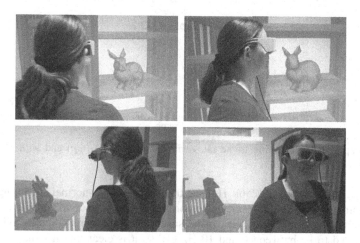

Fig. 3. Changing the GLOD using head tracking. (*top*) The Stanford bunny changes from high LOD to medium LOD. (*bottom*) The dragon rendered at high and low LOD.

More than three discrete levels of detail was not used because for each model that is to be LOD regulated, a version of that model must be stored and loaded for each level. Increasing the number of levels, would cause a larger burden on memory. The time it would take to load an application before it starts rendering would increase.

The use of continuous LOD, the incremental addition and subtraction of vertices to improve or degrade an object's perceptual quality, has been explored. So far the operations required to change the vertex composition of the model has impacted performance too severely to merit the perceptual benefits.

3 Results

A virtual environment with approximately 7 million vertices was created. Five of the models were simplified according to the specifications stated above, resulting in a virtual environment which would require rendering between 24,140 vertices (if all possible models were rendered at the lowest LOD) and 6,945,480 vertices (if all possible models were rendered at the highest LOD, a situation which would not occur unless all of these models are located in the same general area of the scene).

The application was first run in ISU VRAC's C4 CAVE with no LOD switching, so that all of the models would always be rendered at their highest detail, in the manner of current immersive virtual reality systems. The resulting average frame rate was 4.7975 Hz. When LOD switching was enabled for the same environment, the

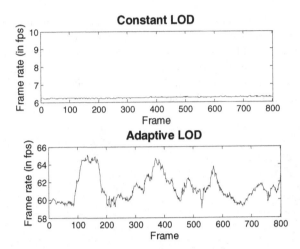

Fig. 4. Graphs of the resulting frame rates with constant LOD (*top*) and with perceptually adaptive LOD (*bottom*)

frame rate improved to 30.2508 Hz, six times faster than normal rendering. Fig. 4 graphs frame rates over 800 frames with constant, LOD_{high} and with adaptive LOD.

The minimum frame rate that can be said to support normal interactivity is has been reported to be between 6 and 10 Hz [4], so it is clear that it is not possible to simply render this virtual environment normally. The frame rate resulting from the GLOD simplification is well within the bounds for normal interaction indicating that using a system which reduces the GLOD in the periphery is a viable method for maintaining interactivity.

Because in our system, the first change does not occur until the angular distance is greater than 57 degrees which it is outside of the field of view for the shutter glasses that must be used when viewing the virtual environment in stereo, the user should be unaware that any changes in the scene are taking place. This larger value is also useful for when the environment is being viewed by multiple users. Since only the person navigating through the environment is being tracked, the LOD will change based on that user's head position. It is standard practice to tell other observers in an immersive environment to align their gazes with the navigator's in order to perceive the scene correctly. Multiple users should then be unaware of GLOD changes in the virtual environment. It is also possible to track multiple users as they are viewing the environment. This would be valuable when there is a small group (2-3 people) viewing the environment simultaneously. Tracking multiple people however, will greatly reduce advantages gained from the use of adaptive LOD because more of the scene will have to be rendered at a higher detail during each frame.

A user study is planned for the near future, but preliminary feedback from users viewing the environment in adaptive LOD mode has been favorable. New viewers of the adaptive LOD environment do not notice any switch between the 3 levels of detail. It is only once they are told what to look for that these changes become apparent. Because the change in detail is not instantaneous, when a user turns his or head quickly, it is possible to find portions of the scene rendered at the lower levels of detail. This means that gaze-contingent perceptually adaptive rendering would not be suitable for applications which require the user to quickly change the focus of attention such as military applications. This system would be much more appropriate for applications which require information of the broader picture but the focus changes gradually such as prototype inspection or visualization of scientific data.

4 Discussion

Perceptually adaptive rendering can save a substantial amount of computational resources while at the same time retaining the perceptual quality of the display. While it is true that the computational power of CPUs and GPUs are exponentially increasing with time, there will always be computationally demanding tasks to which freed resources could be shifted. Spared resources could potentially be used to calculate more realistic physical simulations or scene lighting.

Furthermore, while we have focused here on the reduction of geometric complexity, level of detail reduction techniques can also be applied other places in the graphics pipeline, for example, to shader complexity. Further work needs to be done to explore whether or not the resources spared by having shaders of varying complexities out-balances the cost of loading the shaders in and out of memory.

Though the current system uses head direction exclusively to determine objects' LODs, there are changes that could be made to make the decision-making process more intelligent. Rather than changing the LOD immediately, an object could be marked for change after a certain period of time has passed. Objects that have once been the focus of attention are more likely to again be the focus of attention again, so inserting a delay before changing the LOD, could reduce further the chance of a user noticing any LOD switches.

While adaptive rendering based solely on saliency is not suited to an environment designed for exploration, applying a saliency model in conjunction with head direction could be useful. Like in the previous construction, a delay could be added before changing the LOD of an object. In this case, objects which are deemed more salient could have a longer delay before switching LOD than less salient objects. This would be a further intelligent method of changing LOD to improve interactivity, while still minimizing distractions to the user with blatant, frequent LOD switches.

References

1. Parkhurst, D., Niebur, E.: Variable-resolution displays: A theoretical, practical, and behavioral evaluation. Human Factors 44(4), 611–629 (2002)
2. Ferwerda, J.A.: Elements of early vision for computer graphics. IEEE Computer Graphics and Applications 21(5), 22–33 (2001)
3. Parkhurst, D., Niebur, E.: A feasibility test for perceptually adaptive level of detail rendering on desktop systems. In: Proceedings of APGV 2004. International Conference Proceedings Series, ACM, pp. 49–56. ACM Press / ACM APGV, New York (2004)
4. Watson, B., Walker, N., Ribarsky, W., Spaulding, V.: Effects of variation in system responsiveness on user performance in virtual environments. Human Factors 40(3), 403–414 (1998)

Customized Slider Bars for Adjusting Multi-dimension Parameter Sets

Shigeru Owada[1], Makoto Okabe[2], Takeo Igarashi[3],
Frank Nielsen[4], and Norimichi Tsumura[5]

[1] Sony CSL
sowd@acm.org
[2] The University of Tokyo
makoto21@ui.is.s.u-tokyo.ac.jp
[3] The University of Tokyo / Sony CSL
takeo@acm.org
[4] Sony CSL
frank.nielsen@acm.org
[5] Chiba University
tsumura@faculty.chiba-u.jp

1 Introduction

Application softwares usually support a single set of user interaction tools that are supposed to be optimal. It is satisfactory if the user interface (UI) is really optimal for everyone. However, since the user's intent and the preference vary one by one, such fixed toolkits may cause inefficiency of the UI. For example, if you are performing physical simulation and trying to generate particular animation

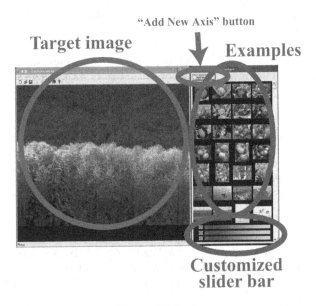

Fig. 1. UI design

A. Butz et al. (Eds.): SG 2007, LNCS 4569, pp. 230–232, 2007.
© Springer-Verlag Berlin Heidelberg 2007

sequence of the object, you need to find a good combination of physical parameters to achieve the desired effect. To support such cases, we focus on customizing UI for independent users, instead of designing a fixed set of UI toolkit.

2   User Interface

In our system, the user explicitly defines the desired number of slider bars one by one. It is performed by giving examples for each slider bar, from the catalog of practical combination of parameters.

The user first creates a new slider bar by pressing the "Add New Axis" button (Fig. 1, the top of the right window). Then the system adds one slider bar under

Fig. 2. Dragging an image onto the slider bar

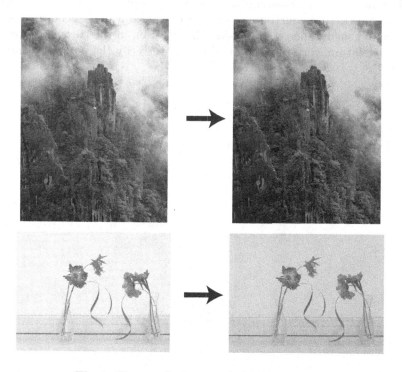

Fig. 3. Change of color specified by our system

the examples area (Fig. 1, the bottom of the right window). The user drops several desired examples onto the newly created bar (Fig. 2). The system internally computes the tendency of the dropped examples and defines the slider bar. By moving the knob on the slider bar, the user can smoothly modify parameter values and the result is displayed on the target image window (Fig. 1 left).

3   Result

We applied our technique for adjusting average color of images. The input of the system is a set of images and we take the average of each in (R, G, B) triplets. The user explores the RGB space by their customized slider bars and finds the desired color, which is then applied to the given image (Fig. 3).

4   Conclusion

We observed that customized tool bar efficiently summarizes the user's intent. However, we have not completely explored the possibility of our system. Especially, we believe that our idea can be applied to other kinds of parametrized models such as textures, bi-directional reflectance function (BRDF) and so on.

One fundamental issue is that we assume that the interpolation between example points in the parameter space can be performed linearly, with Euclidean distance metric. It is our future work to introduce a non-Euclidean distance measure to generate perceptually smooth transition in the parameter space. It is also our future work to perform user tests to verify the performance of our system.

Magical Tile

Maki Terai[1], Jun Fujiki[2], Reiji Tsuruno[3], and Kiyoshi Tomimatsu[4]

[1] School of Design, Kyushu University
[2] Graduate School of Design, Kyushu University
[3,4] Faculty of Design, Kyushu University
[1,2,3,4] 4-9-1 Shiobaru, Minami-ku, Fukuoka, 815-8540 Japan
maki@verygood.aid.design.kyushu-u.ac.jp,
fujiki@gsd.design.kyushu-u.ac.jp,
{tsuruno,tomimatu}@design.kyushu-u.ac.jp

1 Introduction

Many computer games are based on "overhead" two-dimensional (2D) computer graphics which are suitable for displaying planar figure. However, in such graphical engines, three-dimensional (3D) structures are also presented in 2D. In the overhead view, the width of a shape is displayed by a horizontal line, and the height and depth are expressed as a vertical line. Such an expression in not realistic, but is intuitively recognizable, particularly in computer games. In this system, 3D geometry data recognizable by the user is generated from tiles placed on a canvas. The geometric shape created by the system can be viewed from an arbitrary angle by a gradual warping of the geometry, without the user being aware of the conversion to the 3D expression.

2 User Interface

The user designs in overhead view with a view angle to horizon of 45°. The user begins modeling by placing tiles on a canvas in overhead view. The canvas is a uniform square grid, tiles are either green or brown, and the edge pattern has 16 variants (see Fig. 1(Left)). Tile color determines depth and height of shapes, and the edge pattern can create closed domains. The basic generation rule for modeling is that the system creates geometric shapes when a group of green tiles are above a group of brown tiles.

This rule is based on the basic features of the overhead view. Alternating tile arrangements in a row forms a stair (Fig. 1(Right)). In addition, the system infers shapes of locations that cannot be observed in overhead view and interpolates shapes.

3 Algorithm

When a user rotates the canvas, the system creates 3D structure data from the arrangement of tiles, seamlessly converting the overhead view into a 3D expression.

A. Butz et al. (Eds.): SG 2007, LNCS 4569, pp. 233–234, 2007.

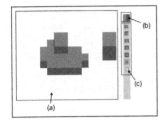 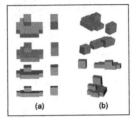 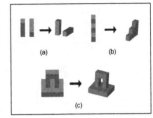

Fig. 1. Left: User interface. (a) Canvas. (b) Panel for changing tile color. (c) Tiles for placement on the canvas. Center: (a) Vertical rotation. (b) Horizontal rotation. Right: (a) Sample shapes with depth and height. (b) Stair shape. (c) Gate shape.

3.1   Creating 3D Structures from Overhead View

The system scans all tiles and calculates the closed domain of green tiles. The green tiles in each closed domain are grouped. Each closed domain consists of a number of vertically -arranged tiles, and the system processes the following algorithm for each closed domain.

1. The depth of the shape is calculated for each vertically -arranged group of tiles according to the number of continuous green tiles.
2. The height of the shape is calculated for each group of vertically -arranged tiles according to the number of continuous brown tiles.
3. After determining depth and height of all closed domains, the height of the shape is modified.
4. The 2D data is converted into 3D data.

3.2   Converting Overhead View into 3D View

In the 3D expression, the shape is distorted depending on the viewpoint. In overhead view, the sizes of top and front of a cube are equal, corresponding the 3D view at an angle (θ) of 45°.

4   Discussion

We expect that users can see the created shape without being aware of wraping of the geometric shape. We are also interested in the shape which users perceive from overhead view. We believe that our system contributes to approach of relation between the ambiguous depiction and the perception of shape.

Invisible Shape: Subjective Surface

Jun Fujiki[1], Taketoshi Ushiama[2], and Kiyoshi Tomimatsu[3]

[1] Graduate School of Design Kyushu University
fujiki@gsd.design.kyushu-u.ac.jp
[2,3] Faculty of Design Kyushu University
{ushiama,tomimatu}@design.kyushu-u.ac.jp
[1,2,3] 4-9-1 Shiobaru, Minami-ku, Fukuoka, 815-8540 Japan

1 Introduction

While, based on shading, shadowing and outline etc, human beings generally perceive a shape, we explore an new representation for perceiving shape. The Invisible Shape is an interactive media art software which has a concept of a new expression for perceiving 3D shapes. Although our work does not draw a shape and the apparent size of the character does not change by parallel projection, the user may be able to perceive the shape by tracking the walking characters on it. Like subjective contour, we expect that the user perceives the surface of invisible shape by motion of the objects related to the shape. In Fig. 1, the large

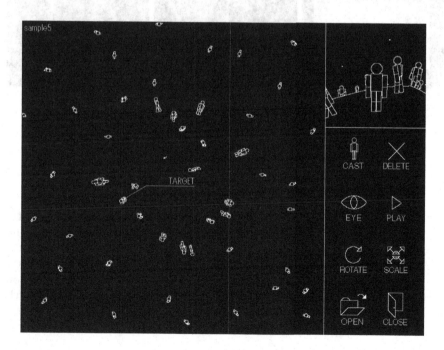

Fig. 1. The screnn of Invisible Shape

A. Butz et al. (Eds.): SG 2007, LNCS 4569, pp. 235–236, 2007.

space at the left is the canvas. The cast icon is used to add a character into the canvas. The delete icon is used to delete characters. Clicking a character after clicking the eye icon displays the sight of the character in the upper right window. The play icon is used to begin the characters walking. After clicking this icon, it changes to the stop icon for stopping the characters. The rotate icon is used to rotate the space. The scale icon is used to change zoom scale of the space. The open icon is used to load a shape model file. The door icon is used to close the session.

2 How to Play

Using the open icon, the user first loads a shape model file, such as DXF file. Although the system does not draw the loaded shape, seeing the filename displayed at the upper left of the canvas, the user can confirm the success of loading (Fig. 2(a)). Next, the user puts characters on the canvas (Fig. 2(b)). When the user clicks the outside of the non-drawn shape, the system puts the character onto the non-drawn large sphere surrounding the scene. Then, clicking the play icon, the user makes the characters walking. At this time, the user may perceive the non-drawn shape by tracking the walking characters (Fig. 2(c)).

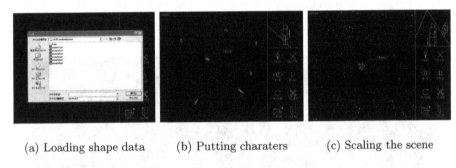

(a) Loading shape data   (b) Putting charaters   (c) Scaling the scene

Fig. 2. The process of using the Invisible Shape

3 Presentation

In our presentation, the user first plays our work without hearing what primitive shape has been loaded. After a moment, we will ask the user what shape he has found in the canvas. We expect that the user says about the invisible shape; he has perceived the invisible shape. We are also interested in how many characters are enough to make the user perceive the invisible shape. We expect that our work contributes to the approach of the relation between the motion and the perception of shape.

Author Index

Lecture Notes in Computer Science

For information about Vols. 1–4465

please contact your bookseller or Springer

Vol. 4508: M.-Y. Kao, X.-Y. Li (Eds.), Algorithmic Aspects in Information and Management. VIII, 428 pages. 2007.

Vol. 4507: F. Sandoval, A. Prieto, J. Cabestany, M. Graña (Eds.), Computational and Ambient Intelligence. XXVI, 1167 pages. 2007.

Vol. 4506: D. Zeng, I. Gotham, K. Komatsu, C. Lynch, M. Thurmond, D. Madigan, B. Lober, J. Kvach, H. Chen (Eds.), Intelligence and Security Informatics: Biosurveillance. XI, 234 pages. 2007.

Vol. 4505: G. Dong, X. Lin, W. Wang, Y. Yang, J.X. Yu (Eds.), Advances in Data and Web Management. XXII, 896 pages. 2007.

Vol. 4504: J. Huang, R. Kowalczyk, Z. Maamar, D. Martin, I. Müller, S. Stoutenburg, K.P. Sycara (Eds.), Service-Oriented Computing: Agents, Semantics, and Engineering. X, 175 pages. 2007.

Vol. 4501: J. Marques-Silva, K.A. Sakallah (Eds.), Theory and Applications of Satisfiability Testing – SAT 2007. XI, 384 pages. 2007.

Vol. 4500: N. Streitz, A. Kameas, I. Mavrommati (Eds.), The Disappearing Computer. XVIII, 304 pages. 2007.

Vol. 4499: Y.Q. Shi (Ed.), Transactions on Data Hiding and Multimedia Security II. IX, 117 pages. 2007.

Vol. 4497: S.B. Cooper, B. Löwe, A. Sorbi (Eds.), Computation and Logic in the Real World. XVIII, 826 pages. 2007.

Vol. 4496: N.T. Nguyen, A. Grzech, R.J. Howlett, L.C. Jain (Eds.), Agent and Multi-Agent Systems: Technologies and Applications. XXI, 1046 pages. 2007. (Sublibrary LNAI).

Vol. 4495: J. Krogstie, A. Opdahl, G. Sindre (Eds.), Advanced Information Systems Engineering. XVI, 606 pages. 2007.

Vol. 4494: H. Jin, O.F. Rana, Y. Pan, V.K. Prasanna (Eds.), Algorithms and Architectures for Parallel Processing. XIV, 508 pages. 2007.

Vol. 4493: D. Liu, S. Fei, Z. Hou, H. Zhang, C. Sun (Eds.), Advances in Neural Networks – ISNN 2007, Part III. XXVI, 1215 pages. 2007.

Vol. 4492: D. Liu, S. Fei, Z. Hou, H. Zhang, C. Sun (Eds.), Advances in Neural Networks – ISNN 2007, Part II. XXVII, 1321 pages. 2007.

Vol. 4491: D. Liu, S. Fei, Z.-G. Hou, H. Zhang, C. Sun (Eds.), Advances in Neural Networks – ISNN 2007, Part I. LIV, 1365 pages. 2007.

Vol. 4490: Y. Shi, G.D. van Albada, J. Dongarra, P.M.A. Sloot (Eds.), Computational Science – ICCS 2007, Part IV. XXXVII, 1211 pages. 2007.

Vol. 4489: Y. Shi, G.D. van Albada, J. Dongarra, P.M.A. Sloot (Eds.), Computational Science – ICCS 2007, Part III. XXXVII, 1257 pages. 2007.

Vol. 4488: Y. Shi, G.D. van Albada, J. Dongarra, P.M.A. Sloot (Eds.), Computational Science – ICCS 2007, Part II. XXXV, 1251 pages. 2007.

Vol. 4487: Y. Shi, G.D. van Albada, J. Dongarra, P.M.A. Sloot (Eds.), Computational Science – ICCS 2007, Part I. LXXXI, 1275 pages. 2007.

Vol. 4486: M. Bernardo, J. Hillston (Eds.), Formal Methods for Performance Evaluation. VII, 469 pages. 2007.

Vol. 4485: F. Sgallari, A. Murli, N. Paragios (Eds.), Scale Space and Variational Methods in Computer Vision. XV, 931 pages. 2007.

Vol. 4484: J.-Y. Cai, S.B. Cooper, H. Zhu (Eds.), Theory and Applications of Models of Computation. XIII, 772 pages. 2007.

Vol. 4483: C. Baral, G. Brewka, J. Schlipf (Eds.), Logic Programming and Nonmonotonic Reasoning. IX, 327 pages. 2007. (Sublibrary LNAI).

Vol. 4482: A. An, J. Stefanowski, S. Ramanna, C.J. Butz, W. Pedrycz, G. Wang (Eds.), Rough Sets, Fuzzy Sets, Data Mining and Granular Computing. XIV, 585 pages. 2007. (Sublibrary LNAI).

Vol. 4481: J. Yao, P. Lingras, W.-Z. Wu, M. Szczuka, N.J. Cercone, D. Ślęzak (Eds.), Rough Sets and Knowledge Technology. XIV, 576 pages. 2007. (Sublibrary LNAI).

Vol. 4480: A. LaMarca, M. Langheinrich, K.N. Truong (Eds.), Pervasive Computing. XIII, 369 pages. 2007.

Vol. 4479: I.F. Akyildiz, R. Sivakumar, E. Ekici, J.C.d. Oliveira, J. McNair (Eds.), NETWORKING 2007. Ad Hoc and Sensor Networks, Wireless Networks, Next Generation Internet. XXVII, 1252 pages. 2007.

Vol. 4478: J. Martí, J.M. Benedí, A.M. Mendonça, J. Serrat (Eds.), Pattern Recognition and Image Analysis, Part II. XXVII, 657 pages. 2007.

Vol. 4477: J. Martí, J.M. Benedí, A.M. Mendonça, J. Serrat (Eds.), Pattern Recognition and Image Analysis, Part I. XXVII, 625 pages. 2007.

Vol. 4476: V. Gorodetsky, C. Zhang, V.A. Skormin, L. Cao (Eds.), Autonomous Intelligent Systems: Multi-Agents and Data Mining. XIII, 323 pages. 2007. (Sublibrary LNAI).

Vol. 4475: P. Crescenzi, G. Prencipe, G. Pucci (Eds.), Fun with Algorithms. X, 273 pages. 2007.

Vol. 4474: G. Prencipe, S. Zaks (Eds.), Structural Information and Communication Complexity. XI, 342 pages. 2007.

Vol. 4472: M. Haindl, J. Kittler, F. Roli (Eds.), Multiple Classifier Systems. XI, 524 pages. 2007.

Vol. 4471: P. Cesar, K. Chorianopoulos, J.F. Jensen (Eds.), Interactive TV: a Shared Experience. XIII, 236 pages. 2007.

Vol. 4470: Q. Wang, D. Pfahl, D.M. Raffo (Eds.), Software Process Dynamics and Agility. XI, 346 pages. 2007.

Vol. 4469: K.-c. Hui, Z. Pan, R.C.-k. Chung, C.C.L. Wang, X. Jin, S. Göbel, E.C.-L. Li (Eds.), Technologies for E-Learning and Digital Entertainment. XVIII, 974 pages. 2007.

Vol. 4468: M.M. Bonsangue, E.B. Johnsen (Eds.), Formal Methods for Open Object-Based Distributed Systems. X, 317 pages. 2007.

Vol. 4467: A.L. Murphy, J. Vitek (Eds.), Coordination Models and Languages. X, 325 pages. 2007.

Vol. 4466: F.B. Sachse, G. Seemann (Eds.), Functional Imaging and Modeling of the Heart. XV, 486 pages. 2007.